Praise for Jon Wells

"Jon Wells is the best true crime writer in Canada. His books are without rival—from the gritty detail to the human tragedy. He is a star in the genre. His books read like novels but are rich in true crime details, and his intimate look at horrific crimes are woven with a human touch that hooks the reader from page one."
—Sue Sgambati, Veteran TV crime reporter/producer

"An excellent, true-crime page-turner."
—Chuck Howitt, *The Guelph Mercury*, on *Sniper*

POST-MORTEM

POST-MORTEM

JUSTICE AT LAST
FOR YVETTE BUDRAM

JON WELLS

HarperCollins*PublishersLtd*

Published by HarperCollins Publishers Ltd

Originally published by John Wiley & Sons Canada, Ltd.: 2009

First published by HarperCollins Publishers Ltd in an e-pub edition: 2013
This HarperCollins trade paperback edition: 2015

HarperCollins books may be purchased for educational, business, or
sales promotional use through our Special Markets Department.

HarperCollins Publishers Ltd
2 Bloor Street East, 20th Floor
Toronto, Ontario, Canada
M4W 1A8

www.harpercollins.ca

Library and Archives Canada Cataloguing in Publication
information is available upon request

ISBN 978-1-44343-834-6

Printed and bound in the United States of America
RRD 9 8 7 6 5 4 3 2 1

This is for Pete Reintjes: Soldier, cop, friend—and a character worthy of his own book.

TABLE OF CONTENTS

PREFACE

I was exploring cases to investigate for my next serial mystery in the Hamilton Spectator, when I floated an email to Warren Korol. He is now an inspector with the Hamilton Police Service in Ontario, Canada, but had been a homicide detective when featured in my book Poison. Were there any recent cases that Korol felt might lend themselves to my extended treatment? "Take a look at the Budram case—there are some interesting issues," was all he wrote in reply. Typical cop understatement, but I'm glad he suggested it. Once into my research, I discovered that the disturbing and sad case of the Yvette Budram homicide was also as fascinating a true forensic crime story as one is likely to find. No doubt that is the reason I have been called by television network producers who read my original "Post-mortem" series in the Spectator and used it as a guide for their own documentary treatment.

As with my other books to date, *Post-Mortem* is written in a novelistic style, but every detail in the story is true, based entirely on reportage—first-hand observation, plus the study of hundreds of pages of court and police documents, and a suspect interrogation videotape. I conducted repeated interviews with sources such as police officers, lawyers, a forensic pathologist, family and friends of the victim, and even the killer himself. Of all the crime stories I've covered, Post-Mortem presented the greatest riches an investigative journalist could mine, in part because forensics was such a big part of the Yvette Budram case, and also because all of the officials who worked it were so open with me. In addition, my eye-witness research took me to the spot where the body had been discovered, and I observed detectives at work in two police forensic labs. I witnessed the magic of luminol illuminating blood droplets in the pitch dark, and I held a cold, rigid, severed digit from the victim's hand, then copied a procedure on the finger (explained in detail in the story) that had been a critical step towards police cracking the case.

Post-Mortem has been billed as a "true CSI story," and that it is. The CSI dramas on television are of course hugely popular, but also riddled with fiction. Real-life forensic detectives either enjoy the shows as pure entertainment or avoid them altogether, while some police officers and prosecutors bitterly rue their existence. As I touch upon in this story, the "*CSI* effect" on jurors at murder trials can even make it more difficult to convict killers. In this book I wanted to show the real thing, take readers into the true world of forensic investigation, where clues are painstakingly hunted over weeks and months, and where "X" rarely marks the spot. Learning how police and other experts—including a forensic anthropologist and forensic entomologist ("the Bug Lady") —worked to find justice for a woman who had been bludgeoned and her body left to rot, I hit upon a phrase that to me captured the essence of the case: Sometimes the mystery isn't just finding the killer, it's finding the victim.

ACKNOWLEDGMENTS

As with all of my serial narratives for the *Hamilton Spectator*, I wrote the "Post-mortem" series in my own mind as a book, with the hope that someday it would find its way between covers. It was Don Loney, the warm and engaging Executive Editor with John Wiley & Sons, who did so much to finally make that happen. We met at a journalism gala in Toronto a couple of years ago, and not long after that we had lunch at a café along Hamilton's beautifully restored waterfront. It was here that Don sketched out his vision for a series of books by Jon Wells. I was both impressed and dubious that it would happen. And here we are, on book number three and counting. Thanks so much, Don.

I want to thank everyone at Wiley, in fact, the public relations and design people and editors, great professionals all. And I want to express gratitude towards those who had a role in the original "Post-mortem" series at the *Spectator*. These colleagues included editor Douglas Haggo and designer Bob Hutton; senior editors Dana Robbins and Roger Gillespie encouraged me to run with the story and contributed suggestions and motivation along the way. Carmelina Prete offered feedback on early drafts and, as always, was a valuable friend. Photographer Gary Yokoyama's images, many of which appear in this book, were spectacular. Gary has a knack for drawing out his subjects and hitting precisely the right tone to match the story. I am a huge admirer of his talent and professionalism.

Most of all I thank the characters in the story whose candor and assistance allowed me to write the narrative with the detail and pace that I had imagined. Homicide and forensic detectives I interviewed, often repeatedly, with the City of Hamilton, Peel Region, and the NYPD, were all open and helpful, and all of these individuals I interviewed are referenced in this story at various points. I take this opportunity to single out extensive assistance from Hamilton Detective Paul Lahaie. (And I don't hold it against him that he ran me into the ground during his regular jog in baking heat, which is referenced in the book, although the reader will note that the author is carefully left out of the scene by name.) Detectives Mike Thomas and Gary Zwicker were enormously helpful, and thanks as well to Crown prosecutor Kevin McKenna and defense lawyer Tom Carey for their participation, and to Lisa Budram, who had the strength to meet and talk to me about an unimaginably painful chapter in her life. And finally, though I will never thank him, I simply note that I'm pleased the killer in this story saw fit to grant me an audience for an interview.

Chapter 1 ~ "Death in the Family"

The images and sounds did not invade his dreams, the snakes coiled in his conscience were kept at bay. At least, that's what he claimed. No flashes of red. No sickening crack. Yvette. White satin. The blood. The rope. *Why? Why the rope?* He loved Yvette. That much, he was sure. A beautiful woman, he thought the first time he met her. Olive skin, dark eyes. He would do anything for her. No, she did not always reciprocate his love, did not always speak to him in the most kindly manner. But that was just her way.

A horrible thing, what happened, he reflected. He believed karma would determine the man's ultimate punishment, because you never escape it—it follows you.

One thing was certain: the killer had shown calculation and composure when it was over. Tried to erase it all, leave no trace at the scene, or, perhaps, on his soul. Run from it. Run, do not look back, and deny, deny until the past is erased. In this, his attention to detail was imperfect, but his goal clear and cold. Only someone with a moral hollowness could go there. Or perhaps someone who has murdered before.

A man approached the travel agent behind the counter, urgency in his voice. Need an air ticket for departure out of Pearson International Airport down the highway in Toronto. Flying out of the country. Tonight. One-way. The travel agent glanced at the schedule. British West Indian Airlines had flights to the customer's requested destination. He checked the time. It was 1:30 p.m.

"There's no flight tonight," the agent said. "BWIA flies out at 2:45 p.m., you won't be able to catch it."

"What would be tomorrow's flight?" the customer asked.

"There's no seat on the special fare, it will cost you more. The next flight on the special fare is in four days."

"No. This is an emergency," he said, and pulled out his MasterCard.

On short notice, for tomorrow's flight, a one-way ticket would cost $1,060. Departs at 11:40 p.m. One stop in Antigua en route.

"Have to be there immediately," the man said. "Death in the family."

* * *

8th Concession, West Flamborough, Ontario
October 4, 2000, 6:20 a.m.

If the dark eyes could see, if the face could turn up to the sky, the
view would offer a peek through tall grass, weeds, leaves of an old
basswood, and the morning's first light filtered through rain clouds.
It is quiet beside the rolling cornfield, the only sound that of wind
brushing leaves, the buzz of insects. A rumble of thunder. Rain
ticks the cornfield, trees. Drops perhaps find their way to that very
spot, through the brush, and dot the cold skin of the neck where
the crescent-moon pendant rests. It had been a bad astrological
period. A Saturn phase. The iron pendant would bring luck.

Summer had never really arrived that year, it was the kind
of summer in which the sky seems a perpetual dead gray, rain is
never far away, and the cool air always seems to betray an end
rather than a beginning.

In the early evening, clouds break, the sun shoots rays of light
between the tree branches. The clarity lasts just an hour. Then
darkness bleeds into the blue sky.

Hamilton Police Services

8th Concession, West Flamborough

* * *

Clop-clop, clop-clop, clop-clop.

A fall morning, Luke stepping along the country road for his daily walk. He was white with brown spots, a 10-year-old jack—a male donkey not gelded, and so constantly in search of a female. Catherine got him out as often as she could for walks that fall so he could burn off energy. She smiled. Poor guy. Typical male.

Three months earlier, Catherine and her husband, Adam, moved to the house on a farm lot out in rural Hamilton, 20 minutes outside the city, just down a bit along Cooper Road from the popular African Lion Safari tourist attraction. They had always dreamt of living in the country. The area was called the Town of Flamborough before amalgamation made it part of Hamilton. An odd duck of a place. Great wads of open space, hamlets, a mobile-home community called Beverly Hills. Some local rebels, unimpressed with the thought of joining Steeltown, put up a creaky display sign on the side of Highway 8 that read, "Free Flamboro."

On occasion visitors passing through the place with something to hide treated it like one giant rural alleyway, a place to sweep things under the rug. Stolen purses and wallets littered ditches near where Catherine and Adam lived. That fireball they saw one night just down the street from their house was a stolen car somebody had dumped and lit up. Their own home had been broken into once already, but they weren't planning on leaving.

Clop-clop, clop-clop, clop-clop.

Catherine and Luke turned left off Cooper Road and walked up the 8th Concession. That's when the smell hit. You live in the country, you get used to strong odors. But this was overpowering, rancid. Luke, he didn't care, the jack's mind was elsewhere. It was coming from over there, the other side of the ditch, somewhere in the thick roadside brush at the end of a cornfield. Couldn't see anything unusual, though. Had to be a dead animal somewhere. Maybe a deer. They headed for home.

Clop-clop, clop-clop, clop-clop.

Most days that fall Catherine walked Luke and couldn't help but pass that same spot along the road. The smell eventually faded. Nothing lasts. Days grew short, leaves, drained of life turned and dropped in the fall winds, returning to the soil. The rain fell cold and hard. Catherine and Adam's house got burglarized a second time. Nobody was caught.

That winter, the winter of 2001, was a nasty one. Unrelenting bitter cold for weeks on end, allowing unusually heavy snow to build, blanketing the country fields and the leaves and other broken remains that had once lived and shone with color.

* * *

Gary Yokoyama

Hamilton Detective Paul Lahaie.

Hamilton, Ontario

The homicide detective's dark eyes stared pensively through the windshield at the nondescript building, as though a clue would miraculously show itself. Twenty-six-year-old male, beaten to a pulp, left to bleed to death right there, in Unit 6. Marijuana grow operation inside. Paul Lahaie thought about the Damian cold case at least once a day. In conversation he usually referred to it by the first name of the victim, rather than wrestle with pronouncing the last name (*Dim-eet-rash...*) of Damian Dymitraszczuk. Even if he wasn't working the case, he would sometimes come here, pull off Rymal Road onto Lancing Drive for a look, in the part of south Hamilton that sat atop the modest elevation of the Niagara Escarpment—which locals had always called, without irony, "the Mountain."

Lahaie did not follow the axiom that you should never look back. On the job, at least, working for the Major Crime Unit with Hamilton Police, he lived in the past most every day. There had been leads in the Damian case, but mostly dead ends. Some in the grow subculture who knew the victim had been hesitant to talk. "The guy lived by the sword, died by the sword," some said. And those were his *friends* saying that, reflected Lahaie. That kind of sentiment always offended him. Everyone deserves justice.

Lahaie liked to think of the Major Crime detectives as thoroughbreds, chasing every case full bore. He felt that some police services went after some cases harder than others, influenced by the status of the victim, public interest in the crime, political optics. Not Hamilton. Should never matter who the victim is. Ever.

His unmarked car descended the Mountain, Lake Ontario along Steeltown's north shore as still and blue as a painting in the distance, and the skyline of Toronto 45 minutes to the east so clear it looked like you could reach out and touch it. Downtown, in the lower city, Lahaie arrived at Central Station on King William Street, mounted the stairs to the second floor and strode into the Major Crime Unit, past the sign on the door that read: *No Witnesses, Lawyers, Media*. Lahaie was 6-foot-1, 190 pounds, lifted weights in the gym and ran to stay in shape. He had short dark hair and his skin bore a faint tanned cast. The surname was French and he looked Italian, he joked. One old-school senior officer seemed to delight in barking out his name pronounced as *Lay-hee* rather than the proper *La-hay*. Maybe an anti-French thing, Lahaie grinned.

He loved talking about his roots. His great-grandfather had come to Hamilton from Quebec in the 1890s, a cigar rolling craftsman who worked for Tuckett Tobacco Company and married an English woman. Policing did not run in the family bloodline, quite the contrary. In the basement of his boyhood home in a part of Hamilton called Saltfleet, next to a large crucifix figurine, sat a black wicker basket. It was a gift, the story went, years ago to his grandfather Jack Lahaie, from legendary Hamilton mobster Rocco Perri. Jack was a bootlegger who helped Rocco run liquor, even once installed an airplane engine for Rocco in a cigar boat to give it a little extra kick for the task.

Lahaie figured perhaps his desire to be a cop had roots in his Catholic upbringing. Wasn't helping people what being a Christian was all about? Not that everyone in Steeltown appreciated the help the way he'd like every time. Once he was at Jackson Square Mall downtown, Christmastime, and there's a teenager outside sitting up on a concrete ledge, high above the sidewalk. The kid had wrapped his belt around his neck and attached it to a railing, threatened to jump, even as the crowd moved back and forth below. Lahaie, in the cerebral way he had of thinking about things, paused to reflect that it was something of an Orwellian moment, this tunnel-vision glazed look on the faces of shoppers, who either were oblivious to the kid's predicament or didn't care. So Lahaie gingerly snuck up behind, trying not to make the ice under his feet crack aloud, and lunged and grabbed the teen before he could do himself in. And then, later, he gets a call from the kid's mother. Thanking him? Not quite. She accused him of *stealing her son's wallet*.

Back when he graduated from McMaster University in Hamilton, Lahaie couldn't find a job. He had simply felt lucky to even have a shot at university; it always seemed to him that for guys like him, it was in their genes to go straight from high school to a job in the steel mills down on the lake. Instead he graduated from Mac, where he'd studied economics, geography, and politics. Didn't help him land a job, though. Applied at place after place, walking door to door. Collected all the rejection letters and made a collage out of them, which he framed and hung in his parents' basement. Got a job with the National Film Board screening movies at a warehouse down on Dundurn Street. Exposed him to some high-brow thinking, felt like he was soaking up wisdom like a sponge each day. The job hunt experience gave him a bit of a chip on his shoulder, though. Maybe that also came from his childhood, when he got called his share of names growing up in Saltfleet, in part because of the olive cast to his skin. Hershey. Nigger. You name it. Or maybe he got the chip from Ma. She was a feminist, quick as a whip, did not suffer fools gladly. She once wrote a letter to Harold Ballard, the bombastic owner of the Hamilton Ticats football team, after Ballard was quoted in the media saying that women were "only good for lying on their backs." In her letter, Ma wrote that, given Ballard's comment, she couldn't very well sit upright enough to attend a football game. She demanded the club cancel her season tickets. His dad, meanwhile, was a simple man, a straight-ahead nice guy, career Stelco steel man. But after the war, Dad also had the nerve to scab for Stelco during a particularly nasty strike in the strongest union town in Canada.

As a young man Lahaie landed an interview down at Central Station. He was turned down. He turned instead to the Mounties, the RCMP, landing a job that sent him out west. And then, in 1987, at 29, he returned to Hamilton and a position with the city police, a confident experienced officer. At that first, unsuccessful, job interview with the Hamilton force, the chip had still been there, the rejection letters fresh in his mind. The interview had not gone well and Lahaie was so ticked-off he stood up to leave and pointed his finger at the senior officer who had sat across the desk from him.

"Someday I'll be the one sitting on the other side of the table wearing sergeant's stripes," Lahaie said. "I guarantee it."

His personality was one of contrasts. The pewter-rimmed glasses he came to wear masked the hangdog weariness that characterized the shape of his eyes. Subtle specks of gray in his hair, conservative dark suits, and the quiet, grave tone of voice he used around those who were neither friends nor colleagues gave him a serious air, belied the manic laugh and offbeat sense of humor that ran just below the surface. During his seven years working on the Hamilton Police tactical unit, Lahaie got tagged with the menacing nickname Ninja. But then, too, he would howl telling a story from his first day working for the RCMP out in B.C., when he forgot to bring ammunition for his gun. Called it his Barney Fife story, a reference to the bumbling sheriff's deputy from the old *Andy Griffith* TV show. Still broke him up.

His first case with Major Crime was in 1997 when he got seconded from the child abuse branch in the middle of what had been a fruitless police hunt for a rapist striking in the Hamilton suburb of Stoney Creek. The case had made big headlines in the *Hamilton Spectator*, which dubbed the predator The Ravine Rapist. He was suspected of having terrorized women off and on for more than a decade, preying in the middle of the night on victims who lived along ravines in that area. One victim died from an assault, another suffered permanent disabilities after being stabbed in the head with a screwdriver, eight other women suffered from attacks and death threats. He also spied through windows of homes and burglarized several of them, where he had stolen pieces of lingerie and other personal items of women. Police had handed out composite sketches of the rapist to more than 2,000 homes in the area. They were feeling the heat on the case. One columnist in the *Spectator* wondered if "lackadaisical police work, underfunding or simple police screwups" had stunted the hunt for the rapist from the start.

"So, *Lay-hee*," a senior officer growled at the detective. "You arrest my serial rapist yet?"

"Sir," Lahaie replied, "I promise you he will be arrested in 21 days."

Why 21? Lahaie wasn't sure, the bold prediction just popped out. As it happened, James (Ted) Wren was arrested in 19 days, and Lahaie played a prominent role, helping develop the profile of the rapist, and uncovering an important piece of evidence, a collage of photos of the victims hidden behind a ceiling panel. Wren was a big-time sexual deviant, Lahaie reflected. He thought the guy had the look of a predator, a cold, bloodless focus to the eyes resembling that of a shark. Felt great to get him off the street.

Losses and unsolved cases stick with detectives more than successes, though. Paul Lahaie often thought of a line from a book called *A Terrible Love of War*: it's harder to kill the dead than the living, because memories live forever. He thought it applied to the job: *I am the keeper of the memories.* They don't go away, not until the case is closed.

"Pauly," one of the detectives greeted Lahaie as he approached his desk in Central Station. Lahaie cracked a cold can of soda water, opened a black binder, and walked the corridors of murders past. Every once in a while when he had spare time, he would look through the department's historical homicide index, listing every case over the years, who investigated, the outcome. He flipped the pages. One of the entries always caught his eye, the question mark jumping out at the eye, a painful reminder of an unsolved case. It read:

Cindy Williams/unsolved
murder-abduction?
July 26, 1974

He turned to the corresponding case file folder. Page 1 was a photo of a little blond girl staring back at him. Four years old. The victim. Cindy. The case had been long before his time, but Lahaie felt his throat tighten. That kind of stuff got to him. The last notes were made in 1996. "So who speaks for Cindy Williams?" Lahaie wondered. She had disappeared one summer day from her family's Fennell Avenue East apartment near Upper Ottawa on the east Mountain. Kids from her neighborhood were haunted by her disappearance for years; some grew up in the same area, had families, and never stopped wondering whatever happened to her. Back then, in the 1970s, police had fewer forensic investigative tools for a case like that. Most notably, they didn't have DNA to work with. But cops were resourceful in the old days, too. Today? Better technology, but the cases got complicated, killers covered their tracks better.

Cases like Damian and Cindy Williams were tough nuts to crack. And yet, as difficult as those unsolved cases are, at least police had a general sense of what might have happened—and to whom. Detective Paul Lahaie was about to learn that there are occasions, however, when the mystery is not just finding the killer. It is finding the victim.

* * *

8th Concession West, Flamborough
Tuesday, April 17, 2001
3:40 p.m.

The jogger's shoes rhythmically scuffed along the 8th Concession. Steve Dmytrus was a firefighter but off-duty that afternoon. His wife was a high school science teacher, and so on his runs he always kept his eyes open for anything interesting for her to bring in to class for show-and-tell. He was a few minutes along the road from his home.

It had snowed on and off that morning. Everything gray—the sky, the lifeless vegetation. This early in the season, the brush did not yet sport fresh growth, although in a few weeks it would be filled in again. Flesh color. It crossed his line of vision, off to the left in the brush. Dmytrus stopped. It was the spot where Catherine and her donkey Luke had smelled something seven months earlier, where even a family doctor had passed on foot earlier in the spring and noticed something, but figured it was a dead deer in the brush.

Dmytrus stopped and wondered. Was it a dead animal? It looked like a deer hide, he thought. He moved closer, just off the edge of the road, standing on the gravel shoulder, just a couple of meters away from it. The firefighter knew anatomy. He could see bones. Leg bones. But it was what was connected to the bones that made his heart jump. They looked like feet. And they were definitely human. And was that black hair? A shirt? Don't get any closer, he thought. He turned and started back for home, his gait quickening.

The phone rang at 5:05 p.m. in the Major Crime Unit at Central Station. Sitting among the cluster of desks in the office, Detective Sergeant Mike Thomas, the senior man on duty, answered. It was a superintendent on the line. Not a good sign, Thomas reflected. Thomas turned to Detective Paul Lahaie. A body had been found out in Flamborough. Major Crime is required to attend at the scene. The detectives stood and slipped on suit jackets over top of their Glock semiautomatic pistols, then their overcoats, and headed downstairs to the carpool garage. It was just about quitting time. And no one was going home.

Gary Yokoyama

The spot along the 8th Concession where the body was discovered.

Chapter 2 ~ Shallow Grave

8th Concession West, Flamborough
Tuesday, April 17, 2001
6 p.m.

The video camera lens panned out. Ditch. Brush. Cornfield. Trees. Yellow tape surrounding the possible crime scene. Now narrowing the focus: a body, lying among short brush, about four meters from the edge of the country road. The body was partly submerged in the dirt, though not apparently from any attempt to dig a shallow grave, but simply from sinking into the soil over time. And in fact this was not the place to try burying much of anything. The entire area was bedrock. Call a guy to come and dig a hole to install a post in that part of Flamborough, and he won't do it.

After the uniforms, Ident was on the scene first—forensic identification. The eye looking through the lens belonged to Gary Zwicker, forensic investigator with Hamilton Police. As usual, Zwicker, who had a lean, compact frame, was armed at the scene with both a camera and a Glock, combination of a cop and a scientist. First rule, always record the scene as you find it. Don't walk in and start handling potential evidence, not until after you photograph and videotape everything. Walk over a crime scene and, one day—if you're fortunate enough to get the case through the system to court—a defense lawyer will try to expose you on the stand. Zwicker knew that's the way the system goes. Police work is put on trial, not just the accused, the O.J. Simpson case being the highest-profile example. Forensics officers take pride in work that requires minute attention to the smallest detail. Some find it disconcerting to be cross-examined with an eye towards discrediting the job you felt was done thoroughly.

They are known by different names. In the United States they are often called crime scene investigators. In Hamilton, the old title was identification officer ("ident officer"), and it has stuck, even though the modern title is forensic detective or forensic investigator. Zwicker, who was an easy-going guy with a dry sense of humor, had been a uniformed cop first, got into forensics later. Some of the forensics types were cut from different cloth than typical cops.

Years back, in a classroom at the Ontario Police College in Aylmer, Zwicker heard the excited voice. "Hey, you gotta come over here!"

Zwicker looked across the room and saw a group of forensic investigators huddled together. What, he thought playfully, is there golf involved? Zwicker was attending an investigation course on forensic entomology—the study of insects and their behavior to help crack crimes. An interesting field. Insects are sometimes the first ones on the scene of a homicide. Know their behavior, and they might provide a lead. Anyway, somebody in the class was pretty excited about something. Zwick walked over to the table. Maggots. In the course they had learned that blowflies lay their eggs on a corpse in any available moist, warm opening—the mouth, a wound. Over time, maggots hatching from the eggs migrate across the dead body, searching for another warm orifice. They leave a trail as they move. You can determine when the maggots started the migration—which can pinpoint the time of death and other timeline details about the wounds, and therefore the crime, even the type of location where the murder took place. One of the guys in class was observing a maggot trail on a pig carcass.

"There it is, there's the trail!" one officer said.

Zwicker's eyes expanded in mock excitement. O-kay. This was interesting stuff, very useful to know, but there were a few things in life that elicited unrestrained excitement from him. His baby daughter. Golf. Maggots weren't high up on the list.

Zwicker had never thought he would gravitate to forensics. Took first-year biology at university, but that didn't spark anything. In his previous life as a uniformed cop, Zwicker made the news-paper for his bravery, received two citations at fire scene rescues, once put his foot through a door trying to save a child inside a burning house, another time carried a man down a fire escape to safety. But when he attended a crime scene investigation course in 1995, he was hooked. This was what he wanted to do.

Forensic detectives need patience, a sharp mind, an eye for detail. And a strong stomach. Cops are a tough breed, but the ident guys see things that most cops would rather not. See rookie ident man Zwicker collecting bagged pieces of a woman's mutilated corpse in a suburban home. A dismemberment case. Zwicker is not just staring into a dark abyss somewhere in the human soul—he's climbing right in and walking around inside. Back then, in 1999, he had been in the forensic department less than a year. He was on the scene with two senior officers, hadn't even taken the basic ident course. Zwick was not yet married back then, did not have a little girl at home. Maybe that was a good thing. No one should have to experience stuff like this, Zwicker thought.

If anybody thought he got enjoyment out of handling body parts, they were nuts. But he knew it was an important job. Has to be done. Take photos. Gather the evidence. Get it done. Zwicker took more than 2,000 photos in that house, macabre snapshots burned into film and, perhaps, his memory.

Gary Yokoyama

Forensic Detective Gary Zwicker.

* * *

Science and technology used in criminal investigation is nothing new—the first conviction based on fingerprint evidence dates back to 1911. What is new is the focus on forensic science in the culture as the ace card in fighting crime; on men and women who chase criminals not down dark alleys but under fluorescent lights in a lab, detecting microscopic residues of foul play, outwitting the "perps" by technology and force of reason. On television dramas these new heroes do not merely complement traditional police work, they are the star players. Popular culture academic Tim Blackmore wrote that, in part, the celebration of the "rationalist scientist hero" or the "scientist-as-priest" comes from society's faith in the scientific method. "We like the idea," Blackmore wrote, "that horrific problems that are initially so bad they seem to be insoluble, can be taken apart and explained at least enough so that the mystery is erased, and in doing so, banish our worries."

So the culture turns to researchers (Tom Clancy's Jack Ryan character), technicians (TV's CSI shows), behavioral psychologists, and even math whizzes (on the show *Numb3rs*) who can, through use of pure reason married to some indefinable, almost magical, instinct, see their way to the truth. That means that a hero is never further away than the local university laboratory—although brainy forensic heroes on shows like *Criminal Minds* and CSI shows also improbably swoop to crime scenes and run roughshod over the uniformed cops and homicide detectives, barking orders and—even more improbably—making arrests. The fascination with cracking the criminal mind perhaps came full circle with TV's *Dexter*, where the forensic investigator/hero is himself a serial killer, as though the only way law enforcement can really get down and dirty with evil is to use evil to understand and combat it.

Real-life forensic detectives laugh off the forensic TV shows. They know that some of the techniques are real, but Hollywood also takes it a few steps further into fiction. No investigator has the technology at their fingertips to sit at a computer, scan in a fingerprint and instantly see a match pop on the screen complete with photo and geographic location, all in less than ten seconds. Forensic detective Gary Zwicker gave talks to students: Sorry to burst your bubble, folks, but in real life CSIs do not interrogate suspects, much less tell uniformed cops to arrest anybody. Police rue the impact of the shows. For one thing, criminals watch TV, too, learn how to better cover their tracks. Hide the body, clean up the scene, bleach to kill the DNA, wear rubber gloves to conceal fingerprints. (Prints can be lifted from the gloves themselves, however.) Forensic detectives constantly upgrade their education to stay ahead of the game, take courses in bloodstain pattern recognition, DNA sample collection, advanced friction ridge analysis—how to use new technology to identify ridges in fingerprints by thickness and shape. There is even a course in footwear identification. Someone boots a door in, it leaves a print. Ceramic is good, too, for leaving an identifiable mark. The key, of course, is having a real shoe to match the print. Shoe prints can have "accidental characteristics," different wear patterns, maybe a piece of glass has nicked a piece out of the tread. Same goes for tire marks: you can make a mold of the print, study it for characteristics to match it to a vehicle.

Another impact of the shows has been to raise the bar in court for prosecutors seeking to convict, to impress juries with evidence, because TV elevates expectations of regular people. Given the technology and brainpower available, shouldn't every crime be cracked? Sharp defense lawyers are well aware of the trend and play on it. There was the time Gary Zwicker was on the stand for an assault case, a drug-deal hit. Someone had used an aluminum baseball bat to attack another person in a parking lot. Zwicker had lifted the accused's fingerprints from a car in the lot, which put the accused at the crime scene.

"Detective Zwicker," the defense lawyer asked, "why didn't you get a print from the handle of the baseball bat as well? If the bat was used in the offense, obviously the prints would also show up on the bat, where he had been holding it"—for effect, before the jury, he now motioned as though clutching a bat with both hands, squeezing tight.

No, thought Zwicker, not obvious at all. Lifting a quality print depends on several factors, among them the type of surface and hand pressure. Squeezing a bat hard, as you would in an attack, smudges prints. Moreover, rubber (used to make the grip portion of an aluminum baseball bat) is not the ideal surface, either.

"The deposition pressure on the bat would be heavy, which causes distortion," Zwicker replied. "And other surfaces are more conducive to the deposition of prints."

It got so prosecutors would remind the jury of the difference between fiction and the real world, right in their opening remarks: *I note, members of the jury, there is no miracle fiber in this case, so don't think we're going to spring it on you at the end.* Police and prosecutors had a phrase for this influence on juries hurting their cases. They called it "the *CSI* effect."

* * *

Gary Zwicker continued filming just off the 8th Concession. The question hung out there. Was he documenting a crime scene? Even that wasn't certain. Body has obviously been here a long time. But could be someone who simply collapsed one day long ago. Old hit-and-run accident? No. Homicide? You're in forensics long enough, you feel when something isn't right. His instinct off the top was to think foul play.

Detectives say the first couple of hours after a possible homicide are the most crucial in an investigation. That's when traces of human evidence are freshest, memories are sharpest among witnesses, and the killer might still be in the area. But if the corpse near the 8th Concession had a story to tell Gary Zwicker, it was probably many months old. Forensic cops are internally wired to be optimistic, their mindset is one that combines scientific probabilities and on-the-job experience. The laws of physical evidence suggest that something should be there. A fiber. Blood. An impression. Zwicker had faith in his training but also faith in the criminal, faith that a killer, no matter how devious or careful, will slip up, somehow. He has broken the rules, violently, brutally. Somehow, some way, he will show weakness, he will leave something, he will be caught.

The area where the body lay was among the worst kind of crime scenes, he reflected. Talk about looking for needles in haystacks; in this one, there were a whole bunch of needles. It was a dumping ground for stolen items, wallets, purses. Everything could be a potential clue. The cime scene is the starting point for most homicide investigations. Comb through the refuse, look for traces of the victim, the killer, look for ghosts, reassemble the story. Zwicker believed that there are always clues left behind at a scene. Always. Maybe, he thought, it's one needle in a whole bunch of haystacks. But it's there, somewhere. The question is can you find it?

Now he could see it through the camera lens, the exposed bones of the remains, skin stretched over part of the skeleton like a tawny sheet. "Who are you?" Zwicker asked himself. "And how did you get here?" He knew identity was going to be the starting point. But was identification of the victim even possible?

* * *

Gary Yokoyama

Forensic anthropologist Shelley Saunders.

"Shelley, it's Warren."

The anthropologist heard the familiar police baritone, informal yet polite, on her voice mail at home. There must be a case. Shelley Saunders was tall and slim—sandy blond hair, green eyes, a gentle calm to her face and manner. Tonight, the eyes met light thrown from her home computer, focused on her work. Dr. Saunders, a professor of anthropology at McMaster University, had developed an interesting expertise on the side, related to her work studying the ancient dead: forensic anthropology.

Science ran in the family. In the 1950s her father had worked on Canada's secretive Avro Arrow fighter jet project and, when the initiative was scrapped in a storm of controversy, he took his family to Ohio where he continued in the field, for North American Aviation. Shelley was drawn to biological anthropology from the first time she heard the lectures as an undergraduate, had a fascination with learning who and what people had been, the biological variability, particularly in the recent past—meaning 10,000 years ago in anthropological history, fitting the pieces together. Saunders elected to spend her career focusing on fossil remains. She was not one of the glamor seekers, the Indiana Jones crowd, as she called them, whose main goal was to make a name for themselves by finding the *ultimate-earliest-human-fossil!*

She built a lofty reputation in the field and was known for innovative teaching techniques. Once, when teaching a course in human evolution, she had students in her class drip their feet in black paint, then run down a hallway, so they could measure gait and stride length. Her research sometimes meant devoting hundreds of hours focusing, for example, on microscopic striations on part of a tooth that had once belonged to an ancient Roman child. Teeth preserve well over the centuries, do not break down, they are perfect for study, capturing a moment in time. Each striation shows a different health stress point in a person's life.

Forensic anthropology, though, that was a different game. These were the occasions when she was asked by police to help unravel mysteries of the past—but quickly, just like the fictional character Temperance Brennan, the hero forensic anthropologist of the novel series by Kathy Reichs, an author and real-life scientist Saunders knew personally. (The series sold briskly, but Saunders was not a fan.) The novels eventually led to a TV series called *Bones*. The show looked pretty bad, from what little of it Saunders had seen, although she joked that everybody in her department wanted to get their hands on one of those magical—and fictional— holographic reconstruction machines seen on the show.

It was in 1987 that she first became involved in this new practical application for her expertise. She got a call from forensic pathologist Dr. Chitra Rao at Hamilton General Hospital, asking if she would help determine the age of a mummified corpse found in a boxcar down near the steel mills. The body had been inside the car for about a year. It was a homeless man who used to panhandle in front of the liquor store on Dundurn Street. One winter day he had sought refuge from the cold in the boxcar, and spent his final moments there. Saunders reported to the hospital morgue, examined the skeleton, cleaned and studied the bones to determine age. Interesting. Her morphological examination suggested the man might be in his late 40s. But using the histological method—examining cell development—he looked significantly older. Heavy drinking over the course of his life had damaged tissue, causing greater turnover in the cells, creating open spaces in the bone. Final answer: he was 58.

Another of her early cases was in the Niagara region, where divers had recovered the remains of bodies after a plane crash and found just a few bones. Saunders studied parts of femurs, a tooth, a hip-bone fragment. She estimated one of the men was 30 to 34 years old, the other 25 to 29. From the femur, or thigh bone, she offered a height estimate for each man. Her findings matched the conjecture of detectives. She had confirmed the identity of the victims.

The message from Warren, on Saunders's voice mail, had continued: "Shelley, we've got a situation here. Got some remains in Flamborough and we're hoping you can help us out." The voice belonged to Hamilton Detective Sergeant Warren Korol. He had first met Saunders in the Hamilton General morgue when he worked the Sheryl Sheppard case. Sheppard, a 29-year-old former exotic dancer and doughnut shop worker, had gone missing in January 1998 and was presumed murdered. Some bones had been found at the bottom of a hydro dam in Niagara. Saunders offered an opinion on the nature of the bones, in case there was some connection to Sheppard. Korol thought Shelley was a dynamic lady, extremely intelligent. Turned out that the bones were not Sheppard's, and her body was never found.

After hearing Korol's message, Saunders knew she would need to drive to McMaster University, where her office was tucked into the end of a narrow hallway on the fifth floor of Chester New Hall. Her office was not much bigger than a walk-in closet, with models of skulls decorating a packed bookshelf. Her kit for attending crime scenes was like a large fishing tackle box, containing trowels and brushes. For this new case, Saunders knew, she would need to take the blue box out into the country. Might need to do an excavation. Her academic work focused on examining clues, meticulously, over years, to gradually unearth answers about those who had died long ago. The death of the person in this new case would not be so ancient.

Chapter 3 ~ Jane Doe

8th Concession, Flamborough
6:10 p.m.

It was an hour before sunset, the April sky cold and gray, temperature just above freezing, the light dusting of snow from the morning still on the ground. Paul Lahaie felt the crisp air on his face, pulled out his pen, the eyes taking mental pictures. The homicide detective wrote in his white soft-cover exercise-style Homicide Case Book. He noted police tape at both ends of 8th Concession West, guarded by uniform officers who protected the scene and documented times of entry for all investigators. Lahaie saw Gary Zwicker and wrote: "*Ident on scene taking photographs and video.*"

When Lahaie was with the RCMP in western Canada, they would take rough notes in the field, then transcribe them as finished notes later. No such luxury in Hamilton. You don't have time to transcribe. Take notes by hand on the fly, at the scene, and that's it. Be accurate, it might end up under the microscope in court, the notes must be unimpeachable, the bible of the investigation. He was a stickler for detail, drew diagrams, attached small documents, made notes on legal points.

Interesting. He could tell the brush where the remains lay had been trimmed recently, all along that side of the country road, down to a height of 12 to 15 centimeters. Probably that's why the body had been spotted.

Lahaie spoke with the uniforms who were first at the scene, learned about the firefighter's discovery while jogging. Soon the other Major Crime Unit detectives working his shift had arrived: Mike Thomas, Dave Place, Donnie Forgan, and the most senior officer, Warren Korol.

18:12. Det./Sgt. Thomas and Det. Forgan arrive.
18:25. Det./Sgt. Korol arrives.

Detectives Paul Lahaie (left) and Gary Zwicker at the scene.

They all noticed the sign up the road a bit, marking the boundary of a city northwest of Hamilton, called Cambridge. If their scene had been just a couple of hundred meters farther down the road, it would have belonged to neighboring Waterloo Regional Police.

"Maybe we should move the sign," quipped Dave Place.

None of them would trade their positions in Major Crime, the most prestigious investigative office in the service. But it was also the most time-consuming. You were never really off the clock. They were ready to engage the new case, but in a perfect world they would all be home for dinner, not on a barren country road staring at a decomposed body. As the senior man, Warren Korol was technically in charge of the crime scene, but he knew his command would not last. He was less than four weeks away from getting locked down as the lead investigator in the first trial for serial poisoner Sukhwinder Dhillon.

Paul Lahaie moved in closer towards the body.

Observations made from the roadway. The body is on the south side of the road off of 8th Concession W. Trees along the road, stone shoulder, ditch. Behind the brush line is an open field for farmers.

The sky darkened as Dr. David King arrived on the scene at 7:20 p.m. There was still a hint of natural light as King walked with the detectives to within three meters of the body lying in the brush. The renowned forensic pathologist from Hamilton General Hospital was slim, had silver hair, and spoke softly and with traces of a British accent, an echo of his childhood in the United Kingdom, where his father had been a family doctor and, for a time, worked as a policeman. No pathologist can say anything for certain by taking a cursory look at a decomposed corpse, but King, who had 30 years of experience in his field, had seen almost everything. The detectives were hungry for any observations he could make.

King saw that the left arm was down alongside the body, while the right arm was bent under the chest. Had the body been rolled or thrown in order to assume that position, he wondered? It certainly did not look like the person had just collapsed and died on the spot.

Gary Yokoyama

Forensic pathologist Dr. David King.

"The remains appear face down," he said. "Some flesh on the back and on one arm but the legs are exposed to the bone. The body remains appear to be mummified." There wasn't much left of the body, but he knew it could have been worse. All that snow from the winter, low temperatures, probably protected the remains from animals, and thus complete decomposition.

"At first glance," King said, "it appears to be a young female."

After dark, the detectives gathered in a Hamilton police command van that had arrived on the scene. Warren Korol looked at the other detectives.

"So what are the possibilities here?" he asked.

Pooling their experience, brainstorming, this was what they did in the early hours at a murder scene. None of them had been thrilled to get a suspicious death call at quitting time, come all the way out here, but now the adrenalin was flowing. A new scene, a new puzzle to put together. Missing persons was the first consideration. If there's someone out there who cares about this dead woman, they will have reported her missing. Phone Waterloo police, get them to check their missing persons files as well. If David King was correct, and the body was female, one hypothetical instantly leapt to the top of the list.

"There could be a nervous boyfriend out there somewhere," said Detective Mike Thomas.

Another possibility was that she was a murdered prostitute. They were dealing with a mummified corpse that had gone through seasonal changes. Should think about getting a forensic entomologist down here—a scientist who studies insect breeding and migration on corpses to learn about the manner and timing of death.

"Let's get the Bug Lady."

David King had taken a stab at general details. He was going to need some help in the light of day. Secure the scene, protect the body by erecting a tent over top, but do not disturb it, wait for daylight to examine the scene, and remains, properly. The body has already been there for a long time. Just before 10 p.m., Paul Lahaie drove back downtown to the Major Crime Unit and finished writing his notes before heading home.

22:00. MCU. Finished.

On the cover of his white Homicide Case Book, in black marker he wrote a case number and title.

1-461723-0
Jane Doe

* * *

8th Concession West
April 18, 2001

The next day, Wednesday morning, the silver BMW stopped along the soft shoulder, and the tall fair-haired woman got out, popped the trunk. She took out a large blue box and carried it towards the yellow police tape. Detective Gary Zwicker was waiting for her. He had never met forensic anthropologist Shelley Saunders before. Zwicker smiled to himself. She looked like the lady next door, and here she was on hand to try to help them crack a murder.

"Dr. Saunders," he said.

Police officers were always so polite, she reflected. In the anthropology department at McMaster, it was funny, women at the reception desk always knew when a plainclothes Hamilton detective had arrived to see Shelley. They would stride off the elevator, always wearing a jacket and tie, carrying a paper bag with bones inside. And it wasn't just how the detectives looked, it was how they sounded. Unfailingly formal, relative to those working in the academic world.

Saunders suggested to Zwicker that they perform a basic excavation of the scene, remove everything around the body for potential evidence, then gradually move closer to the victim. By 1:20 p.m., they were on their knees, meticulously clipping brush. In her academic work, Saunders was accustomed to working deliberately. If you look closely enough at remains of the dead, study diligently, peel back layer after layer of evidence, synthesize what you have, a picture will emerge. But forensic anthropology is different. You do not have months, much less years, to study the bones of a corpse when there's a killer at large. Still, even at a crime scene: patience. A picture will emerge.

After they had cleared leaves and weeds and clutter around the body, Saunders handed Zwicker a small brush. They began dusting the surface of the remains, cleaning off dirt, leaves, vegetation.

"So how fast are we going compared to an archeological dig?" Zwicker asked.

"Indy 500 speed."

Meanwhile, as they had that first night, the Major Crime detectives continued to canvass the area, interview residents, search for clues. With so little known about the victim, every possible angle had to be chased. Paul Lahaie called for an OPP helicopter to survey the area. The detective was noting anything of even remote interest, including a man who happened to stop by the scene in his car shortly after 1 p.m. just to see what was going on.

13:16. Silver Neon [or] Focus, w/m mid-to-late 30s, light brown hair (reddish) mustache with a cocker spaniel stopped and asked me what happened. He walks his dog in the area. Can't relate any suspicious occurrences. 13:17. Left the area driving s/b on Cooper Road.

A spent rifle shell was found in the ditch. A local hunter was interviewed about hunting activity in the area. Detective Dave Place found a bracelet in the weeds near the body. And a watch. There was a serial number on the watch. Could it be stolen, offer an identification clue? Most finds at a crime scene go nowhere, but still require precious time to explore. Every lead must be checked off. Place punched in the watch numbers on the CPIC computer, Canadian Police Information Centre. It was a dead end. They found a ring. Inside were weathered initials that said either MAS or HAS. Did it mean anything?

Lahaie found a wallet with documents belonging to a woman named Caroline, a Humber College student. He ran her information. The woman lived near Guelph, 45 minutes north of their scene. He ran a police check on her. Caroline had been listed on one database as being suicidal. Was that it? Suicide? Could she be the one?

4:45. Entered the inner perimeter to observe the dig.

An hour later, back at Central Station, Lahaie got a call from a police contact looking into the wallet. Turned out the woman who owned it shared the same name, but was not the same Caroline who had been reported suicidal at one time. The other Caroline had in fact already taken her life, but her

Gary Yokoyama

Among the items found by the body was this ring.

remains were not those in the ditch. Meanwhile, yet another purse was found. The ID inside was for a woman named Margaret Anne and her last name started with S. *MAS?*

* * *

By 4 p.m., Shelley Saunders and Gary Zwicker had found and removed pieces of white fabric on the body. Using trowels and small hand shovels, they began removing soil from around and under the bones. The corpse, while still caked with mud in places, was becoming more exposed. Some parts still had pieces of skin and sinew attached. Saunders could tell the body had reached a stage of advanced decomposition, a stage of mummification of most of the outer tissue, she thought, which produced the dry, hard appearance. Most of the internal organs were completely lost, through either insect activity or autolysis—the destruction of cells after death by their own enzymes. Less than half the total skeleton was exposed to view, with bone most visible on the cranium. Some portions of the pelvic and abdominal viscera were present. There was a mass of hair that was becoming separated from the skull.

To Saunders's eye, the body clearly had been there before the onset of winter. For someone to have left the body there after snowfall would have meant having to dig a hole. The body was face down in an extended position, the left arm straight alongside the torso, the right bent under the chest. Zwicker noted that the right hand was pointing in the air somewhat, from underneath the left shoulder. That hand seemed to have a bit more skin on it than the other. Identification was going to be a massive challenge. DNA? Fingerprints? Was it even thinkable? The fingers were hard as rock, the skin was either sliding off the bone or breaking down, eroding the ridges necessary to make a print. It was a long shot, but Zwicker recalled a technique from a forensics course he once took, a way to bring out a print from victims who have suffered major skin damage to their extremities—burn victims, for example. He'd have to give it a try, he decided.

For Shelley Saunders, meanwhile, simply looking at the bones allowed a picture to form. The picture was still cloudy, though, and she was keeping quiet about it, saying little to the police officers. She approached forensic investigation cautiously. She would, before the end of the day, offer investigators a few observations. But she was guarded about getting too specific on her thoughts before she had time to complete her research. Do not make assumptions. Do not offer theories off the cuff. And do not tell police what you think. Wait until you have a chance to study, review literature, double-check, write your report. She had heard the story about the forensic anthropologist who worked the scene after the Oklahoma City bombing to help identify remains. The anthropologist was asked to identify parts from a leg. And, too quickly, he responded, right at the scene, no time in the lab, that it was from a black female. Turned out it was a white male. Completely wrong.

No, force yourself to say nothing. But in her mind's eye, Saunders could see a picture coming together, could not help but make mental notes. The woman was about 5-foot-5. Brunette, but could have reddish dye in her long hair, probably middle-aged. She dusted soil from the skull. While some parts of the skeleton still had bits of tissue, the skull was nearly completely bone. She looked at the jaw. There was distinct alveolar prognathism—protrusion of the part of the jaw that holds the teeth, which tends to produce a receding chin. In combination with the absence of certain other features, this could mean that the person's ancestry was South Asian.

She dusted the hip bone. Forensic pathologist David King had thought the skeleton was that of a woman. And now Saunders was sure of it. If the bones of the pelvis are intact, you can always tell if the remains are male or female—except in the unlikely event the person is a hermaphrodite, someone with male and female sex organs. One of the possible identifying traits is a notch on the inside of the ilium, the largest hip bone. In males, the greater sciatic notch is narrow and shallow, in females it's much wider. The female pelvis is typically wider than the male, which is both narrower and higher. The pubic bone is also a possible indicator. In males it is short and broad, and much longer in females. And the pubic arch, below where the pubic bones come together, is much wider in females, to facilitate childbirth. Signs of pitting on the pubic bones suggested to Saunders that the woman was multiparous—had given birth more than once. Now, it wasn't a sure thing. Marks like that might only suggest variations in hormonal levels. Saunders noticed something else about the skull. An anomaly, something that Dr. King would be examining in great detail at the morgue, no doubt. There was an indentation. This woman had suffered some kind of trauma to the right side of her head.

At 6:20 p.m., five hours after they had started the dig, the body lay on a platform of soil. Zwicker helped Saunders slide a board under the body, then it was lifted and placed into a body bag. The bag was sealed, a sticker placed on it and labeled #1UO7830. It was the first time the body had been moved in months. How long had it been there? No one knew for sure. They would need the forensic entomologist—the Bug Lady—for that. By David King's very rough estimate, the woman's body had been there at least since September 2000.

* * *

Mississauga, Ontario
July 22, 2000

Yvette Budram checked in to the Mississauga Gate Inn, a motel on the edges of the rapidly growing suburb of Toronto. It was 3 p.m. She used a Visa card to pay the $30 four-hour rate. She was with a man named Harjeet Singh—his nickname was Happy. Yvette and Happy were both married, but not to each other. And it was not the first time they had spent time together at that motel. They entered Room 120 and made love.

Lilawattee (Yvette) Budram had recently turned 40. She was born in Guyana, South America, and was a mother of four—two grown kids from a relationship in her home country in the years before she emigrated, and two young ones born in Canada. Yvette had long dark hair, brown eyes, olive skin. There were two men in her life. There was her husband, Mohan Ramkissoon, who was 34 and the father of their two young children, and her lover, Harjeet Singh, who was 31.

Both men loved Yvette deeply. Harjeet had an average build, perhaps 5-foot-11, 170 pounds. He was born in New Delhi, India, had lived in the Punjab in the northern part of the country before immigrating in 1993 to the United States. He had lived in

Orange County, Calif., later Jackson, Miss., where he owned two convenience stores at gas stations. He pleaded guilty to a charge of food stamp fraud while operating one of his stores, a conviction that was grounds to have him deported, so he moved to Canada in 1999 in an attempt to get his papers there.

Mohan Ramkissoon was, like Yvette, originally from Guyana. He was a compact 5-foot-3, 140 pounds, his complexion much darker than Yvette's or Harjeet's, inherited from great-grandparents who had lived in India. Before settling in Canada, Mohan, too, had first moved to the States and resided there illegally. He lived in Brooklyn, N.Y., spent a brief time in Florida, then settled in Ontario without his papers, worked under a false name.

Yvette told family and friends that, even as a girl in Guyana, men in her life seemed to know only violence. Her father abused her. Corporal punishment for youths in the home and in schools has always been a part of Guyanese culture, but perhaps discipline was taken to extremes in Yvette's family. And then, as a young woman, she was also abused by the man with whom she had her first two children. She would show others the scar on her head, the result of a blow with a bottle. The assault had not come from the hand of her partner, but rather from a man he had paid to attack Yvette. Her daughter, Lisa, remembered seeing her mother get into a vicious fight with a brother at a family gathering. The whole family watched as Yvette's arm was broken in the struggle, it just hung there limp.

Lisa always believed that the abuse affected her mother's sense of herself for the rest of her life. Yvette desperately needed to find love. Needed to please. And needed to be a success in life—success defined as a life in Canada, surrounding herself with life's finer things. Growing up, Yvette had not come from poor roots in Guyana. Her father had been well off, ran a hotel. She was able to travel. The poorest of the poor in countries like Guyana cannot even dream of reaching a place like Canada. That luxury is only available to those who have the financial means to make the jump. They are the ones who dare to dream about the good life by western standards. That was Yvette.

She first arrived in Canada, alone, on New Year's Day, 1985. A new start, the promise of the life she craved and expected. She was 25 years old. Her goal was to own a house before she hit 30. Once settled, she planned to bring her two children over, make sure that they made it, too, push them, relentlessly, to be successful. She had heard of the trick for getting status in Canada quickly. Marry someone, on paper. A common trick. She did it, got married, followed by a quick divorce. She was set, could now find a man to marry for love.

Photo courtesy of the author

Lilawattee "Yvette" Budram

CHAPTER 4 ~ "SOMEONE IS GOING TO DIE"

Mohan Ramkissoon's family in Guyana had not been nearly as well off financially as Yvette's. His father picked sugar cane in the fields in a region called Berbice. Mohan had four brothers and four sisters, but he was the baby. He arrived in Brooklyn in 1986 when he was 20 years old, lived with his brother. After the brother married, Mohan briefly dated his new sister-in-law's younger sister. He lived for a brief time in Miami, then arrived in Toronto on December 24, 1989. Yvette and Mohan met at a mutual friend's place in the city. He was instantly attracted to her. Neither of them had settlement papers at the time, but ultimately Yvette got hers and became a Canadian citizen—Mohan did not. They moved in together and married on October 12, 1991, then moved to Mississauga.

Mohan did not have as refined an upbringing as Yvette, did not share her yearning for the good life—but he was more than willing to accommodate her desires. He landed a solid job, working as a supervisor in the lathe department of a plastics manufacturing company. After marrying, Yvette kept her last name, Budram, a sign of her growing confidence and independence. She was strong, did not take anything from anybody, man or woman. In the context of a traditional culture, she had a brazen personality. Mohan said some in his family had urged him not to marry her.

After they wed, Yvette and Mohan bought a house on Benedet Drive in Mississauga, just south of the Queen Elizabeth Highway (QEW) near Oakville. They rented rooms to boarders to make extra money. Yvette seemed to be living the life she had dreamt. She looked after herself. Dental care in Guyana had not been the best, so she had cosmetic alterations done to her teeth, kept her nails in immaculate condition. In her early 30s she went on a vacation with the girls to Chile one year. One of her friends snapped a picture of her. There was Yvette, beautiful, her face radiant, skin the color of caramel, dark hair bundled. Even a measure of success in Canada was not enough, though. Perhaps nothing would ever be enough. She used to fantasize about moving far away, overseas, to a place like Switzerland, some promised land that existed in her mind's eye as though representing a vague notion of beauty and tranquility and achievement. Maybe that was where she would be at peace with herself, would prove that she had made it, beaten her past.

Her relationship with Mohan did not age well. Their arguments got more intense. Everyone could see that Yvette wore the pants in the family. She often talked down to Mohan, even in front of friends. Mohan, though, had a knack for pushing her buttons, too, in his passive-aggressive way. He made her angry. Was she not the reason he even had a life in Canada? She had sponsored him to live here. Still, Mohan never stopped wanting to please her. Wanted to deliver the dream life she craved. He loved her so much. She was his world—that was the phrase he used when talking about her.

In October 1992 Yvette gave birth to her third child, and her first with Mohan. They called the baby girl Preet. In 1993, she aborted a pregnancy. The reason, Mohan told others, was that they felt it was not good timing for them, after moving into a new home. The marriage was not going well, Yvette and Mohan were not getting along. Mohan believed he was doing all he could, buying her the best of everything. Those rugs under her feet? Cost $2,000 each. Bought four of them. He was the one who worked full time, while she had part-time work for a day-care service. He worked long hours but still did all the family's grocery shopping. As for the children, he doted on them, bought them outrageously expensive toys that accumulated in the garage.

When he came home from work, exhausted, he gave Yvette massages. Why? Well, wouldn't any husband do that, he wondered? Any husband who loved his wife as much as he did? Yes, Mohan was glad to do all these things for Yvette, he loved her so much. But he also kept score. It did not help that Yvette stopped responding to him sexually. From Mohan's perspective, he would come home at the end of the day, working long hours, looking for a physical response from his wife, and it wasn't there. But Yvette was tired of the expected sex on demand by Mohan, as though that was her role in life. She told her doctor that her libido had waned, she lacked the desire to have sex with her husband and it was creating stress and friction in the relationship.

In 1994 Yvette was referred to a psychiatrist for treatment of clinical depression, and she complained of minor, undiagnosed physical ailments common for someone who is depressed. She took antidepressant medication. Had a miscarriage, which she attributed to stress. And then in 1995, she gave birth to a boy, their second child, Kevin. During her pregnancies she developed a moderate case of diabetes. She was treated for it and put on weight. Her sex drive continued to flag. In January 2000, her father died in Guyana. She returned to South America for the funeral. While Yvette was away, she phoned home to Canada on Valentine's Day.

"Hi, it's me. Could you call me back? I'm still in Georgetown. I'm calling to wish you a happy Valentine's Day. I'm sorry I missed you."

Yvette had not left a message for her husband. She had left a message for the man called Harjeet (Happy) Singh. It was late in 1999 that she first met him. Harjeet had separated from his wife, Doris, who was an American. She remained back in Mississippi with their baby while he went to Canada. He had heard it would be easier to get his immigration papers in Canada than in the United States. He lived for about seven months in Montreal before moving to Mississauga. At first he stayed at a Sikh temple on Dixie Road, while he called around for a room to rent. One was listed available at 2382 Benedet Drive, the home of Yvette Budram and Mohan Ramkissoon. Yvette met him, but said someone else had already arranged to rent it out. She introduced him to a woman down the street named Maria Raposa, who had a room coming open in about a week. Until the room was ready, Yvette offered to let Harjeet stay in her home. And then, once he moved down the street, Harjeet continued to develop a friendship with her. He told her his story, about the separation, his baby. They grew close. She started inviting him to her house for breakfast when Mohan was off at work and the kids were at school. Yvette would take her daughter Preet to school, come home, and then walk down the street to see Harjeet at Maria Raposa's house. Harjeet even sometimes dropped Preet off at school for her. It wasn't long before they started a physical relationship. Harjeet's landlady, Maria, was not amused when she noticed how much time they were spending together.

"You should watch who comes to see you," she warned him. "You're a single man."

Yvette's sex drive had been in decline in recent years but it had now returned, buoyed by both Harjeet and the hormonal medication she had been prescribed. Harjeet wanted her all to himself, and Yvette shared the feeling. She bought him a ring with a garnet in it, and a watch with the inscription "love you always" on the band. About seven months into the relationship, Yvette took him to her pandit—a psychic in the Hindu religion —to predict their future. In Mississauga, Harjeet held down a job at a factory in shipping, but only for a month. Then he worked nights at Tim Hortons. Mostly, to those who knew him, it seemed he didn't work at all. At one point he drove a truck for work; Yvette even accompanied him to Montreal on some runs. The question was, would Harjeet be able to remain in Canada so they could continue seeing each other? Yvette was determined to help him get his papers. She had a friend he could marry for now. A friend? Actually it was her eldest daughter, Lisa. Or if not—for Yvette surely knew that Lisa, who was developing her own independence of spirit, would not agree to that—she, Yvette, would do it.

"But you're already married," Harjeet told Yvette. "You have two kids, and what would your husband say?"

"I'll talk to him, tell him I'm just trying to help you out."

Harjeet applied for refugee status in Canada. That put his case into the immigration loop, but he needed money to pay a lawyer presenting his case. Yvette loaned him about $3,000 to pay his Montreal-based lawyer. She told Mohan about it. It made him angry.

What was she doing? Harjeet was an attractive enough man— the tanned skin, big smile. He was a Sikh but did not bundle his hair or wear a turban, he kept his hair short and wavy. But what was it, really, about him that so attracted Yvette to him, that drove her to take such risks, to put her family in jeopardy? Perhaps it was his personality, the aura about him. He bounced around from place to place, seemed to make friends everywhere he went. One of his friends had given him the nickname Happy after his live-and-let-live approach to life, and it stuck. He told others, "God wills all, so why worry about anything?"

A photo of the couple shows Yvette in a brilliant blue dress and scarf, and Harjeet in dark pants and shiny pewter sport coat that reflected his raffish personality. He was a trickster, but then he also displayed a hot temper on occasion, and had a tendency to skirt the law. He was a scammer who developed the contacts that provided a pipeline he could use to hop back and forth between Canada and the States, sneaking across the border without his papers, using aliases to ensure his freedom. Some of those he met and lived with considered him a con-man. To Yvette, whose view of men had been shaped so much by violence, Harjeet would have seemed gentle by comparison, just as Mohan had.

* * *

2382 Benedet Drive, Mississauga
September 3, 2000
10 p.m.

The argument escalated, taunts growing into threats. The boarders downstairs in the house could hear it all. Words, insults, spat out like nails.

"I don't want you here!"

"Someone is going to die!"

A black-handled kitchen knife was pulled, waved in the air.

"I will break you! I swear I will kill you!"

A hammer is airborne, striking the glass of the front door, cracking it.

Leave, now.

Rushing from the house, down the street, to the corner, pushing the buttons on the pay phone. A voice answering on the other end.

"Nine-one-one, what is your emergency?"

* * *

Central Police Station
Hamilton, Ontario
April 19, 2001

The homicide detectives gathered for a meeting in Central Station first thing to discuss the female body found in Flamborough two days earlier. It was decided that Paul Lahaie would organize a further search of the scene that day. That ditch would be the cleanest in the region.

Meanwhile, Mike Thomas suggested a new theory. A homicide is sometimes a prelude to the death of the killer—a murder-suicide. So Thomas had considered the puzzle and thought backwards. If there was a murderer at large, he had a few snakes wrapped around his head. Maybe to the extent that he killed himself over it. They should review recent cases of male suicides in the area. Thomas ultimately found a report of a man who lived in the Flamborough area who had taken his life. What about female associates of his? Were they all accounted for? Thomas visited the late man's home, interviewed family, checked up on some names. But nobody from his past had gone missing.

The detectives had all noticed the headline in the *Hamilton Spectator* that morning:

Forensic experts search for body's identity

The story had read: "Scientists and detectives spent yesterday in a west Flamborough ditch delicately removing the remains of a badly decomposed body. Police said it was too soon to offer any details about the body, including gender, approximate age, or how long it had been there."

When things are moving fast in a homicide investigation and the evidence is plentiful, police are less inclined to announce anything to the media. But when they need help from the public, need exposure for a case, the media are their friends. This case was one of those times. A decision was made to hold a news conference about the case that afternoon, depending on what was learned at the autopsy.

At 10:30 a.m., the detectives arrived at the morgue in the basement of Hamilton General Hospital and were greeted by forensic pathologist Dr. David King. The post-mortem—Latin for "after

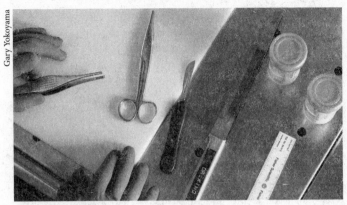

Gary Yokoyama

Tools of the autopsy.

death" —on the victim was about to begin. It can be a sobering experience for an inexperienced cop. The corpse sometimes bloats from built-up gases, requiring incisions from the pathologist to release pressure, making an auditory hiss upon escaping. The stench can be overwhelming. In the past rookies were told to lather up their nostrils with Vicks VapoRub, the pungent fumes knifing into their sinuses as a shield against death's stench.

Sitting on stools around the steel examination table in one of the autopsy suites in the morgue were forensic detective Gary Zwicker and homicide detectives Warren Korol, Mike Thomas, and Dave Place. Paul Lahaie was still out at the scene on the 8th Concession. They had all attended their share of autopsies, but none had been to one like this. There was little odor, the body had already been hardened by mummification, and then kept in a refrigerated locker in the morgue at 10 degrees Celsius.

At 11:07 a.m., Dr. King began. The autopsy would be spread over several days. Forensic anthropologist Shelley Saunders assisted, along with Dr. Ross Barlow, an expert in forensic odontology, who analyzed distinguishing features of the victim's dental work. Few active forensic pathologists had anything close to the experience King had in the field. Over the years he had conducted about 9,000 medical-legal autopsies, including more than 350 homicides. Among these was the autopsy of Tammy Homolka, one of the victims of schoolgirl killers Paul Bernardo and Karla Homolka, perhaps the most sensational and shocking homicide cases in Canadian criminal history.

This new case on his docket would be one of his last prior to retirement and, even for King, it was an unusual one. The corpse lying before him was caked with mud, with traces of fabric visible among the bones and sinew. Mummification, which is the drying of the skin, and skeletonization, which is the loss of tissues from the bones, suggested to him that the body had been exposed for several months. The skin on the back was hard, leathery.

At most autopsies the forensic pathologist follows a standard procedure. Make the incision stretching from the neck down to the pelvic bone, up the other side, as though outlining a zipper on a coat; peel back the slab of skin, unveiling the mustard-colored layer of fat and the pink and purplish viscera underneath. Remove organs, cut them into pieces for examination, look for clues suggesting foul play, discoloration of tissue, bruising, wounds. Send tissue samples for toxicological testing. But in this case, most of the soft tissue had disintegrated, including the organs. He was autopsying a near-skeleton.

Of the soft tissue that remained, he had to make educated guesses at which pieces might be from the heart, the liver, the brain, in order to dissect samples for tox testing. King attempted to examine the genitalia for injury, but those tissues had essentially disappeared from decomposition; he was able to collect some pubic hairs. As the detectives took notes, and Zwicker snapped photos, King reflected that there was no sign of defensive wounds, but with the skin and tissues being in the state they were, it would be impossible to detect such markings in any event. He observed a clue inside the body cavity suggesting it had been lying outside for several months.

"Some of the tissues in the abdomen show adipocere."

Adipocere: an unusual form of decomposition that involves the fatty tissues of the body. In damp conditions the body fats undergo a chemical process that is very similar to making soap, and the fatty tissues develop a waxy or soap-like appearance.

"We see it in drowning victims, where the skin remains intact, but there is adipocere beneath the skin, the subcutaneous fat as well as perhaps the internal organs."

There were insects on the exterior and interior of the body. King removed several and placed the bugs in jars. Shelley Saunders opined that the insects had obviously played a role in the decomposition of the body, but not to the extent one might have expected. She noted that it was as though the body had been protected in its own micro-climate: dry, cold conditions created first by a blanket of fallen leaves, and then the snow, sealed by a long winter deep freeze. There was no evidence of animals scavenging on the bones, although smaller animals might have got to some of the soft tissue.

Saunders examined bones, made some calculations. She needed more time to study them in detail, after cleaning, but for now she could pass on basic information to the detectives: the body was definitely female, judging from the morphology of the pelvic girdle. She was at least in her 30s, was about 5-foot-5, average build, long wavy dark hair. There were two vertebrae missing from the skeleton. Could an animal have interfered with the remains? Possible. Might have even influenced the positioning of the body, albeit slightly. Warren Korol made a mental note: detail the detectives to search the scene for the missing vertebrae.

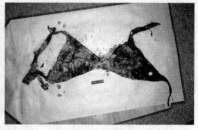

Items recovered from the crime scene.

King removed items of jewelry from the body. She wore a size 8 gold ring with a garnet—the birthstone for January. She had a metal wedding band that had at one time been gold-plated but now looked copper. She wore a 45-centimeter chain of 14-karat gold with two pendants, one gold and the other crescent-shaped iron. Her watch was a gold-colored Citizen Quartz. He removed pieces of fabric from the body that were covered in dried mud.

After cleaning, it was apparent that she had been wearing white panties, a black bra, a white satin nightgown. It didn't take long for Mike Thomas to notice the fingernails. For him it invoked his days working drugs and vice in Hamilton. He knew that fingernails bitten down to the skin was a sign of a woman who may have worked the street. Prostitutes don't spend money caring for their appearance, their nails, their dental work. They buy cheap costume jewelry. Most of the money they earn bankrolls their drug habit, not grooming. But he noted that this was not the case with the female victim on the table before him. Even in the body's decayed form, he could tell the nails had been well cared for. The detectives had wondered from the first night at the scene if the victim was a prostitute. But it was clear she was no woman of the night.

King more closely examined the neck and head area. As the detectives moved in for a look, he pointed to a new piece of evidence. It had been invisible before, since it was caked with mud and embedded deep in the neck of the skeleton. It was intertwined with the gold chain. It was a ligature. A thin piece of rope about the thickness of a pencil. Bone-colored, braided fiber. It had been tied in a slip knot, King observed, the type of knot that can be tightened by pulling on it. He measured the loop of the knot, indicating its diameter as it had been around the neck when the woman was alive and the flesh still on her neck. It was between seven and eight centimeters in diameter. A typical female neck, regular build, would be about 11 to 12 centimeters around, he reflected. The gold chain had been decorative. The cord, a noose.

After the first stage of the post-mortem was complete, police issued a media release, listing the unknown woman's age and size, the jewelry she wore. Pictures of the jewelry recovered from the body were posted on the Hamilton Police Internet site. Nothing was said about the position of the body, or evidence of any possible trauma. The woman's death was described as "suspicious." Nothing was said about the ligature. The detectives would keep those cards a secret. There might be only one person out there who knew that it was a murder, that the victim had been beaten in the head and strangled. And that was the killer.

CHAPTER 5 ~ FINGERTIP

At the scene on the 8th Concession, Detective Paul Lahaie had been helping the search. At noon he got a page from the autopsy suite at Hamilton General. The autopsy had uncovered a ligature around the woman's neck. While suicide seemed a highly unlikely cause of death—why would anyone come all the way out here to hang themselves?—Lahaie had to clear that theory, so checked out the scene to see whether someone could have hung themselves from a tree limb. Later he called in two foresters and a City of Hamilton hydraulic lift to examine the tall basswood tree that had been near the body. In his notebook he wrote that they found no marks on the tree indicating a hanging; the basswood tree had no lower limbs to assist a person in climbing. And he found no evidence of more rope.

At the autopsy, forensic odontologist Ross Barlow examined the victim's teeth. He noted an unusual upper canine, growing outward towards the center. She also had an expensive crown, which was made of porcelain and held in place by a metal post inserted in the root of the tooth after a root canal had been done. From the detectives' point of view, the most interesting observation was that she had good dental habits, and had considerable work done in the past—work that was not available to someone on social welfare, for example. In the days to come, the detectives would discuss the mystery woman. She was no transient. No prostitute. She was a woman with some manner of financial resources, had jewelry that was not extravagant, but not cheap either; she could afford to have her teeth done, took care in her appearance. And the black bra, the nightgown, which was more like a teddy? She must have been assaulted, or killed, in a hotel, a home. Do most middle-aged women wear teddies around the house the detectives wondered?

Forensic pathologist David King examined the skull in more detail. He focused on a fist-sized 10-centimeter depression that ran from the right temple to the back of her head. Later, King laid alternately the end of a crowbar, a baseball bat, and a hammer next to the fracture to see if anything matched. There was no exact match. Could have been something fairly large and heavy.

If it was one blow, it could be something like the head of a bat. If there were several blows, it could have been a smaller object. The angle of the depression suggested the blows had been dealt in a downward motion, with severe force. The most likely scenario was at least two blows. And there was something else. The fracture reached only halfway across at the base of the skull, not all the way. Usually, King reflected, with impact on one side of the skull, the crack goes from one side to the other, producing a transverse basal skull fracture. In this case, the fracture line went halfway. It was an incomplete basal skull fracture. Why? There were two possibilities. One, the victim, and thus the head, was erect, moving freely at the time of the blow. Possible, but not likely. The head would have been bobbing, moving, which would have not been conducive to such a localized fracture area. No, the more likely explanation was that the skull was resting against a surface. But it could not have been a hard surface, for that would have meant the violent blow to the right side of the skull would create its own pressure on the left side, taking the fracture all the way across the skull. That meant the head had likely been on a soft surface when it was struck. Like a bed.

* * *

Forensic Detective Gary Zwicker made his proposal to David King during the autopsy. "I'd like to try to lift a print from the fingers. Right thumb. Right index. Right ring. Right middle."

Zwicker felt the right hand offered the fingers in the best shape. The thumb is always the best bet, with its larger surface. A pathologist will sometimes make incisions and sever digits with a knife, but the fingers had become too hardened for that. King severed four digits using shears, cutting them at the end joint. He placed each fingertip in a small plastic container filled with a phenol-based solution and screwed an orange lid on each. By the conclusion of the autopsy, Zwicker had collected the finger samples along with other forensic exhibits: hair found on the ligature, pubic hair, scalp hair, three fingernails, a dry oral swab and an oral swab with saline, small pieces of tissue that might or might not have belonged to the liver or kidney. He placed the items in a box and carried it out of the hospital, drove back to Central Station, and checked himself in to the forensics department on the main floor and put the exhibits in a storage fridge. He would need to give a quality fingerprint to the AFIS operator. That was Al Yates, who had been a field officer for years but now mostly worked in the lab as the specialist in the Automated Fingerprint Identification System.

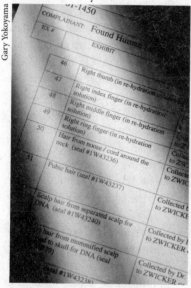

Gary Yokoyama

Gary Zwicker's forensic exhibit list.

Officers brought in prints from crime scenes, partial prints left on door-knobs, windows, documents, and Yates plotted points on the prints on a computer screen, searched databases for a match. Zwicker was excited by the challenge in front of him. There was so little information the detectives had to go on. Identity would be the key. It was his to solve. At the same time, he knew it was a long shot. It would be difficult, perhaps impossible, to ID her. The skin was thin and hard on the fingers, the precious ridges worn. Even if Zwicker could develop a print from one of the digits, the odds were slim it would lead to anything. As with DNA profiles, a fingerprint means nothing to an investigation unless it can be matched to another print.

Fingerprints were one avenue for identification. Dental records were another, although one that was even more unlikely to bear fruit, because there is no central database for dental records. Zwicker put on his white lab coat in the department. Most of the officers had nicknames. A few years back he had jokingly referred to himself, Joe Friday-FBI-style, as Special Agent Zwicker. One of the guys wrote it in black marker on his lab coat. Special Agent it was.

Zwicker retrieved the small box with the finger samples from the fridge, set it down on a metal table in the lab, a small room in the back of the department. There were cabinets, a sink, examination table, and a CA fuming chamber, a device in which cyanoacrylate vapor is produced to react with sweat left on smooth surfaces to reveal latent fingerprints. He saw first-hand, during public tours of the department, people disappointed by the lab. They were used to watching the part-fantasy high-tech wizardry of CSI on TV, where detectives in spacious labs were always bathed in moody darkness, a few shards of neon light showing their way. Zwicker grinned. Right. Funny, he thought, in real life they kind of liked to see what they were doing in the lab. He sprayed the metal table with disinfectant, then covered it with a large piece of brown paper. Pulled on a pair of blue latex gloves. He unscrewed one of the orange lids and pulled the right thumb tip out of the container. There was no fingernail, just an outline where it had been, prior to its removal for DNA testing. The tip weighed little more than a coin. And after having been in the phenol solution, and in the fridge, it felt cold through the latex gloves.

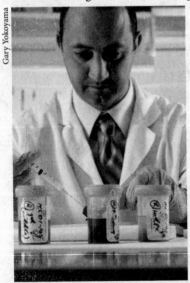

Gary Yokoyama

Zwicker washed the digit, then gently set it down on the paper, and prepared the syringe with a solution of phenol, water, and alcohol. The thumb was so hard, it lacked the softness needed to enable the ridge patterns to make a clear impression on paper. He had to make it soft again. The answer was rehydration. He had never tried the maneuver before, had only heard about it being used to try identifying the deceased from fires. If you can pump up the finger, the ridges can be enhanced enough to roll a good ink

Zwicker with the victim's finger samples.

print on paper. Zwicker held the syringe in one hand, the tip in the other, looked at it from the bottom. There was a core of bone at the center. He gently inserted the needle in between the outer edge of the bone and the skin. The tiny gap was soft, but there was still some resistance from the mummified tissue as he gingerly pressed in the needle. Careful. Don't rip the fragile skin and destroy a chance at a print. Pushing on the plunger of the syringe, he could see a bump from a tiny rivulet of solution journey under the skin of the thumb, pumping up the skin slightly, like a trace of air flowing into a tiny balloon. What do you know—looked like the rehydration was working. He pulled out the needle, filled the syringe again, injected it again.

When he was finished the process, Zwicker placed the thumb tip back in the bottle, screwed on the lid, and put it back into the storage fridge. He knew it would be a few weeks before he could attempt to get a print from the thumb—he needed to allow time for the fluid to settle in the thumb, and only then try to roll the finger. But so far, so good for Special Agent Zwicker.

* * *

Hamilton General Hospital
April 19, 2001

She walked into the hospital morgue, set down her kit, took a net out of it, and started catching flies on the walls and ceiling of the autopsy suite where the detectives were gathered. It was forensic entomologist Dael Morris. The Bug Lady. When the body bag had first been opened in the suite, several flies flew out. Morris needed to catch those that had escaped, and measure the temperature in the room. Then she inserted a probe thermometer into various locations on the body, and removed other insects from those spots. You always work in that order: you first remove the insects and then take the temperature, you have changed the micro environment in the body where the insect had been living.

Her task was to calculate a very big piece of the puzzle—when, and perhaps where, the woman on the table had died. That morning, Detective Dave Place had received permission from the

Ontario coroner's office to bring Dael Morris into the investigation. He phoned Morris at her home in Toronto. She also used the old house as her office, had built an insectarium in the basement. Morris didn't know her way around Hamilton so Dave Place met her in the parking lot of the Fortinos grocery store on Dundurn Street and they went from there. She was driving a black '87 Omni. Fascinating line of work, Place thought, and Morris was one of the few forensic entomologists in Canada qualified to do it. But perhaps it didn't pay all that well. Morris was proud of the old car, though. People tended to stare at it, yeah, she reflected. She figured it had to be because it brought back memories for them. And because she kept it in such good condition.

Even to most police investigators, forensic entomology, while increasingly employed as an investigative tool, seems novel. The field was portrayed in a quirky light in the movie *Silence of the Lambs*, where two entomologists inform an FBI profiler that an insect cocoon is from a death's-head moth. In one scene, the two oddball scientists are playing chess with live beetles. Exposure is good, but the movie made all entomologists look like nutty geeks, Dael Morris thought.

Forensic entomology goes back at least to 1850, in Paris, where, in the course of an autopsy on a child found decomposed in a house, Dr. Bergeret d'Arbois is said to have deduced that the flesh fly *Sarcophaga carnaria* had first deposited eggs on the body two years earlier. He concluded that suspicion should therefore fall on persons who lived in the house at that particular time. Going further back, it is said to have begun in 1247, in China, in the case of a farmer who died of wounds inflicted by a sickle. The story went that a death investigator assembled farmers from the community and requested that they lay their sickles on the ground. To the naked eye, the sickles all looked the same. But the blowflies landed on only one, the one with traces of blood still on it. The owner of that sickle confessed to the murder.

As for Dael Morris, as a girl growing up in the village of Lefroy on Lake Simcoe, just south of Orillia, she got hooked on bugs early, catching and collecting them, and the fascination never stopped. Back then, in the 1960s, in a rural place like that, kids were allowed to roam on their own, discover in the bush and creeks. Her father was an electrician who had served in the Second World War on an aircraft carrier. Her mother used to take the kids for long hikes, camping excursions on foot, go up the creek, make tea and bacon over an open fire. She grew up a country girl but in her adult life lived and studied in cities like Kingston, Quebec City, Guelph, Toronto. Her manner of speaking had a down-home flavor, but was peppered with arcane scientific terminology. As she got older, Morris developed a philosophical passion for insects.

It was their omnipresence, really, that fascinated her. There are more species of insects than any other creature, or organism, for that matter, she pointed out; the incredible diversity, the awesome range of behavior. She said we have learned from insects how to make paper, pottery, and cement. Insects are central to all ecosystems, we depend on them for our survival. She also kept a sense of humor about her passion.

"No, bugs are not cute and cuddly like a kitten or something, that's for darn sure…. Wouldn't quite want to take a maggot to bed with you."

Gary Yokoyama

Detective Dave Place.

Dave Place was the one detective on the case who had in fact worked with Morris before. He had been with Hamilton police for 16 years, the last couple with the Major Crime Unit. Perhaps more than any of his colleagues, big Dave Place seemed cut from the cloth of the classic police officer. His manner was authoritative yet soft spoken. A gentle giant, was how one of the senior detectives thought of him. Six-foot-five, 220 pounds, biceps pushing against his shirt sleeves. Place was not muscled in a bodybuilder way, he was simply big, the physique not in-your-face intimidating, but rather the type you knew could be put to damaging use if required.

Place respected Morris's work, the focus and meticulousness she brought to it. Several months earlier, he had brought her in to examine a woman's body found in a wooded area in Hamilton. The remains showed signs that suggested foul play could have been involved. Place felt that pinpointing when the woman died would help to confirm or eliminate murder. That was his first exposure to Morris's technique—collecting the blowflies and larvae from the body, then rearing flies to adulthood in controlled conditions in her lab. Raw meat was her preferred food for the flies. In fact, after speaking with her on the phone about that first case, the next thing Place knows, he's in legendary Reardon's Meat Market on King William Street, not far from the police station, buying 60 cents' worth of liver for Morris's "little guys," as she called the flies that held the key to the time of death. Sixty cents, way more than enough to satisfy his liver needs, he reflected.

Ultimately the woman in that case was found to have died by her own hand, but Place asked Morris if she'd finish her work, to determine a date of death, give family members a better sense of their loved one's final days, help give them closure. Morris did most of the work on her own time. As it happened, the data she was able to gather from that case would help inform her expertise on cases to come—including the case of the mystery woman found in a field in Flamborough.

Forensic Entomologist Dael Morris.

Chapter 6 ~ The Bug Lady

Even as Dael Morris worked in the autopsy suite, the first thing that struck her when she looked at the body was the hair. The victim had hair that was deep chestnut brown. Beautiful. Luxuriant. But Morris had little time to dwell upon the outer appearance. Her task was to go smaller, work in the microscopic world of insects that had colonized the victim. She saw the thousands of insects on the corpse in various stages of development. The detectives watched with curiosity as Morris noted how much higher the temperature was within a clump of maggots—the "maggot mass temperature"—than at other locations on the remains. The maggots generated an incredible amount of heat, even on a corpse that had been kept in the morgue fridge.

As usual, as she worked, there was some conversation, the detectives asking questions about what she was doing. In her experience, there was usually a comment or two, maybe a bit of black humor. Easier for people to cope that way, she'd done that herself. But Morris found that the atmosphere at autopsies was always respectful. Always. She spent nearly two hours collecting samples and data. She found several species of insects. The most important were four species of blowflies. When she finished in the hospital, Dave Place drove her from the hospital out of the city towards the 8th Concession West in Flamborough.

* * *

Dael Morris had studied entomology at the University of Guelph and flies became her focus. They were such a vital species. In their maggot form, flies have been known as purifiers of wounds for centuries. In the First World War, many soldiers who survived injuries in the trenches had maggots that colonized their wounds—maggots eat dead tissue and leave healthy tissue alone, and they secrete ammonia because they require a clean environment to live. In the days before antibiotics and penicillin, in the 1930s, there was extensive research into their antiseptic properties. After falling out of favor for a few decades, maggot therapy was said to be making something of a comeback in modern medicine as a wound healer in certain cases—for example, for someone with a serious wound in an area with poor blood supply. In fact, the U.S. Food and Drug Administration approved maggots as "medical devices" in 2004.

Gary Yokoyama

Specimen jar of maggots.

After U of G, Morris earned her M.Sc. at Laval University in 1987, then landed a job with the Royal Ontario Museum. She had heard about forensic entomology at school, but it was only in 1990 that she started to train in the field. A forensic detective with the Toronto police approached the museum. He had been at a conference and was exposed to forensic entomology. He proposed that the museum develop a program. Morris learned it on her own at first, collecting specimens, charting bionomic information on different species of flies. She exchanged information with a forensic entomologist in Indiana.

Then it was off to the "body farm." In June 1991 she arrived at the Knoxville, Tenn., research facility where the decomposition of the dead was studied. The body farm was popularized in Patricia Cornwell's novel of the same name. Human bodies are donated to the facility in order to learn how they break down, how insects participate in that process. Morris walked up a pathway on the grounds and there were human skeletal remains on either side. It was her first experience working on a real body. The heat stifling, 100 percent humidity, she was assigned a body to study, collect insect samples. The body was covered by a black tarp, the corpse cooking underneath. When she pulled the tarp off, she jumped back from the ammonia escaping into her face.

She was, after all, a scientist, an entomologist, not a forensic pathologist. But Morris could take it. She learned to focus on the insects, not the body. Morris deepened her expertise, studied the role of Calliphoridae, better known by their common name, blowflies, which are the first insects on the scene colonizing a body after death. Blowflies such as bluebottles arrive within minutes or hours, depending on environmental conditions, and burrow into any available orifice—nose, mouth, ears, open wounds. They lay eggs, which soon hatch into larvae, or maggots. The time at which the first eggs are laid is approximately consistent with the time of death. She learned that blowfly patterns could be used to deduce the post-mortem interval to within about 12 hours—and that was possible even if the body wasn't found for several weeks, or more. Ultimately she presented her findings at conferences for police officers. They took to calling her the Bug Lady. She didn't mind that.

Her first real case to establish time of death was in 1992. Creepy one, she reflected. A father, mother, and daughter found dead in a home in York Region. Looked like a possible burglary. The son, a minor, had escaped injury. Morris determined the bodies had lain there five days. The son, just a boy, had beaten his father to death with a baseball bat as he slept, then his mother in the hallway. Stepped over her body to get to his sister's room, killed her, too. Tried to make it look like a burglary. But the death timeline did not match his story. Another one early in her career was a missing person case, suspected homicide. Police couldn't find the body, but there were insects found in the grille of the car where the victim had last been seen. Where might the car have been? Morris found flies in the grille called midges, flies that for the most part live in a relatively warm, damp area. All of which only proved that the car could have been in a hell of a lot of areas all over southern Ontario, she said. The body was never found.

* * *

Morris and Detective Dave Place arrived at the spot along the 8th Concession. There were uniformed police officers guarding the scene. Soon she was on her hands and knees, inserting a probe thermometer into the soil where the corpse had lain. The detectives had not told Morris much of anything about the case. She didn't want to know, that could be seen to prejudice her findings. All she knew was that the woman's body had been found in that spot, and that it was a suspicious death. Now that she was at the scene, she still didn't know if it was a murder or suicide.

Gary Yokoyama

Tools of Dael Morris's trade.

She dug up dirt about 25 centimeters down, turned it over in a plastic bin, sifted through with her gloved hands, gathering insects, post-feeding larvae or pupae that remained from when the corpse had been there. Broke a shovel, wood snapped like a matchstick. Brand new Home Depot model. "Don't make 'em like they used to." Kept going. She placed specimens in plastic baggies, about a dozen baggies in total, which contained small pieces of raw liver to begin rearing the insects immediately. The baggies in turn went into her large collection bag, which had a thermometer attached to it to monitor the temperature at all times. Too much of a shock in environment to the "little critters" would stunt their development.

After nearly three hours working at the scene, Place took Morris back to the city, she returned to her insectarium in Toronto. Was home by 11 p.m. Then she began the meticulous, time-consuming process of rearing the larvae she had gathered, calculating when the blowflies began colonizing. That could provide the answer to the mystery of when, and perhaps even where, the woman in the Hamilton General autopsy suite had died. David King and Shelley Saunders had guessed that the woman's body had lain in the brush since perhaps the fall of 2000. Morris would need to use the critters as her eyes to revisit the victim's final hours. The way Morris thought of it, in the crucial minutes and hours after a murder, blowflies are often the first witnesses. Sometimes, the only witnesses.

* * *

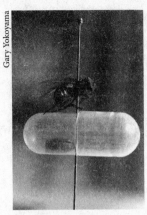

Gary Yokoyama

An adult blow fly from Dael Morris's collection mounted on a pin and capsule.

Mississauga, Ontario
Late September 2000

Mohan Ramkissoon answered the phone ringing in his house. He recognized the voice on the other end. It was Harjeet (Happy) Singh.

"Where are you?" Mohan asked.

"I'm in the States."

Harjeet told Mohan that he was coming clean. He had an affair with Yvette, he admitted, and he was sorry, for the lying, for everything.

"I know it was 100 percent wrong," Harjeet said. "I'm sorry, if you can ever forgive me."

Mohan had in fact known about the affair. He had once spied on them kissing in Yvette's car in the parking lot of a fitness club in town. And there was one day a month earlier when Mohan had dropped by the Mississauga Gate Inn and spoken to the manager there about a credit card transaction that he did not recognize on his card, from that motel. At Mohan's request, the manager looked at his records. Yvette had indeed used her husband's credit card to check in. She charged $30 for the motel's short-term rate. And she had been with a man.

Mohan had long been bitter that Yvette had been so cold towards him sexually, claiming there was something physically wrong with her, taking hormone medication. Turned out she was just saving it up for the other guy, the one who was benefiting from her treatment. All this, and Yvette had hurt Mohan, humiliated him. In one bizarre incident, Yvette was with Harjeet when she had phoned Mohan at home. She disguised her voice, pretended to be a telemarketer taking a survey on sexual habits. With Harjeet listening to the conversation on another phone, she asked Mohan the questions: When had he last had sex? Six months, had been Mohan's reply. Yvette was playing a trick on Mohan, getting him to admit he had not been intimate with any woman, to prove to Harjeet that she was being monogamous with him.

And now, after Harjeet asked for forgiveness, they talked some more on the phone.

"Is Yvette there?" Harjeet asked.

"She's not here, she's with you," Mohan replied.

"What?" said Harjeet.

"She's with you," said Mohan. "Listening on the other line."

"She's not with me," Harjeet replied. "I'm calling from Mississippi. I'm at my wife's place. How can I have Yvette with me when I'm living with my wife?"

* * *

Yvette and her eldest daughter, Lisa, had not been on good terms. In fact, Lisa hadn't spoken to her mother in six months. They had last talked soon after Lisa returned from Guyana where she had attended her father Arthur's funeral in Guyana. It had been a rough month for Lisa. At 19 years old, she had lost her grandmother, grandfather, and father all in the month of February. And Lisa found out that Yvette had said some hurtful things about her to Lisa's father just prior to his death, nasty lies about how Lisa was living her life in Toronto. Lisa was outraged, and hurt. And she told her mother so on the phone.

"How could you say things like that? No matter how much of a bad kid you may think I am, I'm still your daughter and you should love me and respect me and not say mean things like that."

Yvette Budram had always asked—demanded—much of her daughter. She had seen that Lisa made it to Canada and was determined that both Lisa and her brother be successful, take advantage of the opportunity she had given them. Starting in her teens, Lisa had heated arguments with her. They battled over Lisa's weight, her tomboy nature—she was not a girlie girl like Mom wanted. Not unusual things, but as Lisa got older, it seemed that Yvette became more irrational, the arguments got worse. Lisa was aware of her mother's stormy marriage to Mohan. Mom had a sharp temper, Lisa knew it well herself. But she also felt that Mohan sometimes brought it on; he came off as quiet and gentle, but used his words carefully, purposefully, to incite her mother, get her going, play mother and daughter off against each other. Lisa was unaware, though, of the worst of the fights between Yvette and Mohan, the one from September 3: the death threat that boarders heard all over the house, the hammer striking the window, the 911 call.

Lisa woke one morning in early October 2000 with images from a dream she had still branded on her mind. The last she had heard from Yvette was a voice mail left on Lisa's phone a month earlier. Lisa did not return the call, she thought her mother would just go off on her again. It wasn't the content of the new dream that was so terrible. It was just that her mother had appeared in it—wearing white. And that was not a good sign, not at all. Lisa did not usually dream of anyone specific, anyone she knew. There was only one other time it happened—she dreamt of a family member who had just died. She got out of bed, went downstairs, and spoke to her mother-in-law.

"My mother's dead," Lisa said.

"No she's not, how could you know that?"

"I know I sound crazy, but I dreamt my mother. I never dream people. She was wearing white. I just know something's wrong."

As the days passed, the dream stayed with her, and she was shaken by it. She decided to call. In October she phoned the house at 2382 Benedet Dr. No answer. She left a message, and Mohan returned the call. She asked to speak to her mother, then listened as the tone of Mohan's voice quivered on the phone. Then he started to cry.

"What's wrong?" asked Lisa.

He said Yvette was gone, she had left him and the kids. Even took off without her medication, he added, her bank card, every-thing. Left her car, the SUV. Lisa was shocked. It made no sense. How could she do that, most of all, leave Preet and Kevin—Lisa's half-brother and half-sister—like that? Mom adored those kids.

"I can't believe it," she said. "She would never just leave like that."

Mohan said it was true. She had left, probably with her boy-friend, the guy named Happy, he added.

Lisa asked her mother-in-law how Yvette could even get across the border without identification, a passport, money. Her mother was, if anything, obsessive about keeping appointments, being well organized, neat. This would be so wildly out of character for her to pick up and leave her family and adopted country like that. Later, Lisa phoned Peel Regional Police. She wanted to file a missing person report about her mother. But she was told she could not do so, she had not seen her mother recently enough to offer enough information to file the report. After she got off the phone with the police officer, Lisa called Mohan, told him he should file the report.

"I don't want to get the police involved," Mohan said. "And she's not missing. I know where she is. She's having the time of her life with Happy."

Lisa, confused, frustrated, asked Mohan if he needed any help looking after the two young kids. He said he did not. A few weeks later, she phoned Mohan again. Any word from Mom? Yes, he had received a letter from her, from California. She was with her boyfriend, doing fine.

* * *

Mohan attended a meet-the-teacher evening at Elmcrest Public School in Mississauga in the fall of 2000, where Preet had just started Grade 3. Mohan spoke to her teacher and talked about his situation to her, expressed his despair at the burden on him at home looking after the kids on his own since Yvette ran away recently. He grew more upset as he talked.

"If it wasn't for the kids I'd probably kill myself," he said.

The teacher relayed the conversation to a social worker named Kathy Greczi, who decided to pay a visit to Mohan at his home to assess his mental stability. On December 18, Greczi arrived at the house on Benedet Drive. When she entered the home she noticed it was immaculately clean. Mohan lamented the life he was now leading, it was now all about getting up early to get the kids off to school, go to work, look after them at night, homework, baths. It was overwhelming, he said. Greczi thought he seemed extremely depressed, and stressed, although not actively suicidal.

"I should caution you not to let the children hear you talk about suicide," she said. "I do think you should consider counseling."

"I don't want counseling, I just want to know where my wife is," Mohan said.

He talked to the social worker about his marriage; he had done everything he could for Yvette but couldn't seem to make her happy. Bought her a loaded SUV. The house. A gym membership. Still wasn't happy. Not only was she not happy, he said, but she left him for one of their former tenants.

"A guy who is wanted by police in the States."

Less than a month later, in January 2001, Mohan met his *pandit*, the spiritual adviser he had shared with Yvette, a man named Narsingh Anged. He had once blessed their marriage and they had gathered with him for prayers over the years. In the fall, Mohan had called the *pandit* to say that Yvette had gone missing, and now he was seeking more spiritual help, and perhaps a prediction. He told the *pandit* that she had gone missing, left just like that, she had not even taken her medication or clothes with her, even her OHIP card. She had an affair. Mohan was in tears when he spoke. The *pandit* observed that Mohan was not currently in a good sign, astrologically speaking. Did the *pandit* have any prediction on where Yvette was, or what had happened to her? He told Mohan to put his hand on a page in an astrology book, to help him see the future.

"I cannot make a prediction on where she is," he told Mohan. "But you might hear from the police in the month of May or June."

Later in January, Mohan phoned the family's financial adviser, a woman named Lori-Anne. He needed to sit down with her and go over his accounts. Mohan worked for Queensway Machine Products in Etobicoke, a company that made machine components for the plastics industry. Mohan had made a pretty good living over the years, the income from renting out rooms to boarders in their home had helped the family's bottom line as well. Lori Davis agreed to meet him and arrived at the house just after 9 p.m. on January 15.

He wanted to change the beneficiaries on his RSP account from Yvette to his kids. He added that he was stuck doing all the cooking and cleaning, taking care of the kids. Yvette had gone missing, he said. Took nothing with her, no jewelry, credit cards. And no medication, either, even though Yvette is a diabetic. And she just leaves. The police have no trace of her, he said, and a missing person report has been filed. She had an affair with one of the boarders at the house. Probably ran away with him. Guy is wanted in the States for robbery and murder.

"I think this guy has probably killed my wife," Mohan said.

He took Davis into the garage. This is it, he said, the Infiniti SUV he bought for Yvette. Beige, leather interior, TV/VCR. Sixty-thousand dollars. Loaded. Hadn't taken it out on the road since she left. He was too sad. Kept it in the garage, had run it just once, figured he should at least start it up.

They spent most of the time that night talking about Yvette. It was nearly midnight when Davis left. But before she did, Mohan told her that he had been to see his *pandit*, kind of like a psychic, he explained.

"He told me Yvette is dead," Mohan said. "And that her body will be found in May in a wooded area, in a shallow grave, when the snow melts."

Chapter 7 ~ Foul Play

Forensic Pathology Department
Hamilton General Hospital
April 26, 2001

With the post-mortem complete, Dr. David King called a meeting of the investigation team to update the case of the mystery woman found in Flamborough. He had dissected what he suspected were the remains of the liver and kidney and heart, sent them to the Centre of Forensic Sciences in Toronto for toxicological tests. The report would come back showing no significant findings from the drug screening, no barbiturates, no cocaine, no morphine detected. In short, it was unlikely that drugs contributed to her death.

At 10:25 a.m. on April 26, King formally announced his post-mortem findings. The woman was not a victim of a hit-and-run. Typically in a hit-and-run, there are multiple fractures—pelvis, chest, lower legs. But not this time.

"The cause of death suggests foul play," King told them. "It is consistent with blunt force trauma and probable ligature strangulation."

He said it appeared as though there had been at least two blows inflicted into the skull from the side. The victim was most likely taken by surprise, perhaps while asleep in bed. As for the strangulation, it was a debatable point, King thought, whether she was still alive when the ligature was applied. But he felt she had indeed been alive at the time of the skull fracture—because the bleeding had been so severe—so the strangulation must therefore have followed.

Detective Paul Lahaie took in the information. Why would the killer have strangled the victim after she was dead? Perhaps he had been undecided whether to beat or strangle the woman and had, following the fatal blows to the skull, lost control, and wrapped the ligature to ensure she was dead, even as reason dictated it was not necessary. Maybe he had used it thinking the string might slow the blood flow from her head. One thing was certain: there would be blood at the primary crime scene, wherever that might be. In his mind's eye, Lahaie saw the hammer or bat cracking down on the skull. And back up, the wrist cocked again, poised for the second blow, blood flicking back off the end of the instrument.

Typically there is no blood spatter from a single blow, but there is from multiple striking. The blows subsequent to the first project the blood. Nothing like a stabbing case Lahaie had worked, he reflected. The victim had been stabbed several times, not hit, and the blood remained on her sweater, because the material basically cleaned the knife every time the killer withdrew the blade. In this case, though, there had to have been blood spatter. That meant DNA evidence, the holy grail for an investigator, he thought. Assuming, that is, they could figure out who the woman was and where she had been killed—questions they were not close to answering.

David King's finding that the woman had been the victim of foul play was released to the media by the police. With so few leads, and even the identity of the victim unknown, they needed exposure for the case. While they continued to keep details of the murder a secret, the detectives needed to spread the word, perhaps shake some trees out there, get people talking and reacting, or the case was dead.

* * *

The Hamilton Spectator
April 27, 2001
"Police hunt for clues to woman's murder"

"Hamilton Police said a woman wearing a white satin nightie was strangled and beaten to death before her body was dumped in a roadside ditch in Flamborough. Investigators believe the woman was already dead when her body was dumped on the quiet country road. 'If we get this person identified, then a lot of our questions will be answered,' said Detective-Sergeant Mike Thomas of the Major Crime Unit."

Mike Thomas was telling it straight to reporters, but he also did not let on that they were in fact making little progress towards identifying the woman, despite all the work they had logged. Thomas was about to play a more prominent role in the investigation than he had either anticipated or hoped. Warren Korol was leaving the case to prepare for the Sukhwinder Dhillon, double-homicide poisoning case about to go to trial. Korol had to hand off supervision of the new investigation and chose Mike, his old friend and former partner from back in the days when they cruised the lower city in plain clothes hungry to make arrests.

Thomas was the most approachable senior detective in Major Crime. He was a physical presence, went over six feet, 200 pounds-plus, but did not come across as hard-boiled or cynical. Everyone liked talking to him. A good listener, avuncular, he broke easily into a chuckle in the course of regular conversation. Most of the cops had nicknames. Thomas was Jeepers; rumor had it that he used the word in anger years ago and someone tagged him with it as a dig at his clean-cut nature.

He was not especially keen to take over supervision of the mystery remains case. It was not a good time for homicides in Hamilton, he reflected. He already had six murders on his plate—cases that he was supervising at various stages of the judicial process:

One. Rose King. New Year's Day, 2000, the victim, King, a waitress (and no relation to the forensic pathologist), 49 years old. Lived alone. On Wednesdays went to the Prince Edward Tavern on Barton Street East for the 10-cent wings special. That's where she was her final day, before driving alone to a sports bar on Ottawa North. Left at 5 p.m. and, alone in her home later that night, she's stabbed to death in her living room. Man who knew her charged. No trial date yet.

Two. The one-armed man case. A man named Nikola Golubic stabs and kills Polish immigrant Dariusz Derengowski when the man enters Golubic's home, and also maims another man. Police haul Golubic away with his one good hand cuffed to the belt of his pants. Charged with second-degree murder and attempted murder. Trial not yet scheduled.

Three. Gerry Fontaine, attempt-murder. Summer 2000, Fontaine, a 28-year-old father of three has a bullet lodged in his spine from a .38-caliber Smith & Wesson. Happens during an argument with an acquaintance of his, Wayne Lewis, who is the shooter. Bullet paralyzes Fontaine, yet he pleads for Lewis to leave the scene, vows he won't tell police who shot him. Lewis charged. No trial date yet.

Four. Gary Hill. Gentle, friendly, popular local historian Hill, a man with no enemies. Savagely beaten with a metal bar to near death in an apparent robbery at Caroline and Napier streets in August 1999, dies later in hospital. Two men arrested on the day of Hill's funeral. Trial starts in September.

Five. Crazy Horse. Man named Drew Warry shot, dies in hospital after a fight breaks out and shots fired in the Crazy Horse Saloon on John Street South. Warry calls a guy named David Taylor a name, Taylor pulls a .32-caliber semi-automatic, hits him in the forehead with the butt of the weapon, then shoots him. Trial starts in September.

Six. Clark/Del Sordo. Young couple beaten to death, June 2000, Charlisa Clark, 24, and Pasquale Del Sordo, 25, bludgeoned to death in bed sometime after 1 a.m., their bodies discovered by Charlisa's three-year-old son. Cold case. No suspect so far.

And now, the Jane Doe case. As it wore on, Mike Thomas and Paul Lahaie became the engine of the new investigation—Thomas the case manager, Lahaie, the lead investigator. They both chased cases hard but had different personalities that meshed well. Lahaie was emotional, cerebral; Thomas cool, understated. They both grew up in the east Hamilton suburb of Stoney Creek—Mike on the rich side of the tracks, Lahaie joshed him—both went to Saltfleet high school. They used to play road hockey against each other down at Collegiate Avenue Public School. Neither man had police in his family tree to influence his career choice, but there were other common strands in the roots of cops of their generation. Many had fathers and uncles who had served in the military. In the 1970s, police forces—when they were still called forces, not the gentler sounding "services"—weren't too far removed from the military. Most senior officers had served. You kept your boots polished. At Ontario Police College you still practised marching.

Mike Thomas's dad had been in the navy. He wanted young Mike to go to college for business administration. But Mike secretly wanted to be a cop. One of his final exams in the business program at Mohawk College conflicted with a job interview with Hamilton Police. He missed the exam. And when his marks came home, Mom and Dad were not impressed. That's when he had to tell them he wanted to be a police officer. He was a police cadet at 20. It had always felt like a calling for him. Even back in his teens, Thomas had the self-awareness that allowed him to reflect that he was a straight shooter, "pretty good morals, all that stuff." Didn't do drugs, neither did his closest friends. Thought he could make a difference, was influenced by the old shows he watched as a kid, like "just-the-facts-ma'am" *Dragnet* and clean-cut cops on *Adam-12*. No moral ambiguity on those shows, it was clear who the good guys were each week.

In his early days on the force in Hamilton, early 1980s, 6-foot-2, 235-pound rookie Constable Mike Thomas cut his teeth walking the beat downtown, carrying the .38-caliber wooden-gripped Smith & Wesson in the hip holster concealed by a leather button flap they were required to use back then, the nightstick down the inside of his pant leg. He was a member of the "bozo list" as cops called it. Sometimes it took years to get off the bozo list and into a cruiser. But in fact Thomas relished walking the beat, experiencing real police work in a "great crime city". As a cop you never stop learning lessons in a city like Hamilton. Sometimes they are painful ones.

Hot summer night downtown, 1986, the bars emptying at closing time. Trouble is in the air. You can just tell. At the corner of Catharine and King, Thomas sees two guys standing at the corner. They had been in Peaches, in the basement of the Holiday Inn. One of them holding a mixed drink, a Long Island Iced Tea. Thomas allows himself a smile. Cripes, guy's out there breaking the law and it's not even a beer. In downtown Hamilton. Still, by the book, it's the liquor offense, not the choice of beverage, that

Thomas is not about to forgive. Fact was, he enjoyed making arrests. But back then, in the city that was called, without nostalgia, "The Hammer," that sometimes meant paying a price. Fights broke out all the time at bars like The Running Pump, strip clubs like Bannister's, Billy Roses. Thomas had to break up his share of scraps. You get taught self-defense and use of force at the Ontario Police College. But there was a big difference between learning some judo move at school and going up against a rounder from Hamilton, he thought. You get 'em down and it's just the beginning for them. Thomas approaches the guy holding the cocktail and the other guy—his brother, as it happened—with his radar on full alert. He takes Long Island Iced Tea aside and asks his name. Then asks the brother, who gives a different name. They get their stories crossed. Obstructing police. Thomas moves back towards Long Island Iced Tea. *Watch it.* Watch the glass in the left hand, thought Thomas. The guy probably would think nothing of smashing a cop in the head with it. *Crack.* Thomas never sees it, the right cross coming from the free hand, cracking into his face, driving a contact lens back behind his eye, vision going black, nerves in his skull on fire, feeling himself fall to the ground. A nice punch. Then the inevitable boot slamming into his ribs as his partner and more backup bail him out. Worst part was having the contact fished out of his eye at St. Joseph's Hospital. Keep your eye on both hands next time, and expect the unexpected. Here endeth the lesson. It was the last time Thomas got sucker-punched.

In his early years, after he got off the bozo list, Thomas worked a three-man rotation downtown on what was called the special car detail, in plain clothes, or "old clothes" as the cops called it. His partners were Warren Korol and an officer named John Cook. Korol marveled at Thomas's way with people, the way he could talk to anyone. They'd come across a nasty character on the street, and before long he'd be chatting with Mike. Even used Korol and his then-hulking size to his advantage. Mike would nod at Korol and say, "I don't think you want to piss off this guy. You wanna talk to him, or to me?" Korol started thinking, geez, I gotta change my approach here or he's going to get all the interviews. It wasn't just a job. They loved making arrests. Working in pairs, they would work the late shift, straight nights, 8 p.m. to 4 a.m., but refused to punch out until meeting their self-imposed arrest quota, so basically the shift would run till about six in the morning.

That kind of ambition often meant a busy week at court, because you had to follow up on your arrests before a judge. So on court days, you got home at around 6:30 a.m., slept for a couple of hours, got downtown for court for 10, hopefully finished before lunch, went home and slept until the night shift started. And some weeks you'd be in court five days a week. Some cops handled it better than others. Thomas's wife, Lucy, always understood, was always there for him. They had two kids. He seemed to keep a good balance. John Cook was another story. He was a great cop, popular with the guys. But he could not deal with some inner demons. In September 1988, he walked into a washroom in Central Station and ended his life with his own weapon.

* * *

On May 11, 2001, Paul Lahaie met with forensic detective Gary Zwicker, who said that he had made several attempts to roll fingerprints from the mummified digits he had rehydrated. The prints were still not clear enough. Zwicker's senior colleague Al Yates had told Zwicker he needed something more definitive before he could plot a print on the AFIS national fingerprint system, see if it matched anything on the RCMP's database in Ottawa.

After his meeting, Lahaie updated Mike Thomas on the bad news about the fingerprints. Checked his phone messages. He opened his Homicide Case Book and wrote: *Checked for new calls but to no avail.*

"I'm getting pissed off," he said. Lahaie was known for wearing his intensity on his sleeve. He had latched on to the case and its slow pace was getting to him. He chased any and all leads, gathering detail, no matter how apparently peripheral. He interviewed a Flamborough civic worker who drove a weed and grass cutter along the 8th Concession. The worker confirmed that the last time he had cut that ditch area was in the late fall, November 2000, trimming back the growth. The machine could have chopped the body to pieces, but instead had simply uncovered it somewhat, allowing the off-duty firefighter to see it a few months later. That's why the growth had been stubble. The cutters were positioned well off to the side of the machine; he had not noticed anything unusual in the brush.

The grass cutter helped reveal the victim.

Q: *How high would the blade be off the ground when you would cut in this area off of 8th Concession at Cooper Road?*
A: *Probably 8 to 10 inches.*
Q: *Do you recall seeing an abandoned vehicle out in this area?*
A: *No.*
Q: *Can you recall anything suspicious within this area that may assist us in our investigation?*
A: *No.*
Lahaie wrote: *"Roanoke" "The Gregory Mfg Co." made in Lewiston, North Carolina. The cut is about 5', two blades, "flail" (ph) flat that rotate underneath.*

And then there was the ring with the initials MAS that had been found near the remains. Lahaie had found a purse full of ID belonging to a woman with the same three initials. He tracked her down, found her at home, very much alive. The ring was not hers.

He followed up on more missing person reports called in from across the country, other tips phoned in. A Niagara police officer called to advise about a homicide case they had been looking at.

There was evidence of blunt force trauma and strangulation on the victim. They had a person of interest in the case. But the connections didn't hold up.

One man called to say he had been hunting in the area during deer season last November, late fall, anyway. Saw a guy on Cooper Road, out of his car, looking around. The guy had darker skin, maybe East Indian, thick black hair. The car was old, silver. Another called to say he saw two cars in that area in the fall and near the end of the year. One of the cars was a 1970 or '72 dark silver vehicle, one male inside. Parked in a laneway near Cooper Road. Guy looked East Indian, full crop of hair.

And then there was the lingerie angle. At the post-mortem, the white lingerie and black bra the woman had been wearing were photographed, examined. The material was frozen and sent to the Centre of Forensic Sciences in Toronto for analysis. If there was any DNA from the victim on the clothing, the freezing would prevent further decomposition of the evidence. Labels had been evident, Lahaie noted:

1) *Ma Cherie is the night gown*
2) *Private touches by Epsilon is the bra.*

One Monday morning, Lahaie visited a Zellers store asking about Ma Cherie and Private Touches lingerie. Zellers didn't carry it. Then he visited La Senza. And Wal-Mart. No luck. A week later, they found the place that carried it. Lahaie and Detective Dave Place visited Linda Blake, the owner of Ma Cherie Fabrics and Trims, on Plains Road in Burlington. The one-size-fits-all garment was one of her company's best sellers. She sketched a design for him. They showed Blake a photo of the lingerie recovered from the body.

"The fact that our label is on it, it is definitely a sleepwear item," Blake told the detectives. She noted that there was something missing from the outfit, though. There should be a bow attached. Lahaie drew a diagram in his notes. About 4,000 Ma Cherie negligees like the one the victim had been wearing had been sold. Briefs would have had the same trim but not necessarily the same logo. Hamilton, Burlington, St. Catharines were places locally where the garments were sold between 1981 and 1988 at home fashion shows where models would attend.

The lingerie angle was—something. Wasn't it? The detectives were reaching for anything now. They got the names of several women who had held some of the lingerie parties. One in Millgrove, another in Stoney Creek.

"I had one party in the late 1980s, but the clothing sold there wasn't Ma Cherie," one woman told them. "There was lingerie there, but more modest in taste."

The investigation was going to be a long haul.

Chapter 8 ~ Dead Identity

The Bug Lady could sometimes go an entire winter without being approached to work a forensics case, but come the spring and fall she found she was usually tapped for an investigation. In addition to the new Hamilton case, forensic entomologist Dael Morris had two others on the go. She was working a case about a male body found in the Peterborough area, east of Toronto. The man had been set on fire. Even after a burning, insects can still be readily found on a corpse. She knew that when a body burns in most fires, it is not burned to ashes, the fire isn't hot enough for that, not like a crematory. Instead the accelerant burns itself out, exposing even more flesh for the blowflies to colonize.

The other case was one she was working to help provide closure for a family up near Barrie, who had lost a daughter. The original suspicion in the case was murder, but it turned out to be suicide. Morris drove to the death scene, saw a floral tribute to the girl had already been set up. It was very sad. But it was not too late to take insect samples and learn when the girl had taken her own life.

As for the mystery woman found in Flamborough, Morris had been feeling the heat from the Hamilton detectives. "They had ants in their pants" about her work, clearly anxious to get her findings right away. But these things take time, she reflected.

She reared the maggots she extracted from the woman's body into flies in her basement in the insectarium she built, with the aluminum-frame cages lined with wire mesh. The environment was tightly controlled; she had timers set up to simulate day and night light exposure, and temperature fluctuations to mirror climate changes. Inside the cages she placed fresh beef liver in a dish for the flies to lay their eggs on, and also small dishes containing water, and pebbles for the flies to land on, and dishes with white sugar—a carbohydrate source—to eat. Whole milk for protein. Within a couple of weeks of her April 19 visit to the morgue at Hamilton General Hospital and the scene on the 8th Concession, she had already noticed something about the flies that had hatched from the larvae she collected. Far too early to jump to conclusions, but she could tell that black blowflies—*Phormia regina*—the ones usually first on the scene of a body, had colonized only the head of the victim. That was curious. They should have colonized everywhere, should have been present in other parts of the body, but were not. Something had retarded their development. It was as though the body had been colonized in two environments. Could be as simple as the body being rolled over into a different position, after death. Or the body could have been moved to an entirely different environment at some point after death.

Morris sent Detective Dave Place an e-mail on May 16 informing him of her preliminary speculation. The body might have been moved, she told him—say, from inside a building, to the spot in the countryside. And if you want to keep an eye out for something, she added, if they ever found a building where the woman had been, look for fly pupae, shells of the fly pupae, which are usually left behind after colonization. In a residence, you might find them on the floor, along the edges of rugs, along baseboards.

* * *

"*Determination of sex based on observations of the morphology of the pelvic girdle. Sex: female.*" Forensic anthropologist Shelley Saunders had already come to some general conclusions in her own mind about the victim, but in the days and weeks following the post-mortem, she worked on her final report in her office in Chester New Hall at McMaster University. In order to examine the bones in minute detail, she first had to ensure the skeleton was cleansed of all remaining tissue and dried mud. One of her graduate students, John Albanese, volunteered for the arduous job of cleaning the bones in the morgue using a bleach solution brought to a boil. The room in which he cleaned was ventilated, and he wore a mask, but it was still not a pleasant task. He had to be careful when scrubbing the surfaces so he would not create misleading marks. Saunders then examined the clean bones in the morgue, took measurements, made notes. There were strict tracking restrictions on the skeleton—it could not be removed from hospital—and she would not have wanted to examine the bones back in her lab in any case, as the location was not secure enough. Upon closer examination she was able to confirm her initial suspicion—the woman had borne one or more children. Saunders arrived at an age estimate.

The first test she used entailed making observations on the right fourth rib: "No central arc, no regular scalloping, sharp, irregular rim, costochondral pit is V-shaped. Identified as Stage 5-6." The average age of a white female in Stage 5 would be 40; in Stage 6, 50. The right and left pubic symphyses, meanwhile, suggested an average age from 38 to 48. Saunders and her graduate student took 38 measurements from parts of the skull. The cranium is often used as a guide to help determine age, since it is often the best preserved portion of a skeleton. There is no consistent change in the thickness of cranial bones from aging, but there are other indicators. The texture of a young adult skull is smooth on the outer and inner surfaces, but as it ages, markings become evident, matting of surfaces, depressions deepen. Also, the junctions between the bones of the skull, called cranial sutures, slowly close and disappear over time. The degree of cranial suture closure is one indicator of age.

Saunders found that study of the victim's skull indicated "no evidence of any cranial suture closure, either ectocranially (outside the skull) or endocranially (inside.) Since this individual is clearly an adult—all secondary growth centers are fused including the medial clavicle, first sacral vertebra, and spheno-occipital synchondrosis—then the observation of open sutures suggests, at least, that the individual is probably not older than 50 years. There is no evidence for any cranial suture closure which would suggest that this individual is not likely to be much past early middle age, i.e. forties."

She estimated the age range to be 38 to 48 years old. Saunders also studied the skull to help arrive at conclusions regarding the woman's ethnicity. The absence of certain cranial and dental features eliminated the possibility she was of African ancestry—such as a post-bregmatic depression (a depression behind two sutures at the top of the skull), Quonset hut (half-moon) nasal shape, and pinched ascending ramus (narrowing of the vertical portion of the lower jaw, just below where it meets with the base of the skull). And there were features absent that would have suggested her ancestry was North American native—such as Wormian bones (accessory bones in the sutures where the major cranial bones meet), tented nasals (a prominent root of the nose), and everted gonial angle (sideways flaring of the back of the lower jaw on each side, where the vertical and horizontal portions of bone meet).

Several features suggested a European background—towered nasals, prominent bilobate chin (two lobes in the chin bone structure), but most of these were also in common with South Asian or East Indian groups. One of the dental features that suggested she was not European was the absence of "Carabelli's cusps on the maxillary molars." (A cusp is a raised round part on the chewing surface of a tooth. A Carabelli's cusp is a prominent feature seen in up to 85 percent of some European populations.) On the other hand, the woman had a prominent degree of alveolar prognathism, which is frequently seen in skulls of those from the Indian subcontinent who otherwise show similar skeletal features to Europeans.

"There are several features of the cranium which indicate to me that this individual is likely of Asian background, perhaps East Indian," Saunders wrote. Her initial thoughts on the bones had been borne out by further study. And in Saunders's final report she hit the dead woman's ethnicity perfectly. She sent her report to regional coroner Dr. David Eden, with copies to the forensic pathology unit at Hamilton General Hospital.

A portrait of the victim was emerging piece by piece. The detectives needed to get the best hypothetical picture possible of her out in the public eye to encourage more tips. Late in May, Paul Lahaie spoke with Frank Daulby, who was based at the Ontario Provincial Police forensic identification section in Orillia, north of Toronto. Daulby was a composite artist and expert in facial reconstruction. Daulby told Lahaie he could assist in producing a two- or three-dimensional drawing of the unknown victim. The fact that a skull was available, and the sex had been established, was a big plus. You can work, if imperfectly, on a skull if you do not know the approximate age, height or weight of the victim, said Daulby. Helps a great deal to have the ethnicity. But if you don't know the sex, it's virtually impossible to reconstruct the victim from the skull. Obviously the more physical information about the woman available, the better.

Towards that end, Lahaie followed up on testing at the Centre of Forensic Sciences. He phoned CFS analyst Joanne Almer. "Can you examine the scalp hair?" Lahaie asked. "We're creating a bust of the victim and need to get the detail as accurate as possible."

Almer told him she would test hair samples and have an answer to him by the next day. "The original color of the hair will depend upon the growth between the last time the hair had been dyed," she added.

She called Lahaie at home on May 25. The CFS had determined the hair color was black with some gray. The dye streak was auburn-orange, and appeared to have been applied shortly before death, but most of the hair is black. Some curl detected. Longest strand measures 22 centimeters. The nails are long, but no nail polish present. On the morning of May 31, Lahaie entered a new Canada-wide homicide investigation alert into the Canadian Police Information Centre system:

> The deceased is a female, between the ages of 30 to 45, height 165 centimeters, average build. Predominantly black hair with some gray. Length of hair is above the shoulders. Dental work for the deceased is distinctive having the front left upper eye tooth growing towards the center incisor tooth. High-end expensive dental work is present. The deceased was found wearing a gold color Citizen watch, a size 8 garnet ring in an ornate 10-k gold setting. Inside the band is the stamped letters "MAS". A 14-k Figaro Link chain, 18" long with a "lucky horn" pendant attached along with a metal crescent shaped pendant that has the appearance of a fishing sinker.

Photos of the woman's jewelry were posted on the Hamilton Police Service website. It was the first time Hamilton police had ever posted evidence online to encourage public tips. At 9:30 a.m. that same morning, Lahaie met with TV and newspaper reporters to publicize the information. Later in the day, after the media started to broadcast the latest news on the unknown victim, the phone rang in Lahaie's office. The call display said it was from a pay phone. It was a 25-year-old Hamilton man who said he had not seen his mother, Mary Ann, since 1996. She was 5-foot-2, had dark hair, brown eyes. She used to wear a garnet ring like that all the time. Lahaie met and interviewed the man. Showed him photos of the teeth, the ring. Dead end. It wasn't her.

That same day, Detective Dave Place visited forensic pathology at Hamilton General Hospital. Place picked up a square box, carried it out of the hospital, put it on the passenger seat beside him, and hit the 403 highway, his large hand wrapped around the box in case he had to brake quickly. The box contained the victim's skull. He drove north to the Orillia OPP detachment, entered the forensic Ident section, and turned over the skull to Frank Daulby, along with all the latest information about the woman's appearance. Place watched with fascination as Daulby began.

Facial reconstructions had been attempted as long ago as the 19th century; in 1895 an anatomist used the skull of Johann Sebastian Bach to reconstruct the composer's face. Daulby had been doing facial reconstructions for 13 years, had once trained at the FBI Academy at Quantico, Virginia. There he reveled in learning about the great Clyde Snow, the genial Texan who, in his childhood, learned to identify skeletons when he accompanied his physician father on trips to accident scenes and morgues. Snow became one of the most famous of all forensic anthropologists, one of those who helped identify bones from a Brazilian grave as those of the infamous Nazi Josef Mengele. He also performed skeletal confirmations following the Oklahoma City bombing. "You do your work in the daytime, and cry at night," he was once quoted as saying.

Daulby had done the first facial reconstruction ever from a skull in Canada, back in 1986. A fascinating case, Daulby reflected. City police in Barrie found a decomposing body in a pine grove. Daulby examined the skull, built a composite of the victim, and when the story of his work aired on TV, a grandmother watching the show in British Columbia thought she recognized the composite as her daughter, although in fact it was her granddaughter. She phoned police and it led to the arrest and conviction of her granddaughter's boyfriend.

With Dave Place looking on, Daulby pasted tiny rubber pegs on the skull, allowing for different elevations and contours based on her projected ethnicity. Then he spread acetate over the pegs, smoothed it out. Daulby would still need to consult more specific details about her ethnicity and appearance, examine the pictures of the necklace and pendant she had been wearing. The work would not be completed for several days, at which point Daulby could fax a copy of an illustration from the reconstruction to the Major Crime Unit in Hamilton. Meanwhile, forensic odontologist Ross Barlow was preparing to help police canvass dental supply houses to build a database of Hamilton-area dentists who had purchased the specific brand of metal post that had been inserted in one of the victim's teeth after a root canal had been done. The post was an uncommon brand, Barlow said.

Tips continued to come in from the public and police services in Canada and the United States. More than a few people phoned wondering if the body might be that of Sheryl Sheppard, who had gone missing in January 1998. Police had suspected foul play, and Sheppard's body was never found. The public defender in New Jersey wrote a letter asking if it was possible that the body was that of Dede Rosenthal, a woman from Hamilton who had been murdered in the U.S. In that case, a man had confessed to the homicide, and would eventually be sentenced to death for it. He had claimed that he dumped the body in a rural area, but the body was never found. The lawyer said that if the remains turned out to be Rosenthal, it would at least bring closure for her family. But the ethnicity and other identifying factors proved that the body was neither Rosenthal's nor Sheppard's.

Cutting-edge forensic techniques had so far produced a clearer picture of who the woman found in Flamborough had been, what she looked like generally. But so far the homicide investigation was making little progress figuring out who she was, where she lived, and why she was murdered. Her identity was still dead.

Meanwhile, Mohan Ramkissoon opened his mail at home on Benedet Drive in Mississauga. One of the envelopes was addressed to Harjeet Singh—the man who Mohan knew had had an affair with Yvette. He opened the envelope and saw that it was a court summons dated from April, a Notice of Failure to Appear from a court in Evanston, Wyoming. The original offense had been a speeding ticket in March, going 13 mph over the posted speed limit.

The fine was $120. The driver's license Harjeet had been using listed 2382 Benedet Dr., Mississauga, as his own address. Even though Harjeet no longer lived in the city, or country, Mohan contacted Peel police and passed along the summons for their records.

Mohan told police, and most everyone he spoke to, that Yvette had an affair with Happy. Maybe she was with him. Happy was trouble, Mohan told friends. Police were after him in the States. Might have even killed somebody down there.

Mohan had already met once with the social worker from his daughter's school, and now he agreed to meet her a second time, a follow-up to the first meeting when she had considered him suicidal. After the second meeting, the social worker filed a new report. She noted that Mohan Ramkissoon said he suspected that his wife was in the U.S. with a man who recently got a speeding ticket in Wyoming. And she sensed that he seemed to be feeling better. Said he planned to focus on the children, get on with life. The social worker concluded that she could now close Mohan Ramkissoon's file.

"He seems to be moving on as a single father nicely," she wrote. "Feels it's time to move on."

CHAPTER 9 ~ "TELL ME WHO YOU ARE"

It rained on and off through the night of Saturday, June 2. Thunder cracked. The next morning, Paul Lahaie woke in his home on the Mountain in Hamilton, got up, and checked his pager. There were several messages. The investigation had lurched on through the wet and dark spring of 2001. It had now been 44 days since the body was found, and many more months than that since the woman had been murdered. They had tried everything and there was no apparent break in the investigation on the horizon. That fact offended Lahaie's high-octane personality, his belief that if you turn every stone over, you'll find the answer.

He walked to the kitchen, picked up the phone, and dialed, looking out the window at the morning gloom and also his prized tomato garden. He listened to the messages. Woman named Judy had called to ask about a missing young female. A "Reverend Tony" who had heard the description of the mystery woman on the radio said he had a "curious bit of information you might want to check on." Another called to say the garnet ring looked familiar: "Let's talk tomorrow. It may be I know something, I'll leave it at that."

Another caller, an area police officer, said he remembered back last October seeing a woman out in that area who asked him for directions to Guelph. She was white, might have been wearing a garnet ring, and a necklace, too, might have had some charms on it. Lahaie hung up the phone and returned to his family. It rained the rest of the day. Monday morning, another gray day, the temperature barely rising out of the single digits, Lahaie met with Mike Thomas and Dave Place. Reviewed the tips and calls, the case. There were precious few avenues to explore. At 10 a.m., he spoke with Rev. Tony and made notes on the conversation.

Tony advised me that a female had cancelled an app't with him in late Jan/early Feb. without explanation. She never contacted him back. W/F light complexion, late 20s early 30s, slim build, dark hair but not black, resided at an apartment Concession Street Hamilton. She was attempting to sponsor a boyfriend into Canada.

Late January, early February would not have left enough time for the body to decompose as it had. At 10:40, Lahaie tried phoning Judy. No answer. He visited another contact that afternoon.

Was advised that the red garnets are from Czech mostly. Doesn't know the lady that is under investigation. "MAS" has no meaning. Was shown the teeth and said he doesn't recognize them as someone he knows. The horn and fishing sinker was something like gypsies would wear. Otherwise he was unable to assist the investigation further at this time.

He followed up on a tip left by a woman who said that last August, around 8 p.m., she observed a white Subaru parked on the side of Cooper Road. Just after 5 p.m. Lahaie drove out to Lynden to visit the woman. She said she had a 19-year-old daughter who worked at the African Lion Safari.

She says she saw a car with a trunk open on Cooper Road between Safari and Highway 8. An Asian fellow and a girl in the back seat of the car. She was crying. We went back and wrote the license plate down. By the time we got back they were in the front seat driving slowly.

Q: How old were they?

A: They were about 26 or 27 years. He wore glasses and she had long hair pulled back in a ponytail. It was dark and they were Asian.

Q: Any injuries observed?

A: No, we just went to see if they needed more assistance. He wasn't hitting her, she was upset.

Lahaie returned to the station to update his notebook. The last woman's account didn't mesh with the age of the remains as determined by Dr. Saunders. Another dead end. Lahaie burned. On one level, he took pride in the community's response to the plea for help in the investigation. In some investigations, where drugs are involved, for example, you're dealing with a narrower underground community of sorts, where no one wants to get involved. But this one was different, people were at least coming forward, even if nothing was panning out. One guy even called in to say he recalled a pack of possums walking near that area of Cooper Road at Concession 8 in the spring. Perhaps they had gathered there because of the body? Might that help establish a time of death?

Yes, people were taking the time to remember, phone in, try to help. That was positive. On the other hand, it made more work for Lahaie and the other detectives to follow up the tips that had amounted to mostly nothing. Even Lahaie, crime dog that he was, had to concede that the investigation was in the process of winding down, or at least of being relegated to the back burner. Major Crime Unit detectives who had played a role that first night along the country road were getting assigned to pursue other homicide cases in which the victims' families wanted justice.

That's what continued to nag Lahaie, he could not shake it: Where were the people from this woman's family, those who had actually known and loved her? Why was no one coming forward? Was there no one who cared if she was living or dead? This woman, this mother, had taken pride in herself, in her appearance; they had to deliver her some dignity, he thought.

* * *

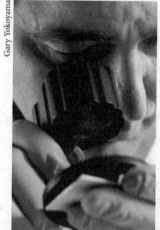

Gary Yokoyama

Forensic Identification Department
Hamilton Police Service
Wednesday, June 6

It was foggy when Al Yates woke Wednesday morning and drove to work downtown at Central Station. The ident officer signed himself in at forensics, put on his white lab coat over top of his shirt and tie—top button undone, as always. Never liked wearing a tie, that had been one of the benefits when he was a uniform. He walked into a small room and opened the door to the fridge. Inside, among other evidence, were the

Ident officer Al Yates.

severed fingers from the mystery woman found in the brush in Flamborough—fingers whose skin had been rehydrated by Gary Zwicker in the hopes of developing a fingerprint.

Yates took the container out of the fridge and carried it into the lab, slid on a pair of latex gloves. Yates didn't get out of the station as he had earlier in his career. These days field officers collected fingerprints at crime scenes and brought the paper to Yates, the AFIS operator—Automated Fingerprint Identification System. It was up to him to scan the prints into the computer, plot the points of the print on the screen, submit the print to the RCMP's identification system in Ottawa, and try to find a match. It's a highly specialized job. If the plotting of the points on the print is off, or the AFIS technician's eye is faulty, a fingerprint match might not be made. It can kill a case.

Yates grew up in the old heart of Hamilton, on Melrose across the street from the football stadium before it was renamed after Ivor Wynne. His dad had worked at Stelco for 35 years; Al worked summers at the Parkdale Works bundling bales of wire. You had to reach down into these big coils, the wire was hot, you got cuts up and down your arms. Not his idea of the way to make a living. He eventually started hanging out at the police station every morning, bugging them until they hired him in 1973 at 22 years old. He was promoted to Ident in 1989, and as soon as he started in forensics he loved it. So much to learn in the science of breaking down crime scenes to the smallest units, putting the puzzle together. Plenty of grisly crime scenes, multiple homicides.

In his career, Yates had attended probably 75 autopsies, been to crime scenes studying putrefied remains. He worked autopsies for a triple homicide in Stoney Creek, observing the post-mortem on a mother, son, and daughter. When you have kids at home around that same age, as Yates did, lots of thoughts go through your mind. You deal with it. Photograph, collect evidence. Don't forget what your purpose is. He also worked the Staples murders, the case of a Binbrook man and woman who were murdered, their bodies ultimately discovered in the covered bed of a pickup truck down at Toronto's Pearson Airport's Park 'N Fly.

There was one case where Yates had to personally transport the clothes worn by a victim to Ottawa for further study. The body had been found in such a bad state of decomposition that the clothes were put through a special freezing process to remove the odor. But the smell was so bad when he was examining them inside a federal building in Ottawa that employees complained and he was asked to leave. Yates drove the seven hours back on the 401 Highway with the windows down so the smell would vent out the back of the car.

Of course, most of the time guys like Al Yates didn't make the newspaper. Like the quarterback on a football team, the homicide detectives get most of the attention, not the ident field officers. The understated nature of the job suited Yates's personality, though. His family roots went back to the Ukraine, and Saskatchewan, where his parents had been raised before being attracted to jobs in Steeltown. Yates inherited a homey, western-style tone to his voice. But he was intensely proud of his work, driven to perfection. That's the way you had to be if you wanted to be a good ident officer.

Yates's specialty, with his 30-year career now winding down, was fingerprint identification, he discovered that he had an eye for it. He was the one who plotted the match for a print recovered off a lamp in a case in 1997—a lamp used to beat to death the bus driver of a visiting choir staying at a city hotel called the Admiral Inn. The accused was sentenced to life in prison. Few officers shared the knack of staring at the finely contoured ridges of a fingerprint, recognizing the subtle changes in arcs and peaks that distinguish one fingerprint from another, differences that can make or break an entire case. Yates figured it was a left brain/right brain thing. Not everyone was cut out for that kind of work.

It had been about a week earlier, late May, that Yates had first stared at the unknown woman's prints presented to him by Gary Zwicker. Yates had scanned the print and viewed it on his AFIS computer, tried to plot points. There were areas where ridge detail was identifiable. But it was not continuous. One print would show an area with ridge detail. A different print of the same finger had another area with ridge detail, but the first area was blurry. There was distortion on the prints because the fingertips were in such rough shape, even after the rehydration Zwicker had done. The skin was beginning to slip off the bone. The best print so far had perhaps as many as five points of identification visible. Hypothetically, if the Major Crime detectives had found a print to compare it with, Yates would have enough points to make a comparison, to determine if it matched or not. But there was no print to compare it to. So, with only partial prints to examine in isolation, Yates could only compare the five points against the huge RCMP database, with a very limited number of points of comparison.

He emailed Zwicker, told him that he needed a better print, needed more points. But Zwicker had been tied up in court on another case, had been unable to give it another shot. On the morning of June 6, Al Yates was ready to start fresh on his own. He had met with Zwicker and they agreed that Al, the senior man, would take a shot himself at getting a better print. Zwicker understood the learning curve in forensics. Al had a lot of years under his belt, knew a few more tricks of the trade. And so he retrieved the fingers from the fridge.

The homicide detectives usually left the forensic detectives to their work. But on occasion somebody might pop downstairs and see how a case was coming along. Paul Lahaie came down to see Al and check on his progress. If nothing else, he told Yates, they needed to officially advance the investigation by making a decision on whether the fingerprints were a dead end. If fingerprinting the victim was a nonstarter for identification, they needed a report that said so. Yates was an easygoing guy. But he didn't want to call it game over, not yet.

"I'm just not able to do it with what I have here," he said. "I need a better print. I think I can go further with this."

Yates took one of the digits out of its container, the right thumb. It was blackened with fingerprint powder. Alone in the lab room, Yates ran warm water from the tap, took the thumb tip and washed the powder off. Zwicker had rehydrated the thumb, inflating the skin like a tire, which brought out ridges. But Yates tried to encourage even more detail in the skin that might accentuate more identifiable ridges. He applied a lanolin-based waterless hand cleaner to the thumb, and began massaging it, rubbing the oil in, trying to soften the hard ridges. He massaged it for nearly an hour, kneading at the skin, feeling the ridges.

"Come on," he said to himself, staring at the woman's thumb as he rubbed it. "You gotta tell me who you are. Talk to me."

He later applied fingerprint powder to the clean digit, leaving some of the lanolin on the tip to help the ridges adhere to the powder. Zwicker had used a hard surface under the fingerprint

Post-Mortem   83

paper. Yates placed a rubber pad on the table, put white fingerprint paper on top of it, and started rolling one finger, then the next, applying different pressure each time, the rubber pad forming to the contours of the fingers. A clever move. He rolled 30 to 40 impressions. Of those, he was pleased with two or three. There was still distortion; the skin had stretched, and when you plot points on the computer, distance counts. If an ending of one ridge is too far away from where it's supposed to be, your score for a match will be lower. He put the thumb and the other fingertips back in the fridge, locked it, removed his gloves, and took the paper to the cramped AFIS computer room, the mint-green walls cold and bare.

"OK. Let's see what I can do for you," he said in the empty room.

He scanned one of the prints he made into the computer, the right thumb. That alone would eliminate a whole swath of fingerprints in the RCMP database—the fact that it was the right thumb, and that it was a female right thumb. Now he saw the victim's scanned print appear on his screen. He could see that he had rolled a decent print, it looked to be in reasonable shape magnified on his screen. It was a whorl pattern. Fingerprint patterns include the arch, tented arch, left loop, right loop, whorl. Sixty to seventy percent of patterns are loops. Yates started plotting characteristics on the screen, following the tiny black lines of the fingerprint, moving the computer mouse from spot to spot, clicking here, and there, marking dots and lines on the screen, measuring distances between locations, building a blueprint for the woman's fingerprint.

He plotted the core delta, a tiny triangle. Ridge endings. Bifurcations, trifurcations, lakes, islands. He plotted 10 to 14 characteristics, and then submitted the search through to the database in Ottawa for comparison. Fingerprints that exist on the RCMP AFIS databases include only those individuals who have been charged in Canada with a criminal offense and not cleared, and also those who have recently claimed refugee status in the country.

The Major Crime File (MCF) and the Latent Crime File (LCF) are the two major databases. The immigration database is part of the MCF. The LCF lists those who have been charged recently.

Yates searched all of it. In the fictional world of forensic investigation, a print is submitted and the computer instantly spits back a
matching photo and personal information. In real life, a forensics
officer will, if he's lucky, get a list back from the computer of many
possible matches, perhaps hundreds of them, in order of probability. The computer is not infallible. The officer must use his eye
to make the best match from that list. It can be a long, arduous
and sometimes fruitless process.

As he worked, Yates imagined that the woman he was looking for might well have been someone who fell between society's
cracks. Might have a criminal record. Why else would no one be
looking everywhere for her or filing a missing person report for
her? Either that, or, if she was involved in some kind of criminal
activity, maybe there were people out there who didn't want her
to be found. Either way, it had no impact on his motivation to
identify the victim. No one deserves to die like that, be beaten,
dumped in a field, he thought. No one.

On the first search he submitted, Yates requested all possible
fingerprint matches for individuals in the database who lived
within the Hamilton area. In a couple of minutes, images of prints
from a list of possible matches came back. To Yates's eye, none of
the matches looked solid. He expanded the search to the Golden
Horseshoe, larger cities in south-central Ontario surrounding
Hamilton. Back came a series of prints. Again, nothing.

CHAPTER 10 ~ DECEPTION THEORY

Al Yates was getting back 100 responses—100 prints—with each submission he made to the database. Names do not appear alongside the submissions that come back, just code numbers. The Number One response on a list is, in theory, the best match, but usually the computer is not that precise. Sometimes the 50th best match might turn out to be the right one.

Now he expanded the search wider, to Ontario-wide. And still none of the potential matches were jumping out as a match to his eye. Yates returned to the woman's original right thumb print on his computer screen. He replotted several of the characteristics to account for distortion, eliminating a point here or there, added another, changing the mix. Then he resubmitted to the database. Again, he stared at the original woman's print on the screen, and then over at each of the responses coming back, focusing on the points in each, looking for a match. Some were close. But he didn't need close. Fingerprints are all or nothing. He needed an exact match.

He replotted points again, a new combination, and resubmitted to Ottawa. Yates toiled on the search database for at least four hours in the tiny room, alone. He stared at the thin dark lines on the glowing screen, his eyes tiring, burning, the inevitable headache building. Just before four in the afternoon it was near quitting time, and he felt like his retinas were scorched, the original fingerprint now tattooed on his mind's eye. He continued scanning a list of responses on an Ontario-wide search.

He stared at the 24th position on the latest search. Counted the points that matched. One. Two. Three.

"OK," he said tentatively. "Keep going."

Four. Five. Six.

He felt a chill. Yates spent the next 15 minutes focusing on the two prints, the original victim's print, the possible match on the database, back and forth, back and forth, staring, watching them merge. Were his eyes still working properly? Was his mind playing tricks with the blur of narrowly spaced swirling black lines? He saved his search information, logged off the system, and stood up from the computer, drained, head throbbing.

He hung up his white lab coat, said nothing to anyone in the office, got into his car and drove down the road home, a town just outside the city called Mount Hope. Yates walked in through the door of his home and saw his wife, Dori.

"You remember the lady they found out in Flamborough?" he asked.

"Yes."

"I've identified her."

* * *

Gary Yokoyama

Al Yates.

Al Yates went to bed that night hoping morning would come quickly so he could get back to the station. He had stared at the fingerprint of the mystery woman so intensely, for so long, that it was branded on his brain. As he lay in bed, he could still see the ridges, deltas, and other points of the original, matched with lucky No. 24 on the AFIS list. He was certain it was the one they were looking for, positive that he had found her. The reason he had left the office before doing his final checks, or telling anyone what he had found, was to rest his eyes so he could look at it fresh the next day. He definitely wasn't going to call Paul Lahaie until he was certain of what he had.

Gary Yokoyama

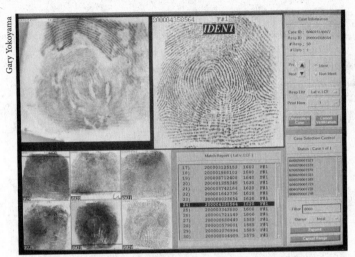

The fingerprint from the severed digit (top left) and the match (middle).

Overnight, as he tried to sleep, the clouds finally parted, the sky cleared, and Thursday morning broke crisp and blue. Yates was back in the office downtown by 7:30 a.m. He logged on to the computer, opened up the fingerprint file he had saved, and spent 10 minutes comparing the two prints all over again. Absolutely. Not a question in his mind.

"You did talk to me, didn't you?" he said under his breath. "Now we'll see what we can do for you."

He phoned the RCMP in Ottawa. He knew they would have another version of the same print, and it might even be of better quality than the one he was looking at. They sent it to him and, in fact, it was even clearer on the points of comparison he had plotted. He asked a colleague named Dave Doel to have a look, offer his opinion. Doel confirmed it. Finally, Yates paged Lahaie. He was at court and returned the call.

"Paul, as soon as you're done you should come down here. Got some good news for you."

Lahaie felt adrenalin course through him. This could be huge. Meanwhile, Yates typed in the number of fingerprint match No. 24 to the RCMP database, then ran the database code number on his computer and detailed information raced across his screen. Their victim had a criminal record:

Budram, Lilawattee
DOB 1960-04-26
Non-white female 160 cm, 5'3, 144 pounds
L.K.A. 2382 Benedet Drive, Mississauga, Ont.
Assault with a weapon/Threaten death

Assault? Threaten death? What happened? Whom did she threaten? The profile offered no further details.

Lahaie parked at the station and hurried to the Ident section. Yates showed him the fingerprints on the screen, and the personal information of Lilawatte Budram. Lahaie was pumped. Just like that, he reflected, the victim had become someone. She was human again. Ms. Budram. But he also instinctively knew that solving the identity riddle was also just a beginning, and no more than that.

In nearly all homicide cases, you have the identity from the start, but it means little as far as getting an arrest and a conviction —the only real litmus test for the homicide detective, Lahaie well knew. Later that morning Lahaie met with Mike Thomas, who had not heard the news right away. The others had been looking for him to pass the word, but Thomas had been holed up writing an essay. It was for a training course in financial management in police organization. Nice bedtime reading, he cracked. After the essay he dragged himself back to the Major Crime Unit, then perked up when someone told him that an identification had been made. But Thomas grew skeptical, as he hurried downstairs to see Al Yates.

"What do you have?" Thomas said. Yates and Dave Doel told him about the match. Thomas knew how sure the ident guys would have to be before telling him, the case manager, such a thing. He had worked with Al and Dave before, trusted their judgment. And yet.

"Are you sure?" Thomas asked. "The finger was in pretty bad shape. Any possibility there is a mistake?"

"There is absolutely no doubt that this person is Lilawattee Budram," Doel replied.

Now Thomas believed, was excited. Experience had taught him to never get too high or too low, but at least part two of the investigation had finally begun. At that point, just four of them knew who the victim was. They had to learn her history, and fast. When word got out who the woman had been, people would start reacting: her family, friends. And, perhaps, her killer. The detectives had to be in a position to monitor the reaction, learn from it. Who was Ms. Budram? Who had she threatened? When was she last seen alive? Who knew her? Who had motive to kill her? The information on the database said the arrest of Ms. Budram had been in Peel Region, 40 minutes east of Hamilton. That was the place to start.

At noon, Lahaie checked out a car and drove to Mississauga, exited north off the 401 and headed to the Special Services Bureau of Peel Regional Police on Matheson Boulevard. He met two Peel detectives named Jamie Davis and Jennifer Dinneen, who pulled a file on Ms. Budram for him to view. Lahaie learned that Lilawattee (Yvette) Budram and her husband, a man named Mohan Ramkissoon, had a stormy marriage during their 12 years together. Lahaie opened his homicide notebook labeled Jane Doe and started writing:

—*Mohan Ramkissoon DOB: 26 Jan. 1966*

—*Yvette Budram aka Lilawattee Budram DOB: 26 Apr 1960*

—*Previous complaints involving these two for domestic. Verbal argument, clothes strewn outside upon vic return.*

—*14 March 1996. Domestic. Niece was a witness. Yvette 8 months pregnant, threw a picture and struck M.R. M.R. grabbed his wife and pushed her on the bed.*

—*Domestic 13 Oct. 1999 Complainant Yvette is attempting to leave the home, husband is refusing to let her remove any of her belongings or their children.*

—*04 July 1999 Complainant advises minor verbal dispute with husband. They have not been getting along for the past several months due to him working long hours and not coming home. She told her husband that she had enough and was leaving. He told her she was not going anywhere and she called police.*

Lahaie noted the most recent item in the file was from September 3, 2000, police occurrence #00-149595.

—*Accused threatened to kill the vic several times. Acc'd grabbed a knife and pointed at him.*

Yvette Budram.

And now Paul Lahaie understood the origin of the criminal charge against Yvette Budram. She had allegedly threatened death and assaulted her husband. And as it happened, her actions were also the key to cracking her identity in death. Had Yvette not done these things—or, at least, if Mohan had not run from the house and made the critical 911 call against his wife—she never would have been charged, her fingerprints never added to the AFIS system, and Al Yates would never have found them.

Lahaie read that, following the arrest, Yvette had been taken to jail, fingerprinted and required to attend court. At some point she had also been taken from jail to the ER at Credit Valley Hospital in Mississauga, complaining of shortness of breath in the cell. She was released. Yvette was in custody for five days, from September 3 to September 8. On September 8 she had headed to court first thing in the morning and was released on bail at three that afternoon.

Lahaie read Mohan Ramkissoon's statement, his version of what had happened leading up to the night of the arrest. There was a reference to a man named Harjeet Singh. Yvette had once loaned Harjeet some cash, $3,200. And they had been having an affair, and Mohan knew about it:

My wife started going to Planet Workout in May/00. Once I went there ... I saw my wife and Harjeet in a car, when she should have been in the gym. I was very upset and had an argument with her. My wife asked me to divorce her so she could marry Harjeet for landed status. She said she would stay with me but set up an apartment for Harjeet. I disagreed with her and said this would never happen. She told me with or without your consent I will do it for him. My wife then spoke to a lawyer about getting a divorce.

On Sept. 3, 2000 ... I returned home at 10 p.m. and saw all my clothes on the stairs outside the house. I brought them inside. She grabbed some from my arm and threw it back outside, she told me to get out I don't want you here. I said this is where I live, I pay the bills why should I go outside. She said if you don't go, I will kill you.

She ran into the kitchen and returned with a black handled short kitchen knife. She pointed it at my face five times. I went outside to pick up my clothes in my hands. She pushed the knife three times, once on my right arm below the bicep and two times in the left rib area. She was screaming I will kill you. I told her to cool off you are not yourself. She ran downstairs and grabbed the hammer and threw it at me.

I ran outside, locking the door behind me. She couldn't get the door open so she started breaking the glass on the right side of the door. I ran and called 911 from the phone booth.

How did Mohan Ramkissoon feel about his wife after the incident? There was a note in the police file dated September 6, which was three days after he filed the charge against Yvette. It said Mohan "is fearful for his safety as well as that of his children; accused called him from custody and told him he is finished. Victim stated that accused upset the children by telling them to lie to police. Accused told them to tell police their daddy kicked and slapped her." But then a subsequent note, dated September 8, said, "(Mohan) states not afraid of accused, wants her back and loves her, etc."

It was on September 8 that Yvette had been released from jail on $2,000 surety posted by a man named Vijay Khurana, a friend of Yvette's. One condition attached to the bail was that she stay away from the family's Benedet Drive house. A court date for her case was set for September 20. That day, Khurana showed up at court to witness the hearing. Mohan Ramkissoon told Khurana that he would also attend, that he was going to move that the charges be dropped. He loved his wife, thought they could patch things up. But Mohan did not attend court. And neither did Yvette. Vijay Khurana revoked the surety he had posted. A Failure to Appear

Notice was issued for Yvette. A bench warrant for her arrest was issued on October 13. No missing person report had ever been filed.

She was never seen again.

* * *

Lahaie was thinking suspects, and there was no shortage of them. The husband, Mohan, was obviously one. He had been threatened by Yvette, assaulted by her. The fact is, the spouse is always a person of interest. Her friend, Vijay Khurana, had revoked the surety after telling a judge that he no longer felt in a position to supervise Yvette. He no longer wished to be held responsible for her. On a form asking about Yvette's whereabouts, he had checked off "Unknown." What did he know? Also, Yvette was not a popular person with several tenants who rented units in her home. The police file indicated that several former tenants had been angry with Yvette—she had argued with them, had even changed locks on them. Were these tenants bitter enough at Yvette to bludgeon her and leave her in a country field?

What about her family? There was a note in the file about a heated argument in May 1995 between Yvette and the two teenage children she had from a relationship years before in Guyana. And then there was the other man, Harjeet Singh. He had boarded at the Benedet Drive house. Had a relationship with Yvette, was her lover, a fact of which the husband seemed clearly aware. Where was Harjeet now? They had to find him.

The review of the file and briefing by Peel Police lasted into the early evening. Jennifer Dinneen told Lahaie about a social worker who had spoken to Mohan Ramkissoon. The social worker had reported that Mohan talked to her about committing suicide, said he didn't know if Yvette was dead or with a man with whom she had been having an affair. Clearly Mohan was not shy about telling others about his wife's affair, reflected Lahaie. But then, at a subsequent visit, she reported that Mohan was adjusting to life as a single father, was coming out of his depression, felt it was time to move on.

Lahaie was introduced to Peel Constable Warren McPherson. In the days following the domestic on September 3, the officer followed up on the bench warrant issued for Yvette. He spoke to Mohan in the driveway at 2382 Benedet. Mohan told him that Yvette had been having an affair with another man, a truck driver who had been involved in some violent altercations during some travel in the U.S. He suspected that Yvette was with that man now.

"Mr. Ramkissoon advised," concluded the officer, "that he was in the process of attempting to locate Ms. Budram."

Just before 8 p.m., Lahaie finished reviewing the file. It was time to shut down for the day. He was keeping an open mind, but clearly Mohan was the prime suspect, and Harjeet definitely a person of interest. He needed to interview Mohan, and soon, but be careful not to telegraph where they were at in the investigation, or that he was a suspect. As far as Mohan knew, Yvette was still missing. Lahaie drove back to Central Station in Hamilton, checked out and went home to bed, his mind swirling with possibilities.

Just after 9 p.m., Mohan Ramkissoon answered the door of his house on Benedet Drive. It was his financial adviser, Lori-Anne Davis. He had phoned her and asked for a meeting. Their most recent meeting had been five months earlier, in January. Davis was apprehensive about coming over for the new appointment, to his house at night alone, knowing that Mohan was now a single man with Yvette gone. She decided to keep the conversation strictly business, get right to the matter of his request to liquidate his financial holdings.

"How are the kids?" Mohan asked her.

"Fine—I have an appointment at 10, have to pick up a cheque. We should get to business."

Mohan said he had recently received a traffic ticket in the mail—addressed to the man who had been sleeping with his wife. "It's from Kentucky. The guy is still using my address."

Mohan said he forwarded the ticket to Peel police. And he reiterated his interest in liquidating his account. Davis suggested Mohan not liquidate his RSP account, at least not until later, after he had sold his house. She presented a note for him to sign. It read: "Please close out my RSP a/c and forward to my agent the cheque to deliver to me."

She could close the account and liquidate his assets later if he decided not to return to Canada, and then forward a cheque to wherever Mohan happened to be living without needing his signature again.

"I can't stay in Canada any longer," he said. Mohan said he wanted to move to Guyana, take the kids with him, of course. Maybe come back to Canada in a couple of years. Sure, Guyana lacked political stability, he added, but it would be a chance to start over—he didn't have much of a life any more. With Yvette gone, he just took care of the kids, although he had hired a nanny to help. He was ready to take the kids out of school. Had his lawyer ensure everything was being done properly. A friend of Mohan's was going to buy the house. And he had sold Yvette's SUV.

"Took a $14,000 loss," he said.

The next day, Friday, Lahaie phoned the regional coroner, David Eden. He told Eden they now had a name for Jane Doe, the unknown woman found in April along the 8th Concession in Flamborough.

"The next of kin will not be immediately contacted," Lahaie told the coroner, "pending further investigation."

CHAPTER 11 ~ WORST CASE SCENARIO

Friday night, Lahaie took Peel detective Jamie Davis to visit the scene at the 8th Concession where the body had been found, got him caught up on the case so far. Davis had been assigned to play the lead role on the Peel side of the investigative team. Davis had worked for Peel police since 1984 but lived in Hamilton, commuted the hour to work from his home on the east Mountain. Starting today, his daily commute would be a short one—driving down the Mountain to work out of Central Station in downtown Hamilton. Davis grew up in Ancaster, his father was a career steel worker, his older brother Ted served with Hamilton Police. Fresh out of high school he worked at a bank and stayed there nearly 10 years, but he always had the itch to try police work and made the jump when the opportunity came.

The detectives drove around the area in Flamborough, recorded driving distances from the spot the body was found to major transportation routes, such as the distance between Highway 6 and the 403. On Sunday, the detectives conducted surveillance outside Mohan and Yvette's Benedet Drive residence in Mississauga. Lahaie recorded the license plate numbers of six vehicles that were parked in a driveway at the house; some of them belonged to boarders. White Acura. Blue Cavalier. Red Intrepid. Blue Isuzu. White Firebird. Gold Nissan Maxima. Lahaie ran the plate numbers through the CPIC computer database, read the names and addresses for each car owner. There were no criminal records listed for any of them, although a restraining order was included with one name.

After returning to Central Station, Lahaie turned his attention to writing search warrants so they could begin checking phone and financial records for Mohan Ramkissoon and Yvette Budram. That meant writing a history of the investigation to date for a justice of the peace. Lahaie reviewed notes, drew up a flow chart in his notebook listing Yvette's family members, boarders of interest, suspects. He noted that in the investigation to date, Yvette's last known time alive was September 8, 2000.

On Monday, June 11, Lahaie swore before a Justice of Peace to three search warrants for documents that he had written. When he obtained financial records he examined charges to Mohan

Ramkissoon's Visa card. He noted there had been a charge for a stay at the Mississauga Gate Inn. Lahaie had asked that the warrants be sealed from public access; he didn't want the media spreading the word of Yvette's death and tipping off the prime suspect, Mohan. They couldn't keep the secret for much longer, but had to try to keep it quiet in order to take the measure of Mohan Ramkissoon. And it was critical that he be kept unaware that Hamilton Police was involved in the investigation. If, in fact, Mohan had dumped his wife's body near Hamilton, he would get suspicious if Hamilton detectives started contacting him. But Yvette's husband had been in touch with Peel Police about her disappearance—best to keep his contact with Peel cops only.

A Peel officer named James Laing was assigned to contact Mohan. The two had met before; Mohan had spoken with Laing several times in the past about Yvette, he was clearly comfortable with him, would assume that Laing was simply phoning regarding the outstanding bench warrant that had been issued for Yvette's arrest for failing to appear in court. The officer phoned Mohan at home and suggested he come in to the station for a meeting about the case.

On June 11, just after 4 p.m., Mohan showed up wearing a casual, blue, short-sleeved shirt and silver watch, at Peel's 11 Division, located at Dundas Street West and Erin Mills Parkway. But it was Peel Detective Jamie Davis who greeted Mohan at the station instead. Davis explained that he, not James Laing, was hosting the meeting. The reason, Davis lied, was that he had been assigned to coordinate a campaign to look for his missing wife.

"We're ramping up the search," Davis told Mohan.

Meanwhile, in an adjacent room the size of a closet, Hamilton Detective Dave Place and veteran Peel Detective Doug Grozier secretly observed the interview on a monitor, studied Mohan's reaction, made notes.

Davis asked Mohan where he thought Yvette might be. Mohan told Davis what he had already told several acquaintances. Yvette had left him, just like that; he didn't know where she had gone, but suspected she was with a man named Harjeet (Happy) Singh. She had been having an affair with him.

"I think she's in the States, somewhere in California with him," Mohan said. "For 10 years, we're having a good life, then

Happy came along. This guy, he's evil. The whole thing makes me sick inside."

He talked about the domestic fight with Yvette on September 3, 2000, and the phone call he received from Harjeet about three weeks after that, when Harjeet had told him that the affair happened because Yvette came on to him, it had not been his fault. As the conversation moved along, Mohan asked Davis if he could take a break and use the washroom. That meant he'd have to pass through the monitoring room next door. Dave Place and Doug Grozier jumped out of their chairs, scrambled out of the room so he wouldn't know they were eavesdropping. The interview resumed minutes later.

Mohan talked about Yvette's family, said she had two sisters, her father had good money. When her father died in January 2000, she went back for the funeral in Guyana. Mohan agreed to provide credit card information to Davis, phone records, whatever the police needed.

"I just want a quiet life," he told Davis. "I don't smoke, don't drink, don't party. Don't have many friends. Just my family. I don't know what went wrong. Bought her the best things. Bought her a $62,000 SUV. Gave her too much. Whatever she wanted."

The interview lasted just over an hour and a half. Dave Place tried to get a read on Mohan Ramkissoon through his answers, and how he offered them. Place had a keener eye for that than most. He had a reputation as an excellent interviewer, one of the best first-three-hour detectives around—the early hours being the most critical window for talking to a suspect. His expertise was detecting deception, and in this regard he was probably the best trained in the Hamilton Police Service.

Detectives schooled in the art know there are telltale words and phrases that those dodging the truth often use. For example, there was the case of Scott Peterson, the man who killed his pregnant wife Laci in the sensational murder case near San Francisco. When Peterson was asked, "Why did you murder your wife?" he replied, "I had nothing to do with it." That, say the experts, is a dodge. The more believable denial is more direct: "I didn't do it," or "I didn't kill her." The key is assessing the extent to which the subject is showing commitment in his wording. Is he using the pronoun "I" in his answers—I did this/ I did that? Using "I" is indicative of commitment, responsibility, but if he began the interview using first-person singular, and later slides into losing the "I"—"did this," or "did that," or "whoever did it," the change might suggest something.

Dave Place knew it's often challenging to detect a lie, but at the same time, it's nearly impossible for someone, anyone, to seamlessly keep a lie going for an extended period of time. Near the end of the interview, Mohan continued answering questions, his hands folded on the interview table, gesturing here and there. And now Davis asked the payoff question.

"There's something I have to ask you," Davis said. "It's my job to ask you."

"Sure," Mohan said, and he raised his right hand up and leaned it against the side of his head as Davis spoke.

"Did you have anything to do with your wife's disappearance?"

"Oh no, absolutely not," Mohan said in an even voice.

"Why should I believe you?"

"I know that's your job," Mohan said, gesturing now again with his hand, to himself. "But I have never, never laid my hand on my wife, never asked her to leave or whatever. She was the one having an affair and wanted to get out of it—oh, and I forgot to tell you, she asked me before, 'Can we divorce?' She wanted to leave, and I said over my dead body I can't do that. But all this time I never had a clue she was having an affair. But I'm not going to divorce my wife so someone else can marry her."

Place wrote the phrase down in his notes. *Oh no, absolutely not.* Wordy, repetitive denials, rather than a straightforward "I didn't do it," can be the sign of a guilty mind, Place reflected. "Oh no, absolutely not/ Never laid a hand on her, never asked her to leave," added up to four denials in one answer. And the phrase "Oh no": it was, Place thought, a weak response. This was his missing wife they were talking about, who, to Mohan's knowledge, could very well be dead. Where was the outrage at such a question? Why didn't he react with anger, disbelief: *"How could you even suggest I would be responsible?"*

But did Mohan's performance scream guilty? In the past, Place had had moments like that, when a suspect's responses provided instant clarity of a man's guilt. There had been that night the previous year when waitress Rose King was killed, and Place interviewed a man named Michael Griffin. Just the way Griffin had responded to his questions, Place knew something wasn't right. The way he answered was not consistent with a truthful person, the words, the body language. And if he wasn't being truthful, why was that? Griffin was ultimately convicted for the slaying.

And Mohan Ramkissoon? By the conclusion of the interview, his phrasing had sounded evasive in spots, but he also seemed to have an answer for everything. Even his answer to whether he had anything to do with her disappearance—it was as though he answered in the context of Yvette simply having left him, the way he immediately took off on a tangent to her desire to divorce him. Was he speaking like a man who knew she was dead? Or speaking like the one who killed her? Moreover, the detectives all knew, the verbal component accounts for only about seven percent of what a person is communicating. Body language, facial expressions, often tell the story. And on this score, Mohan was not offering strong signals, he seemed relatively calm answering the questions. To Place, as well as Jamie Davis and Doug Grozier, his first interview with police had not tipped the balance. To all of them, the jury was still out on Mohan as the prime suspect.

* * *

The next day, Paul Lahaie and a Hamilton detective named Terry Hill appeared at the front desk of the Mississauga Gate Inn.

Gary Yokoyama

The Mississauga Gate Inn.

"I'd like to see your guest registration books," Lahaie told the manager behind the desk. The manager, a man named Sonny Uppal, went to the back office to retrieve his records. Lahaie looked at the entries from the previous summer. There was an entry for July 22, 2000, someone signed for a room rate that day of $30, a four-hour stay. Lahaie couldn't make out the signature. He asked Uppal to read the entry.

"Is it Harjeet Singh?" asked Lahaie.

"I know what this is about," Uppal replied. "The one who's screwing the other guy's wife. Why didn't you guys say it before?"

"Mr. Uppal," Lahaie said, "let me obtain a proper statement from you."

Uppal began again, told Lahaie about the time Yvette Budram's husband, Mohan Ramkissoon, had come by the hotel. The husband was short, had a mustache, West Indies appearance. He had demanded to know who had charged a room to his credit card.

"He noticed it from his bank statement," Uppal added. "Said his wife was having an affair with a guy who signed his credit card. Told me the guy was a friend and a truck driver."

Hamilton Detective Mike Thomas, who was supervising the overall investigation, and Lahaie had talked it over. They needed to turn the heat up on Mohan. They were going to have to release Yvette's name to the public soon. They had to shake Mohan a bit and see what happened. Peel Detective Jamie Davis was assigned to phone Mohan and arrange for a second interview with him, and once at that interview, in person, Mohan would be told they had found Yvette's body. If Mohan had nothing to do with her murder, the news that his dead wife had been found would be a shock and he should be given the courtesy of hearing it in person. And, if he had something to do with her death, they could read his reaction better face to face, try to get information from him on the spot. On the phone, though, Davis would only tell Mohan that they needed to meet simply to update their investigation into Yvette's whereabouts. He would not tip his hand.

The next morning, Wednesday, June 13, just after 7:30 a.m., Davis phoned Mohan Ramkissoon's home. A woman answered. It was Mohan's day-care provider. He wasn't there, she said, he had already left for work. Thanks, said Davis, he would try him at Queensway Machine Products Ltd., where Mohan was a supervisor in the lathe department. He worked a 6:30 a.m. to 4 p.m. shift there each day. Davis tried the work number. A call was transferred to Mohan. It was 10 minutes to eight. Davis reintroduced himself on the phone.

"Mohan, I need to speak to you this morning," Davis said.

"Oh shit," Mohan replied.

Detective Jamie Davis.

Davis felt the blood drain from his face. Had he been too direct? It was not the reaction he expected. They had met just two days before, and as far as Mohan knew, they were simply continuing the search for Yvette. *Oh shit?* Mohan Ramkissoon sounded very nervous.

"I'll have to make some arrangements at work," Mohan said. "Maybe we can meet at four-thirty or something. I'll call you right back." He hung up the phone and called back a few minutes later.

"I spoke to my lawyer the other day," Mohan said. "He said I've been very cooperating, and that if I come back in again I should bring my lawyer with me."

"What is your lawyer's name?" Davis asked.

"Kevin."

"What's his phone number?"

"I can't find it right now. I want to wait to hear back from him and then get back to you and come in later."

When Davis got off the phone he told Lahaie and Thomas about the conversation. Lahaie thought Mohan was acting like a guilty man. He wants to speak to his lawyer? Sure, lawyers will say, there's nothing that should imply criminality about that. Common sense, though, says something is up.

"What?" Lahaie said. "You try to portray yourself as a grieving husband and now the police want to talk to you about your missing wife, and you put them off? Why isn't he asking police for new information about his beloved wife?" The reason, thought Lahaie, is that Mohan knows the answer already, knows the real reason police want to see him. Needs to buy time to think out his strategy for what to do next.

But Lahaie's analysis of the situation was now overcome by a sick feeling in his stomach. Oh, no, he thought: they had been building the case, putting their ducks in a row—and now they had spooked Mohan. The case was in the balance now. The suspect might run, or do something far worse. His two young kids could be in danger. Murder-suicide. It crossed the detective's mind. Everything was in jeopardy now. It was the worst-case scenario.

CHAPTER 12 ~ ONE-WAY TICKET

Just before 10 a.m., Mohan Ramkissoon left work. After making a brief stop at his lawyer's office, he drove home, picked up his youngest child, Kevin, and his nanny. He took the nanny back to her home, then drove to Elmcrest Public School, went to the office and asked to pull his daughter Preet out of class. He drove to a strip mall, took the kids to a passport photo outlet. Then he drove home. That evening, he changed cars, took the kids out for pizza.

Just after 8 p.m. Mohan dropped in to see a friend of the family, a woman named Avian Kalliecharan. Avian had lived in Canada for many years, was originally from Trinidad. She was a personable, outspoken woman with a colorful personality, had known both Mohan and Yvette for years. The kids called her Auntie Avian. Several months earlier Avian had listened to Mohan express how upset he was that his wife had left him for another man. Avian had invited Mohan and the kids to her place for Christmas, bought them all presents. She always felt for the kids, missing their mother. She had thought Yvette was an odd woman, could tell she treated Mohan poorly, even as Mohan clearly had an obsessive love for the woman. Bought Yvette everything, and the kids, too. Mohan stacked thousands of dollars' worth of toys in the garage. Who needs so many toys, she wondered? All that stuff just sitting there.

That night when Mohan dropped by her house, he told Avian that the police had said they wanted to see him for a second time.

"So did you go see them?" Avian asked.

"No."

"Why not? I don't understand you, Mohan."

"I think the police are following me."

"You're paranoid—why would the police follow you? I don't think they're following you."

"Yeah, they are."

Mohan looked over at Avian's husband.

"I need a break," Mohan said. "Under a lot of stress. I'm going to go on a holiday."

"What do you mean you're going on holiday?" Avian interjected. She couldn't believe how he was talking. "This is the greatest thing, the police have been doing nothing since September, now they're finally starting to do something. You should be happy—and the kids are in school, you want to take them out of school?"

"I'm just tired. Stressed out."

Just after 10 p.m., Mohan drove the kids back home for bedtime. They had a busy day ahead of them.

The next morning, just before 6:30 a.m., a man in the neighborhood named Richard Cyr returned to his house after walking his dog, Chase. He noticed a short man with two little kids outside his house. It looked like they were hiding in the bushes. Bizarre. Never seen him before. The man walked over to Cyr from the bushes.

"What the f--- are you doing?" Cyr asked.

"My daughter has to go to the washroom," Mohan Ramkissoon replied.

Earlier Mohan had taken Preet and Kevin out the back door of his home, asked one of the boarders, a man named Seelan, to help lift the kids safely over his back-yard fence, then hopped it himself, walked a couple of blocks from his Benedet Drive home, over to Sandgate Crescent.

"So why don't you just take your daughter home?" asked Cyr.

"It's too far."

Cyr agreed to let the girl use his bathroom. Mohan led the two kids into the house, Preet used the bathroom downstairs. Mohan took off his shoes as if to follow her down.

"Whoa, you stay here, my daughters sleep downstairs."

Cyr looked at Mohan. The small man was acting weird. Why was he out walking with his children at six in the morning?

"I have to get to the GO station, can you take me there?" Mohan asked.

Cyr said no. Where does the guy need to go with his kids on a GO train so early? He seemed to be in quite a rush. He was carrying a kit bag of some kind.

"Please, can you take me? I'll give you 20 bucks. Please."

The guy was acting very odd, but Cyr gave in. Cyr, Mohan and the two kids squeezed into the two seats of Cyr's '87 Ford

Thunderbird. They drove three minutes to the Clarkson GO Station and he dropped them off. Mohan thanked Cyr, offered him $20 but was refused. Cyr pointed over to where they would catch the train, and pulled away.

But Mohan did not get on a GO train. He called a taxi. He rode with his kids to Queensway Machine Products. He was there by seven-thirty.

"Mohan has just showed up at work in a taxi, with his kids," Mike Thomas said to Paul Lahaie.

Thomas had received the latest news from his officers in the field. He had ordered a surveillance team, or "spin team," into action to follow Mohan just in case. The team had watched him hitch a ride to the GO station, and now taxi his kids to work. Lahaie made a notation in his notebook. Mohan's odd behavior didn't make sense—unless he was running. Mohan usually took his own car to work. And he brings his kids with him this time?

The detectives held a meeting. It was decided that Peel detectives Jamie Davis and Doug Grozier would go to Mohan's work and bring him in for an interview. Tell Mohan they just want to give him new information about his wife's disappearance. Davis and Grozier drove to the workplace and entered the building. A manager told the detectives that Mohan was not there. He wasn't sure he had even been in at all this morning. The detectives contacted Mike Thomas. It made no sense.

Thomas checked in with the surveillance team leader. Where is Mohan? He had gone into the building, all right, with his kids, Thomas was told. The team had waited in the parking lot ever since that point for nearly five hours. No sign of Ramkissoon, or his kids, making a move. A spin team officer went into the building and spoke to a worker. The worker said he had seen Mohan and his kids enter, but leave quite soon. In a hurry, too. Thomas heard the words from the spin team leader, who was beside himself. Sorry, sorry, sorry. They had blown it. They had lost the subject. Mohan was gone.

The railway tracks behind Mohan's workplace.

Thomas's heart raced as he listened to the news. The word from inside the office building was that Mohan and the kids had left from a little-used back door, crossed some railway tracks, through a gate and through brush on the other side. Worst of all, co-workers said Mohan seemed not only in a rush, but very agitated, sweating profusely. The workers actually thought he might harm his kids. They were so worried they went outside after him and searched the brush for them, but found nothing.

The detectives shuddered at the implications. Mohan, their prime suspect in the murder, might well get out of town. He might kill himself or his children in his agitated state of mind. They had scared him, and he had burned their surveillance. Mohan's death would be bad, thought Thomas, but two innocent children? Thomas was angry. But he didn't yell at anybody. Wasn't his style. His cool rationality, even at a time like that, took over. Nothing he could say would make them feel any worse than they already did. Fact is, sometimes in surveillance you lose the subject. This was not a good time for that to happen, certainly.

"We gotta try to find him," he told the team leader.

"We'll find him."

The surveillance team cars, about six of them, now split up, everyone whizzing around a different part of Mississauga where

Mohan was known to go, searching. They could not find him. Thomas's stomach churned. It was going to be a long day. And night.

* * *

"I've decided I'm leaving," Mohan said on the phone.

After leaving work through the back door with his kids, he had taken them in a taxi to the Fort York Motel in Mississauga and checked in. And now, at 4:30 p.m., he phoned Lori-Anne Davis, his financial adviser. He told her he was going to Guyana after all. He needed to give her instructions on what to do with his RSP account cheque once he gave the green light to liquidate it.

"You can mail the cheque to my brother in New York," he said. "Roobnarain Ramkishun." He gave her his brother's address in the Bronx. Unlike their previous conversations, Mohan was not chatty. It lasted only about three minutes.

"Good luck," Lori-Anne said.

That afternoon Mohan and the kids stayed at the motel. Mohan had arranged for his friend, Seelan, to load Mohan's luggage into Seelan's car and deliver it to him for the trip. Mohan would pick up the car at the gas station where Seelan worked prior to heading to the airport. He told Seelan he was taking his children to visit relatives in Guyana.

That night, Mohan and his two kids headed to Pearson Airport undetected by police. He had booked seats to Guyana for the three of them. They arrived at the airport at 9:30 p.m., leaving enough time to check in for their 11:40 p.m. flight. They walked in through the automatic doors carrying their bags, could see the check-in counter at the front of Terminal 3, made their way through the crowd of people.

It was a busy night in the terminal, people everywhere. Mohan Ramkissoon was so close. He felt a hand on his elbow, turned and saw the police. He recognized Jamie Davis, and Detective Doug Grozier had his arm. Mohan did not say much, did not register an outpouring of emotion. But the air seemed to go out of his body, his face sinking.

Grozier stood 5-foot-11, weighed 220 pounds, Mohan was much smaller. But the worst fight Grozier ever had was with a guy who was 130 pounds. Under stress, anyone can panic, experience an adrenalin dump. The detective maintained a firm enough grip that if Mohan tried to escape or make an aggressive move, he'd be ready. A Peel police children's services official was there to talk to the kids, spare them any shock. The detectives led Mohan through the doors outside. They didn't want a hundred witnesses in the terminal listening in on their conversation.

"Your wife has been found," Davis told him quietly outside, out of earshot of the kids, who waited off to the side.

"Where is she right now?"

"She was not found alive. She was found murdered."

"That's not what I wanted to hear," Mohan said. An odd response, thought Davis. Did he mean he didn't want to hear that she was dead, or didn't want to hear that the police now knew what he already knew?

"Did he shoot her?" Mohan continued. "Because that's what he does, he shoots."

Grozier, who had seen Mohan in action in one interview so far, thought his reaction to the news suggested a man who already knew his wife's fate. Where was the shock, the emotional outburst?

"Look, Mohan," Davis continued, "there's been a lot of things happening over the last few days. We need to talk. Can't talk here, let's go back to the station."

"What about the kids?"

"They're being taken care of."

"What about my flight?"

"You're not going to be able to make your flight."

"Cost me $4,000. Was going on a two-week vacation."

The detectives ushered him to the parking lot. The kids were still in view, so Davis opened the door to his car, subtly frisked Mohan behind it, and did not cuff him when directing him inside the vehicle. Then he read him his rights.

"You are under arrest for murder."

"Yes, sir."

"This is regarding your wife's death and the person responsible is going to be charged with murder. The last thing I want to say," Davis continued, "is that I don't want to talk about it here. We'll talk when we get back to the station because we want to record it on video. If you have any questions, though, go ahead."

Mohan said nothing. They headed for the highway and back to 11 Division. Mohan Ramkissoon had very nearly made his flight, had lost the police surveillance. What had happened?

The travel agency where Mohan bought his tickets.

The day before, on Wednesday afternoon, the spin team had watched Mohan enter the Orient International travel agency with his kids. Shortly after he left the agency, Detective Paul Lahaie had come calling in person, and interviewed travel agent Tahir Khan.

"Do you recall meeting Mr. Ramkissoon earlier today?" Lahaie had asked.

"Yes."

"What were the circumstances surrounding this?"

"He came in, he asked for a seat to go to Guyana for tonight's flight."

Khan said the flight left at 2:45 p.m. and he wouldn't be able to catch it, but there was one leaving at 11:40 p.m. the next day. It was not a special, would be more expensive. If he could wait four days, there was a deal for the flight of June 17.

"He said, 'No, I have to be there immediately, there's an emergency, a death in the family.'"

"Did he describe the death in the family to you?" Lahaie asked.

"No."

Lahaie examined the credit card statement Mohan had signed for the airfare. It was for three tickets, total cost $3,179.10. The flight would leave Toronto Thursday night, BWIA West Indies Airways Flight 601, to Georgetown, Guyana, via Antigua. One-way tickets. When the surveillance team lost Mohan, Davis and Grozier were assigned to wait at Pearson Airport. They arrived at Terminal 3 at 8 p.m., learned that Mohan had not yet checked in. They waited at their post to see if he would follow through on his plans. And he did.

* * *

By 10:30 p.m. Thursday, Mohan Ramkissoon was in a holding cell at 11 Division of Peel Regional Police. Then he was moved to an interview room. He waited alone, sitting in a chair in the corner, motionless, staring at nothing. He let out a deep sigh. Hamilton Detectives Dave Place and Mike Thomas prepared to monitor the interview in the next room. Meanwhile, his luggage had been checked. Thomas called Paul Lahaie to give him an update.

"They searched Mohan's luggage at the airport," Thomas said. "Found photographs of the kids, and Mohan, and in the background is African Lion Safari. Kids look to be not too far from the age they are now." African Lion Safari. Just around the corner from where Yvette was dumped in Flamborough. Not a good photo for Mohan to have in his luggage, Lahaie thought.

In the interview room, Doug Grozier opened the door and strode in, sat in a chair and shook Mohan's hand, and spoke quickly.

"A drink—" Mohan began.

Gary Yokoyama

Detective Doug Grozier.

"I'll get you a glass of water and we can go from there. First of all, my name is Doug Grozier, you can call me Doug. I'll be dealing with you, I have some questions if you choose to answer them…. The first thing I want to tell you is, I'm very sorry I had to give you that news at the airport."

"I wish I had known earlier," Mohan said. "I wish Jamie had told me when he called me before."

"Mohan, we've been working around the clock on this, and we didn't know all the details ourselves until recently, we know an awful lot more now. And we certainly wanted to speak to you before tonight…. I want to cover off a couple of things first. I have told you, you are under arrest, you can't go anywhere, we are investigating a murder right now, right? And I told you that if you are the person responsible for killing your wife you will be charged with murder, right?"

Mohan nodded.

Grozier outlined his rights, Mohan gave the phone number for his lawyer, and the detective exited the room, reappeared to hand him a glass of water, left again, then returned. This was the pattern for the next few hours: Grozier making Mohan wait alone for long stretches, then more questions, and more waiting.

"Are my kids OK?" Mohan said.

"Yes, I can assure you they are getting the best treatment," Grozier said. "I'm a father, I understand."

Grozier left and returned with a phone for Mohan to call his lawyer, then left again. Mohan sat in the corner. It was kept frigid in the room and he wore only a short-sleeved shirt. He sat with his arms crossed, then bent over at times, appearing like he might break down, holding his head with his hand, then sat back up again, at times with his hands clasped behind his head, until Grozier returned. With all the delays, it was now after midnight.

"You all right?" Grozier asked. "I have a couple of things to ask you about. We have lots of information now about what happened. That is clear in my mind."

"Can I ask you a question?"

"Sure."

"Do you have my driver's license?"

"Yes, we have your license."

Grozier took Mohan's personal information then launched into questioning.

"When did you come to Canada?"

"It was 1989—are we going into details? I don't want to be rude, I want to cooperate, but based on my lawyer's advice, he said let's wait to talk about the case."

"I don't want to talk to you about any of that, I told you I have lots of evidence about that. If you don't want to talk about the incident, that's up to you. But I can tell you right now, sitting here in front of you, there is no doubt in my mind that you are the person who did this to your wife."

"No, sir."

Mohan Ramkissoon's police mugshot.

Chapter 13 ~ "Everyone Is a Suspect"

"There's no doubt in my mind," Grozier continued. "We've spoken to lots of people, gathered lots of evidence in the past seven months." He explained that his expertise was studying human behavior: "A few days ago, you spoke to Jamie Davis in here, when I listened to it, I thought, you were not the type of person I expected to see. You love your children—"

"I am loving father. I would give everything in life for my family. My happiness in life was when they were happy. Love my wife, I could kiss the ground she walks on."

"Now just a minute, Mohan, that's the only thing I know is not true, because there is no doubt you're the person who did this."

"No, sir."

"There is no doubt, I'm telling you."

Grozier, Mike Thomas, and Dave Place had discussed how to approach it. They agreed that Mohan's weak spot might be his kids.

"After meeting you today, there's a reason for why this happened. I'm a father, I would do anything for my children … I know you loved your wife. You tried desperately to keep her. And I know she did some bad things to you. You raised your kids, went against your family to marry this woman because you loved her so much. And she had an affair, attacked you, threw away all the promises and vows she made to you. You kept your side of the bargain and made things better, for the sake of your children. Preet and Kevin. You did your best to try and protect your children from the things your wife was doing. And you did something out of character for you, if you could turn back the hands of time you wish you could, you reacted out of pure emotion. Everyone who has children knows how far they'll go to protect them, do things we wouldn't normally do, even act out of violence and rage."

Mohan was sitting quietly, arms folded, staring at Grozier, saying nothing. Maybe it was an accident, Grozier said, but Mohan did what he had to do, in anger.

"No, sir."

"Mohan, maybe it was an accident, but you did what you had to do."

"No, sir, I never—"

"I know you want to tell me that, because you are acting out of fear, and are a bit embarrassed. It's a normal human behavior. But I need you to understand that I see you as a different person than others are making you out to be.... Let me tell you, we know what was going on back in September. And we've been watching you for the last three days. The one thing that is clear is you are responsible. The only question is why."

Grozier tried to steer Mohan into admitting responsibility, offering him reasons for killing Yvette, offering empathy,

"You bought that woman cars, gave her everything, treated her well, and in return she has an affair with a man you had tried to help."

"That is why I'd really like you getting hold of him—"

"Look, you have come to a crossroads right now. I'm telling you, there is overwhelming stuff here, the walls are crumbling around you. The only person that sees something good in you is me. Lying is not going to change the facts."

Grozier brought up Bill Clinton. "Everyone knows he's a liar, he comes forward and says he knew he made a mistake, I had sexual relations with another woman. I am sorry for lying. And what do they do? They left him in power. Everyone understands when a person makes a mistake, but at least the guy has courage to admit doing something wrong ... there are reasons why people do wrong things in life. I think there's a reason why this happened here. I don't think this is something you planned and did on purpose."

"You are thinking wrong."

"Are you willing to bet on that?"

"Yes."

"Well, then, you're not the person I thought. It's not going to go away, you're going to have to live with this the rest of your life. What are you going to tell your children when they grow up?"

"I don't know because it's bothered me that my wife has left and I don't know where—"

"Mohan, you and I both know that's not the truth."

"Sir, no, I have no idea what you're talking about."

"You're having trouble dealing with this, Mohan, everyone has been concerned about you."

"I'm having trouble dealing that my wife went away and I have no idea and you're making it tough on me—"

"No one's making it tough on you. I'm willing to swear on a bible that you're lying. Are you willing to swear on a bible?"

"Any time."

"You can look me in the eye and tell me I'm wrong?"

"I'm not saying you're wrong. I'm saying you are making a false judgment on me."

"No, I'm not."

"You are."

Grozier floated evidence they did not have to jar Mohan into an admission. He said they could track everywhere Mohan had been by his cellphone.

"For the past eight months I haven't had my cellphone."

"Well, I hope you're sure about that because it's going to tell us."

"And what do you think the satellite pictures will show when we get that, from the scene where she was left?"

"I would like to see."

"Well, believe me they are coming. What are you going to say to me when it shows you at that scene?"

"I would like to see … it's impossible, how can I be there when I've never seen her since September the third when she left?"

"Mohan, when do you think this body was found?"

"I don't know."

Grozier also asked if Mohan had ever heard of "retinal imaging." He explained that it's technology that allows forensic detectives to extract the final image recorded in the retina of a murder victim. The image is branded on the inside of the eye. It would offer forensic proof whether or not Mohan killed Yvette. It wasn't true, of course. Scientists have, in the past, conducted experiments to determine whether an "optogram" might be taken from a dead person's eye, to reveal the last image seen at death. But the technology is still science fiction.

Standard interrogation technique is all about shaking up a suspect, jarring him into revealing his level of truthfulness, even if a suspect's response to such approaches is rarely allowed in court for a jury to hear. Even simply asking a suspect if he'll agree to take a lie-detector test is part of that process; the answer to that question alone is often indicative of something, although, as with polygraph results themselves, it almost certainly won't be allowed as evidence in court, but is useful for the police investigation to focus on a prime suspect. But Mohan did not show fear about the concept, nor relief that such technology would prove his innocence. He just ignored it.

Mohan was tired, his voice shaking at times, eyes welling with emotion, and he got colder. Grozier told Mohan he would be staying in the station for the whole night, although the decision on whether to hold Mohan in custody was Mike Thomas's to make, and Thomas had not yet made that call. Grozier then left the room, again for a long time. Mohan kept his arms folded, shivering. He pulled the empty chair next to him and lay his head on it.

When Grozier returned, he brought Mohan a yellow tarp-like blanket with a felt liner that crackled whenever he shifted in the cold silence of the concrete room. Now Grozier was the comforter, offering him warmth, his tone less confrontational, offering more empathy, encouragement. He reviewed Yvette's mistreatment of him, the affair with Harjeet, suggested Mohan had perhaps been a victim of abused husband syndrome.

"I wouldn't blame you if you did something to him. Let me tell you something, he comes and steals my wife, I'd do something. You don't touch my children and you stay away from my wife. Mohan, listen, everyone I know would. You touch my wife, sometimes you can't control yourself … I notice you have a watch on, when did you get that?"

"She gave it to me, 1985. A special watch she bought for me." Mohan's voice cracked.

"Even though this woman ripped your heart out, you still wear it?"

"That's because I still love her."

Now is the time, Grozier said, for Mohan to own up to what he himself had done. Take control of his life and the things others were saying about him.

"At some point you'll come from denial to acceptance, Mohan. There are things there that can't be explained away. In the end you have to stand up and take responsibility."

But Mohan kept sticking to his story: She disappeared. Doesn't know where she is, but suspects she is with Happy. And Happy—Harjeet Singh—probably killed her.

"You're talking to the wrong person," Mohan said.

"Are you going to help me find the person who did this then?"

"With all my strength…. Ask him all these questions. Why did Harjeet leave? Why did he run from police?"

"You know what? I don't think we'll find Harjeet."

"Why not?" Mohan said, in an exasperated tone.

"I don't think Harjeet is alive. I think the same thing happened to him that happened to your wife, and I think it happened at the same time. And I think a big story has been put together to make us think he did this. I have a bad feeling that I'm going to find out you are not being truthful with me."

"Sir, on the life of my kids, you are wrong."

"If I do prove you were lying in the end, and that it was you, will you come and apologize to me?"

"I will not apologize to you because I have done nothing wrong."

* * *

Mike Thomas had closely studied Mohan on the monitor. He knew deception theory, body language, words, phrases that suggest someone is lying. The simplest way to explain deception recognition is to imagine when a child is lying. As children, we don't know how to hide lies. Facial expressions, body language are dead giveaways. We learn to mask these signs better as adults. But to the trained eye, they are still visible. Sometimes at home, when he was casually fishing for information to see if his teenage kids were fibbing, Thomas would ask them the telltale questions, test them. "Mike, come on, you're not trying to get a statement out of them," his wife would tease. Hey, figured Thomas, if they're out late Friday night and you can drop a question in there to get the right answer, why not? Pretty handy for a parent.

Through the intense questioning, Mohan did not crack, seemed to have an answer for everything. What about the attempted trip to

South America? He insisted he was going on a two-week vacation. One-way flights? Guyana Airlines was on strike, he said, the one-way flight was cheaper than booking return. Why go to work in the morning and suddenly leave? To tell the boss about the trip. That's why the kids were with him; hadn't seen his boss in the building, so he left. But why leave out a back door, go through a field and crawl through a hole in the fence? Just taking a shortcut, to catch a taxi back to the hotel; faster to go out the back door than out the front. Why not take your own car to work? Didn't want to take his car to the airport and pay for long-term parking.

Some of Mohan's answers were obviously a stretch. But some others had some commonsensical basis. Grozier felt Mohan was clearly being deceptive. As for Thomas, he had heard and seen some things that suggested a guilty mind. Some of Mohan's evasions were beyond the pale. He showed signs of being a professional liar. But on the other hand, he would say things that suggested sincerity, too. Detective Dave Place, an expert in detecting deception, was of the view that Mohan had not tipped the scale, that even with his evasions, had not yet clearly shown his guilt, and that the boyfriend, Harjeet Singh, was someone they had to explore further before resting their entire case on Mohan Ramkissoon.

Just after 3 a.m., with the interrogation over, the question kept going through Mike Thomas's mind: Do I have enough to hold him in jail? Even at that hour, tired, frustrated, Thomas coolly reasoned it through. What he had, the detective reflected, in terms of evidence, was a man who was avoiding the police. Thomas could all but hear a lawyer picking him apart in court for holding a man based on thin circumstantial evidence. *"So, detective, you arrest and hold a man in jail because he's running scared from you? A man who comes from a Third World country where the checks and balances on police corruption are not as stringent as we—purport—to have here?"*

Thomas did not believe that theory, but it would be a legitimate point to raise in court, and one that he was not, at that moment, in a strong enough position to counter. Thomas asked himself again, "Do I have enough to hold him?" His mindset did not allow him to contemplate, in the absence of more evidence, bending the rules slightly in order to hold their number-one suspect. It was simply a reflection of who Thomas was and how he saw the job. Not every senior cop works that way, but he did. He felt that you work in the system, and sometimes it works against you, but you still play by the rules.

"The fact is, you're dealing with people who themselves don't play by the rules, and that makes it difficult. But that's the real world. You gotta believe in the system."

In homicide investigations the key is building a mountain of evidence, because the court system chips away at your case, waters it down, which means there's only so much of your evidence a jury will hear in court. Thomas knew there were loose ends to tie up: they needed more physical evidence to prove when, and where, Yvette had died, and whether Mohan had opportunity to kill her. And then there was Harjeet. Thomas thought that Mohan had done everything possible to set up Harjeet as the perfect alternative suspect, planted the seed in the minds of friends and family. They had to explore that angle. He made his decision. Not long after the sun rose that morning, Friday, June 15, Mike Thomas watched his lead suspect in the murder of Yvette Budram walk right out the front door of 11 Division.

Thomas drove back to Hamilton. After the surveillance, the interrogation, he was going on no sleep, mentally beaten down from letting Mohan walk. He checked back in at Central Station, talked to Superintendent Bruce Elwood. The senior man wanted Thomas to hold a media conference that day to announce the identification of Yvette Budram's body. Thomas knew that news now had to be made public, they could wait no longer. With Mohan himself informed of the news, and released, the rest of Yvette's family needed to know. But right now, and by him? He had been up for nearly 40 hours.

"Bruce, I'm kind of wiped here." Elwood was unmoved. Thomas went home, showered, put on another suit and sat at the kitchen table to gather his thoughts. What should he tell the reporters? What should he keep quiet? He returned to the station, reviewed notes, and headed to a boardroom for the news conference.

Thomas stood at the lectern, still exhausted, looking pale in the wash of the television lights. Just get out the necessary facts, nothing more: The body found in rural west Flamborough in April is a 40-year-old mother of two children. Her name is Lilawattee (Yvette) Budram. As Thomas spoke, he scanned the faces of the reporters. He had dealt with most of them before. He saw veteran *Hamilton Spectator* crime reporter Paul Legall. Folks like that, crack investigative journalists, would have plenty to ask. Great, he thought ironically.

As Thomas made his statement, he could feel their curiosity building. There was so much he wasn't telling them, and could not tell them. He had some dancing to do. Thomas finished reading his news release and was about to open the floor to questions. His face was calm, but he was dreading the imminent inquisition. OK, he thought, here it comes.

Where is the victim from?

How did you identify her?

Who reported her missing?

Has her family been notified?

Guyanese-born, Thomas said. Identified by her fingerprints. No one reported her missing. Her husband has been told the news. Thomas felt like a duck on water, he reflected: calm and cool on the surface, but his legs spinning furiously underneath.

How did the husband take it?

"He was—visibly upset," Thomas said. "We are trying to respect the family's wishes at this time as funeral arrangements are being made."

Any motive?

"Too early to speculate on motive."

Thomas allowed that they would need to try to find out why no one filed a missing person report for her.

"We do know that people around her were—comfortable that she'd be safe."

Any suspects?

"Everyone is a suspect."

Everyone, sure—but some perhaps more than others, said Thomas's inner voice. *You know, there's the guy who was having an affair with Yvette. Oh, and the husband who was visibly upset— did I mention we had surveillance on him, he tried to fly out of the country to Guyana, we arrested him but I had to release him?*

Lori-Anne Davis, Mohan's financial advisor.

"The identification gives us a place to start the investigation," Thomas intoned. "Thank you, everyone."

That night, when the rest of her family was in bed, Lori-Anne Davis turned on the 11 o'clock news. Mohan Ramkissoon's financial adviser was channel surfing. She saw the name Yvette Budram appear on the screen. Yvette? The news report said Yvette had been identified as the body found near the African Lion Safari back in April. The story said that Yvette's husband had never reported his wife missing. Lori-Anne Davis had heard differently from Mohan, he had told her that he filed a missing person report. Either the news got it wrong, or Mohan lied to her, she thought. She decided to call the police and tell them about their meetings, Mohan's plans to leave the country, and his statement that he had filed the MPR.

The next day, Mohan and Yvette's young children, Preet and Kevin, were interviewed by a Peel police officer. Detective Dave Place monitored the interview, took notes as the kids spoke. Had the kids been coached, or at least conditioned over time by their father? At times, Place thought that was obviously the case.

Preet was now eight and a half, with a birthday coming up in October. Her little brother was six. Preet was interviewed first.

"What do you remember about your mom?"

"She was nice to me," Preet said. "We went to the mall, she bought me clothes. When I was seven she was living in the house. Then she left. Then my birthday came. She left the month before my birthday."

"Miss her?"

"Sort of. I'm having fun with Dad, don't miss her that much."

"Did you ask him about Mom?"

"He said, 'You'll forget her one day because now you're having fun with me.'"

"You don't ask any questions?"

"No, I don't even ask him one single question about my mom. Not one."

"How come?"

"I don't know."

"Don't you miss her?"

"Sort of."

"Mom never called the house?"

"No, she never did call after she left."

"Where were you when your mom left?"

"I was downstairs playing Nintendo."

"What was happening?"

"I don't know. She was just saying goodbye. She said: 'Goodbye, Preet. Goodbye, Kevin. Goodbye, Mohan.' And then she left."

"She ever come back?"

"She never did."

"Does she call the house?"

"Never did."

"Do you have any secrets?"

"None at all."

"Anyone tell you to keep a secret?"

"Just my brother when he wets the bed."

"Mom and Dad argue?"

"Not at all."

Next up was Kevin.

The boy said that his mother never told the family where she was going. Does he miss her?

"I like my dad the most, he's special, he brings us everything we want."

"Was Mom special when she was with you?"

"Yeah, a little bit, but Dad was the best the most."

Both kids had scrapes on their legs from their journey through the brush behind Mohan's workplace, when he had evaded police surveillance. Kevin was asked about that, and the journey that took them to Pearson Airport.

"First this guy drops us at the GO station. The taxi takes us to work, shortcut went into the mud place ... Then train tracks. Went to our car. Found taxi then we were out of there."

He talked about the night his mother was arrested for threatening death on his father.

"She was taking the knife. Almost killed my dad, but he didn't get killed."

"When?"

"A long time ago. Me and my sister were there eating pizza, went to bed to watch TV."

"What happened with Mom and the knife?"

"She ran it into Dad's stomach, he didn't get killed. The next day she left us. Now the motorcycle police are looking for my mom."

"Who knows where Mom is?"

"Uncle Happy, which my dad hates. They still have to look everywhere. In Canada and New York City."

"Where were you going yesterday?"

"Guyana. Never been before."

"How long were you going for?"

"Three weeks."

CHAPTER 14 ~ BLOOD WORK

Paul Lahaie did not hide his bitterness upon hearing that Mohan had been released from custody. The guy was clearly acting like a guilty man. Surely they could make the case to a judge that Mohan was a flight risk, literally. He had tried to flee the country on a one-way flight! But Lahaie did not envy Mike Thomas's position. Having to decide whether to hold or release him had been a tough call. Lahaie wasn't sure the right call had been made. But then he reflected that you can't let yourself get angry in an investigation, you'll get tunnel vision, won't be able to see the evidence for what it is. Later, in hindsight, Lahaie agreed that Thomas made the correct decision. They needed more evidence, additional details to the pattern of behavior, more physical evidence from the crime scene, more timeline details, before locking Mohan up. It was time to go to work. Priority number one, search the house at 2382 Benedet Drive.

Like Thomas, Lahaie was exhausted. He had worked 16 hours straight on June 13, and 32 hours from the 14th through the 15th. On Friday morning, June 15, after Mohan had been released from custody at 11 Division in Mississauga and Thomas drove back to Hamilton, Lahaie worked on completing a search warrant application for Mohan's house. He needed to meet with a justice of the peace to get it approved. But first, that morning, he met Mohan, for the first time. Lahaie handed over some of the belongings taken during the arrest.

"There's a red bag missing," Mohan said.

"I'm unaware of the bag, but we'll contact CAB [Child Abuse Branch] and see if it went with your children."

Lahaie and Jamie Davis drove Mohan to a home belonging to a family member. There was a van parked nearby. Mohan volunteered that it belonged to his relatives, from New York. At the house, an elderly woman came out the door, and also a younger woman. Mohan got out of the police car and spoke with a few family members. Lahaie listened, picked up stray bits of conversation, made notes.

"What's going on?" a younger woman said. "You're supposed to be in New York next week."

"You know the problem with him," said another. "He cries all the time. He doesn't face his fear and just runs."

"I wanted to go for the kids," Mohan said. "They have no life now. I work, they come home and go to bed."

"You should have waited for school to finish," an elderly woman said. "They have projects."

Lahaie took Mohan's measure. The suspect's eyes looked focused, intense, as though Mohan, not the detectives, was studying everyone around him to record their expressions, including the detectives themselves. Despite the long night, the nine-hour interrogation, the news that his wife's murdered body was found and he was being pursued by police, Mohan Ramkissoon was in control. His guard was up. He's a player, Lahaie thought. Even now Mohan has the presence of mind to continue to justify his actions, for the record.

Lahaie spoke up.

"If you have conversations with Mr. Ramkissoon it's my duty to record those conversations," he said.

"You have nothing to fear, Mohan," a woman added. "Yvette wanted the divorce. She said she didn't love you, she wanted a new man."

Lahaie wrote the quote in his notebook, and left the family and headed to the courthouse to swear to his search warrant for Mohan's house before a justice of the peace. The importance of getting the warrant had, to Lahaie, skyrocketed. The house might hold the key to the investigation. Have to get into the house. Now.

He waited outside the JP's office at 9:15 a.m. Closed his eyes to catch some sleep. He was called in at one minute after 10 a.m. Lahaie gathered his thoughts. He presented the warrant, swore to its veracity, and then waited, the words he had written on the warrant—a play-by-play account of evidence in the investigation to date, from that April night on the 8th Concession to the present, and Lahaie's argument why the house must be searched—running through his mind. Lahaie's words were the narrative of the investigation. If he was sloppy in his written account, the investigation would be stunted, the team let down. His stomach knotted.

At 11:35 a.m. on Friday, the JP approved the warrant. Lahaie left the courthouse for 11 Division. At the station he presented an outline of the case to Peel's forensic detectives, a summary of the investigation. The remains of the deceased, Yvette Budram, found in a ditch, wearing a nightgown. She had been dead at least since the fall, had suffered blunt force trauma to the skull. And she had lived at 2382 Benedet Drive in Mississauga. Lahaie handed over the warrant. The house might be the primary crime scene. If there is blood in that house, he said, they have to find it, he said. Have to.

* * *

Benedet Drive, Mississauga
Friday, June 15, 2001

Nine months. It kept running through Dave Emberlin's head. The potential crime scene the Peel forensic detectives were turning over was at least nine months old. He was usually at a scene before the blood had dried. Nine months? Emberlin did not feel optimistic they would find anything. If someone had been murdered here, there was plenty of time for the killer to clean the place up, Emberlin thought, sand and refinish the floors, paint the walls.

The victim had been wearing a nightie. So start in the bedroom. Before touching a thing, they photographed the room. Then peeled sheets off the bed, examined the flower-patterned mattress. Didn't see anything. Flipped the mattress. You always flip the mattress. A hole. Someone had cut a hole out of the bottom of the mattress. It was at the top part of the mattress, near where the pillow would be. The hole measured 60 centimeters by 45 centimeters. There was no sign of blood, though.

The victim is beaten while lying in bed? Killer takes a bat or a hammer to her or something. Blood soaks into the mattress. Killer cuts the hole? They continued to search. As Emberlin anticipated, the house was clean, immaculately so.

Forensic entomologist Dael Morris had suggested investigators look for fly pupae in and around the baseboards, a sign that blowflies had colonized the body after death. But the baseboards in the bedroom had been freshly painted. They searched on their hands and knees, shining flashlights into every crack in the hardwood floor. Didn't see anything unusual. They searched for two more hours. No sign of blood. It was discouraging.

By now it was dark outside. Dave Emberlin sat on the floor in the bedroom, resting his elbow on one bent knee, staring at nothing, frustrated, holding his flashlight. In the hand resting on his knee, he started absent-mindedly turning his flashlight off and on. Click-click. Click-click. Click-click. Their job is to find evidence. Someone's been killed. There's a body. Nine months? Still, someone has to find the goods. The case is nothing in court without the evidence. Click-click. Click-click. There—right there. On the TV. The flashlight beam had inadvertently illuminated a smear, on the bottom black plastic portion of the TV set sitting atop a stand. He moved closer.

"Hey, Frank," he said to his partner. "Look at this. Jackpot."

Blood. Emberlin didn't have a hemastick with him, couldn't test the stain to prove it, but he'd seen enough blood to know. Under regular light, it hadn't been visible to the eye. The harsh beam of the police flashlight did the trick. In forensics they call it oblique lighting. People are so used to seeing objects lit by overhead lights. But turn the light at a different angle, use a flashlight, it's amazing what you might see. A good way to find your car keys if you lose them.

The next morning Paul Lahaie took a call at home just before eight, heard the news. Blood. He got dressed, went to Central Station, checked out a vehicle and drove to 11 Division in Mississauga. Adrenalin fired through his system. Times like this, he was all but jumping out of his suit. The case had begun with a pile of bones, he reflected. No name, *nothing*. And now they were on the brink of processing the primary crime scene. Or at least they'd better be. The entire case could sink or swim based on what they could prove happened in that bedroom.

Mohan Ramkissoon had killed her there, Lahaie knew it. He was juiced to hear that Dave Emberlin had found blood on the TV. But he also knew there were miles to go. Could they get DNA from the blood? Could it be matched to Yvette? Could they put Mohan in the room? The fact was, Lahaie was so wired, everything was a question mark. He was not entirely at ease with having to continue working with the Peel investigators. It was an unusual case in that respect, rare that two police services worked together on a single homicide. But because the body was found in Hamilton, and their detectives had done so much work on it, while the location of the primary crime scene remained an open question, senior police officials decided it made sense to collaborate.

Nothing against Peel, Lahaie thought. Peel is a large force, plenty of experience in forensic identification. It was just that he knew his own ident guys best, their strengths, weaknesses. All Lahaie knew for sure was, if Mohan's house contained critical forensic evidence, the Hamilton ident detectives would find it. Lahaie was in a zone, it was no time to give anyone the benefit of the doubt. But then again, he had not yet had the opportunity to work with the Peel investigator who had just been seconded to the case: the blood man.

* * *

With his shaved head and dark eyes, Detective Bernie Webber exuded intensity. He been had been on the Peel Region Police Service 10 years and had been consulted as a blood analyst at crime scenes more than 100 times. His father—also Bernie —worked in the civil service when the family lived in Ottawa. The son, in fact, was named Bernard, with the British pronunciation (*Bernerd*). He never did appreciate the handle; fortunately it evolved into Bernie.

Early days as a uniform on the force, and Webber attended his first post-mortem, along with two other rookies. They had heard the horror stories about the sights and sounds and smells of the autopsy room. What struck Webber most was standing there, waiting for the pathologist to enter, and the corpse just lying there. It was the lack of movement. You stare at the chest, as though waiting for it to rise and fall, and it never does. Soon Webber became intrigued by forensics, the science of murder detection. He wasn't squeamish around blood or body parts. Even back in high school biology he used to volunteer to do additional pig and cat dissections for extra marks. He loved discovering how everything works.

The first homicide he worked with Ident was in July 1996. He reported to the home of a 94-year-old woman named Irma Seale, who had been sexually assaulted. The man who did it had broken into a string of apartments undetected, but this time, when he entered the window of the ground-floor apartment, Irma confronted him. He raped her repeatedly nearly to death and stole her goods. She later died in hospital from her injuries. Webber was able to lift lip prints off the outside of the apartment window. The prints were quite high up on the glass, where the perp had been peering in—just shy of six-feet-seven inches high—close to the height of the accused. He was convicted.

Two years after that, Webber worked the case of Jayweera Yathra, a Mississauga woman who was murdered in her home. He reported to the scene and noticed what looked like water marks on a couch, and burn marks on the woman. Later, he conducted experiments to deduce how the woman was burned. He heated water and applied it to couch materials. When the water was below 30 degrees Celsius, the coating on the couch caused the water to bead. When the heat was increased, fibers in the fabric started to melt. It was around this time that Webber attended a bloodstain pattern recognition course in Miami. In his final report on the burn case in Mississauga, he used bloodstain pattern terminology to describe the movement of the water on the couch and on her body. In the end, he was able to prove that she had been sitting on the couch, and boiling water had been applied to her in a left-to-right motion on her torso, and that the water temperature had to have been in excess of 70 degrees Celsius. Her husband was convicted for having sexually assaulted and asphyxiating his wife, and torturing her with boiling water.

At that scene, Webber had to photograph the woman, who lay naked on the floor, her skin bloated and leathery from the burns, bloodstained as well. A sickening sight to the average eye, but he learned to harden himself to what he saw on the job. He was married, with three young daughters. He told himself that death is a natural part of life—although not the way Bernie Webber had to witness it. He carried with him the motto of the ident man. Mundane though it is, its logic is inescapable: It's an important job and somebody has to do it.

He developed a specialization in bloodstain pattern analysis, and at one point was just one of 13 certified in the field in Canada. Got called for assistance by other Toronto-area police forces and trained other officers, too. He collected blood samples and created spatter patterns for students to analyze—put a small amount of blood on a white board, drop a hockey puck on it, chart the pattern. Even used his own blood when he needed a sample. Later he got to know a vet who gave him horse blood samples. Blood spatter pattern analysis involved studying the shape, size, and locations of bloodstains to interpret what had happened at a crime scene. Projected bloodstains radiate outwards from the source of blood and impact. The laws of physics tell the journey the blood took to arrive at its final destination—on a floor, wall, table. The size of a projected stain is related to the speed it traveled; if the droplets of blood are tiny, it means a higher level of force was applied. Direction of the blood is determined by examining the shape of the drops; a drop starts out as a perfect sphere, changing shape on impact. If it retains its round shape, it is a "passive" drop, from a drip pattern. A "pool pattern" means blood flowing from gravity, for example, oozing from a wound. A "transfer" or "contact" bloodstain happens when a bloody object touches a surface. But when the speed of the blood drops increases, there are projected bloodstains, when drops change their shape, smudge. When this happens, the wispy "tail" of each drop will point in the direction it was traveling on impact. There is low/medium/high velocity impact blood spatter. But also, gravity comes into play, can cause blood drops to curve and slide.

Webber taught officers how to examine the drops, the pattern, and ultimately develop a hypothesis about what happened by calculating how far away the impact point was using trigometric calculations—measuring the width of stain, dividing by length not including the tail. Arrive at the angle of impact. Illustrate the findings by tacking pieces of string from the drops to the source. Webber's expertise was in demand at a time, thanks to the TV shows and movies, that forensic investigation's profile grew. Eventually, the macabre but popular show *Dexter* hit the air, about the twisted forensics detective who himself is a serial killer. Colleagues started calling Webber "Dexter." He smiled, took it in stride. He did, he joked, know how to commit the perfect crime.

And he wasn't about to tell anyone.

It had been Saturday morning, June 16, when Webber got the call that he was being brought into the Yvette Budram case. At 9 a.m. he reported for duty at Peel police headquarters, packed his equipment, and drove to 11 Division. Soon after that, he met Paul Lahaie for the first time and listened to the Hamilton detective brief him on the case, talking in urgent tones. Lahaie was pumped and still going on little sleep.

"We gotta get into that house, find every speck of blood. We have to find this crime scene. The stakes are very high."

Lahaie was an intense guy, Webber reflected. He instinctively respected him. At 1 p.m. Webber arrived at the scene on Benedet Drive, slipped on the protective white forensics jump suit, entered the house and started to look around the bedroom. He examined the stain that Dave Emberlin had detected on the lower left-hand corner of the TV, then outlined it with a white marker. He photographed the stain, took a hemastick out of his kit. The stick will turn green in the presence of hemoglobin. Physicians will place a hemastick in urine to determine if there is blood present.

Webber wet the hemastick with distilled water, placed it against the stain. The stick turned green. Blood. Webber measured the stain. It was 20 centimeters high, 20 centimeters wide. It was not a projected pattern, was not spatter from an impact of some kind. It was a transfer stain. Whatever had made contact with the TV, it had been heavily stained with blood. Bedding, perhaps? A towel? No. There was a wispy appearance to it. He opened his notebook and sketched a diagram of the TV, wrote the word "transfer" with an arrow pointing to the left side of the TV. Then he wrote "swipe" with an arrow, and wrote: "Wet bloodied person/object has made contact with side of the TV, max. 9 cm, then across front, a swipe, in an upwards direction. Nothing on the screen. Very wispy. Clothing. Or hair."

How many times, Webber wondered, had someone sat right here watching TV in the bedroom, long after the victim was dead, looking right at the evidence, this stain, but not actually seeing it? Webber figured the blood had to be from the victim's head. The wispiness, for one thing, but also the volume. The head bleeds more than other parts. All the hair follicles, temporal veins, and arteries. People have died from small cuts to the head, alcoholics taking a fall.

He also looked at the large hole in the bed mattress. He needed to examine the entire mattress more closely, with luminol. The search warrant he was working under permitted investigation of items readily visible. He would need a new warrant to dig deeper, to find the invisible. He took a cursory look at the floors. They had definitely been redone, covered in polyurethane. If the TV had been a big oversight in an attempted cleanup of the scene, perhaps the job had been more thorough elsewhere.

Meanwhile, something else in the room had caught Webber's eye the moment he had entered. The bunk beds. Dark speckled dark dots on it. To his eye, it resembled a blood pattern. Couldn't shake it out of his mind's eye when he worked on the TV. But then he looked at the dots closer. Applied his hemastick to them. Paint. Just a paint job. As for the TV, Webber swabbed the stain in order to submit a sample to the Centre of Forensic Sciences in Toronto. He was certain it was blood, but there is a process to follow. CFS technicians had to confirm it. More importantly, they would analyze the sample to develop a DNA profile.

Five hours after entering the house, Webber packed up his equipment and left. He knew the hunt for blood was just getting started. He needed to top up his supplies. The next day, Webber drove to the Peel station, a sprawling complex across the street from the courthouse in Brampton, just north of the 401. He walked through the homicide office and into the forensic lab, a plain concrete room, a fan droning overhead to vent the place of chemicals, opened a container no larger than a fishing tackle box containing several small bottles. A note attached to the box said: "If you use, you shall notify Webber so the kit can be restocked. Thank You. Bernie."

He consulted the recipe for luminol he had written out. He retrieved a jug of distilled water, measured 500 milliliters into a plastic container, then emptied some white powder and separated 3.5 grams of the sodium perborate with a spoon. He grinned. Always felt like he was back in high school playing chemist when he did it. He placed the new solution on top of a metal mixing plate and dropped a plastic magnet inside. He turned on the switch and the magnet whirled inside the container, stirring until dissolved.

He let the solution sit for 15 seconds, added 5 grams of luminol powder, and 25 grams of sodium carbonate, stirred again. Luminol has a short shelf life; you have to pretty much use it right away. But he was mixing several spray bottles full of it for this case.

Monday morning, June 18, Webber met with Paul Lahaie at 11 Division. Webber briefed the detective on his preliminary findings on the TV. "A bloody person or object came into contact with the side of the TV," Webber said. "And it moved across the face of the TV in an upward direction." He said the movement had been in a left-to-right direction, across the speaker portion of the TV. There was a combination—first the transfer, followed by a swipe along the front of the TV.

Lahaie processed scenarios in his mind's eye. The killer bludgeons Yvette to death. Carries the body out of the bedroom, but is clumsy, her head brushes against the TV. And then what? Into the bathroom to clean the blood? And then to the car, transport the body to the country ditch by African Lion Safari? They had to examine Mohan Ramkissoon's car. Lahaie had obtained a new search warrant to widen the search in the house, allow Webber to break out the luminol. And the day before, Lahaie had also recorded license plate numbers of cars in the driveway at the house. One of them was a red Intrepid. Mohan's car.

CHAPTER 15 ~ A GHOSTLY GLOW

So much blood on that TV, thought Bernie Webber. If it was a sign that the killer had tried to move the body, in an effort to cover up the murder, he had done a very poor job of covering his tracks. So what else had the killer missed? Had to be evidence of blood elsewhere, from the cleanup, or the murder itself. Monday morning, Webber examined the bed mattress.

To the naked eye, under regular light, there was no sign of blood near the hole that had been crudely cut from it. The luminol test would show the invisible. When luminol is sprayed on a surface where hemoglobin is present, there is a reaction, a chemical luminescence in the form of a blue-green glow. The light is not powerful; the room must be in complete darkness to see the reaction—which is sometimes difficult to achieve. A new luminol-style chemical agent was about to come on the market, called Bluestar, which would cause blood to luminesce even in regular light, but police services did not yet have access to it.

If there was more blood in the room, how long had it been there? How old was the blood in that room? As far as Webber was concerned, the older the better. When blood is exposed to air over time, oxygen breaks down the hemoglobin molecules further, exposing them, creating an even stronger reaction to the chemicals. Webber had worked a five-year-old case where the old dried blood showed up very well. And he read an article in a bloodstain journal that said floorboards known to date back to the Civil War were sprayed, and a strong blood reaction recorded. There are, as defense lawyers point out in court, sometimes false positives for luminol blood tests—although an experienced bloodstain expert can tell if the reaction is a false positive. Luminol can react with things other than hemoglobin in blood—the surface of copper pipes in a bathroom sometimes show a reaction, as do phosphates, for example, as they occur in decaying vegetables, or bleach and other cleaning products.

When you spray luminol on bleach, there is what forensic detectives call a "Fourth of July reaction." In pitch dark, on contact with the spray, the bleach bursts and crackles with brilliant neon blue light, as though the molecules are on fire. When Webber taught students about luminol, he would darken a room and put a bit of bleach in the sink, spray, setting off the crackling blue reaction. Upon rinsing the sink, the bleach flowed down the drain like a neon blue river, even visible in dim light. But the bleach reaction, while dramatic, does not last more than a few minutes. Luminol on blood, however, is a less brilliant, but more sustained reaction, lasting as long as a few hours—although it's best to photograph the reaction immediately, at its brightest.

Webber reflected ruefully that these days, killers know that bleach is one way to cover up DNA at a scene. Although that, too, can backfire on a criminal. He did a case where a guy used bleach to cover up a murder. He killed his wife, cleaned up, dumped the body in another city. When Webber sprayed that scene, he found signs of blood, but also bleach all over the place. That's the thing when a killer tries to cover tracks: you might erase much of the blood, but in doing so, when you dilute a scene, you end up moving the blood around. When it shows up, it looks even worse than the original crime scene. The entire kitchen glowed. In court, the defense tried to nail Webber on what was bleach and what was blood. Since much of it was mixed together, it was difficult for Webber to definitively say which was which. Either way it was damning to the accused. The killer was convicted.

Webber sprayed the mattress. He killed the lights, his pupils dilating, adjusting to the blackness. A ghostly blue-green glow started to radiate from the mattress around the edge of the hole. Blood. He was sure of it. If someone had tried to hide a bloodstain in the mattress, they had not cut a big enough hole. Clearly they had not banked on the blood seeping beyond the perimeter of the cutout. He outlined a rectangular area of the upper left corner of the bed with a black marker, in the vicinity of the hole, and cut the material out, a piece measuring 114 centimeters by 73 centimeters, to be sent to CFS. With the discovery of blood on the mattress, and the TV, they had a possible primary crime scene, if it could be established that the blood was Yvette Budram's. In order to accomplish that, however, they needed a DNA profile from the blood, but just as vital, a DNA profile from the remains of Yvette's remains. Was that even possible?

* * *

Webber continued his search in the house. Surely there would be signs of blood spatter from the attack itself, of the blunt force trauma injury. In the bedroom he sprayed the half-moon-shaped bed headboard, and the end tables, with luminol. He killed the lights. Nothing. No reaction. He sprayed the walls, sprayed the baseboards, the floor. No sign of blood. Webber was surprised. And disappointed. How is it possible, he wondered, that the bed stain was so large, and the transfer stain on the TV so prominent, but nothing else in the bedroom? You see blood like that, you expect to find traces of spatter. The luminol should work right through new paint to get some reaction. He moved on to other rooms, including the bathroom.

It was more difficult to control the amount of light elsewhere in the house. He used a different chemical, a carcinogenic product called Leucomalachite green, which glows green when reacting with blood even in regular light. Sprayed all over. Nothing. In the main bathroom, there was a slight reaction on the carpet, but it was not blood. The small ensuite bathroom showed no reactions at all. There was no sign of a bleach reaction, either—no sign of a bleach cleanup in the bathrooms. In fact the bathrooms were messy. There were hairs still floating in the toilet, appeared to be mustache hair.

Webber was frustrated. He spent seven hours in that house. When Paul Lahaie and Mike Thomas heard the news of Webber's findings, they were excited. Despite the lack of blood beyond the TV and mattress, they had their crime scene. Yvette is murdered in the bedroom, perhaps on that mattress; blood seeps into the mattress, Mohan tries to cover it up, carries her body out of the house and her head and body brush against the TV. The lack of blood spatter elsewhere in the bedroom? Had there been some suppression on the victim to prevent it? If a blunt object had been used to kill Yvette Budram, while you'd expect to find spatter, it was not a certainty. The detectives knew that, with the first blow, there is no projection away from the victim on impact—it is the subsequent blows that spray blood, the "castoff" blood from the instrument when the killer cocks it a second time, and then from continued impact on the wound.

But in theory, if only one blow was needed to kill Yvette or render her unconscious, there may have been no spatter. Did the killer strike Yvette in her sleep, just once, knocking her unconscious, wrap the ligature around her neck to finish the job? Or did he wrap a blanket or tarp around her head and strike it again and again? The blood in that case would have been substantial but contained; it would pool on the mattress.

The lack of blood found at the scene made Mike Thomas think of the Rose King homicide that he had worked. She had been stabbed multiple times. And yet, there was no evidence of a drop of blood on the walls. Just traces from a table near where she lay. But that fact hadn't hurt their case against her killer. Rose King had been wearing a heavy sweater and was underneath a comforter as well. With each blow of the knife, the sweater and comforter essentially cleaned the blade off upon withdrawal. The lesson for the detectives was, even in a violent beating or stabbing death, spatter was not automatic, other factors could mitigate it. Thomas knew they might have to make that very argument in court to account for why there was no further blood evident from Yvette's bludgeoning murder. Perhaps the killer put a blanket over top of her that prevented spatter. Then, the killer throws out the blanket, along with the bedding. But he also makes mistakes, allowing her to bump against the TV while carrying her out of the bedroom, and cutting a swath from the mattress rather than getting rid of the entire thing.

Paul Lahaie shook his head at the mattress omission. Lahaie had spent time searching in Mohan Ramkissoon's garage. The guy had kept piles of financial documents, all filed in place. He was meticulous and organized in some respects, but clearly not in others. "Mohan was a neat freak. But he was also too cheap to buy a new mattress."

* * *

Paul Lahaie was briefed by Detective Terry Hill, another Hamilton officer assisting with the case. Hill had spoken with Lori-Anne Davis, Mohan Ramkissoon's financial adviser. She said Mohan had told her back in January that he had filed a missing person report for Yvette with Peel Police. Mohan had also told her that he spoke with a *pandit*—a spiritual adviser—who had predicted Yvette's body would be found "in the spring in a wooded area." And Davis also related how, on June 14, Mohan had called her and asked about liquidating his financial holdings and having the money forwarded to his brother in New York. June 14—the same day he tried to leave for Guyana.

Just before 10 a.m. on Tuesday, June 19, investigators again entered the house on Benedet Drive looking for more evidence. The search warrant expired that afternoon. Lahaie joined Dave Emberlin and others in the search. Emberlin resumed luminol spraying of the kids' room, bathroom, with swabs taken. Lahaie searched a family room, found a couple of small stains, asked Emberlin to spray them. No blood. Lahaie searched the dressers and the closet in the master bedroom, sorting through clothes, family photos. Just before 3 p.m., the investigators left the house, in anticipation of Mohan Ramkissoon's arrival. Minutes later, Mohan returned, along with family friend Avian Kalliecharan. He had been lamenting his situation to Avian, a woman who was not afraid to speak her mind. The police were still there. Mohan moaned that he was still not able to return to his house.

"Shut up," Avian retorted. "The police have a job to do."

Mohan walked up to Lahaie outside and shook the detective's hand. Before police left the property for the last time, they impounded his red 1995 Intrepid. It was towed to 11 Division. On Wednesday, Bernie Webber examined it inside a police garage. Under normal lighting nothing appeared suspicious, although there did appear to be darker coloration on the rubber molding around the trunk. Webber sprayed luminol on the weather stripping, and the garage was darkened. Blood. He noted bloodstains on the lower left side of the rubber molding, and on the upper right side. He removed the carpeting that lined the inside of the trunk. And found more blood. He stuck identification pins into the spots of note, photos were taken. Patches of rubber were cut out for the CFS to process. On the carpet in the trunk he recorded six stains. A piece measuring 35 centimeters by 30 centimeters was cut from inside for CFS. The car was later returned to Mohan Ramkissoon.

Gary Yokoyama

Bernie Webber spraying luminol.

Just after noon Thursday, Lahaie spoke with Mike Thomas. Even as evidence continued to point at Mohan Ramkissoon, the case of Yvette's lover, Harjeet (Happy) Singh, had to be explored. They sat down and watched a four-minute video Thomas had received courtesy of the Wyoming Highway Patrol. It was the traffic stop involving Harjeet back in March 2001. The rental car he was driving was a silver Dodge, New York state plate. And Thomas had an update on Harjeet's history. Harjeet was not his real name. His legal name was Harpreet Makkar. But he had used many others. Lahaie opened his notebook and wrote.

Harpreet Makkar
AKA: Harjeet Singh, Harpreet Singh, Harjinder Singh, Harpreet
Singh Makkar
Arrested 4 Dec 96—food-stamp fraud, Mississippi
29 Oct 97 U.S. Immigration to be deported.

Meanwhile, Lahaie heard from Peel detective Jamie Davis. Mohan had previously agreed to take a lie-detector test. But now, Davis said, Mohan had changed his mind, had canceled, on his lawyer's advice. The next day, Friday, Lahaie received a call from Monica Sloan, a forensic biologist at the Centre of Forensic Sciences. Sloan was an expert in DNA analysis. DNA test results in the course of a homicide investigation are never made instantaneously, and the results are not always illuminating. Sloan had worked at CFS for 10 years and her services were increasingly in demand.

Deoxyribonucleic acid had become the gold standard in murder investigations, the sure thing, but a tool that had only started to be used regularly by police in the early 1990s, as big a splash in criminal trials as fingerprints had once been. DNA is "the blueprint of life," containing the code that distinguishes one human being from another. Most of the DNA is the same from person to person—99.9 percent of DNA is identical. It's the other 0.1 percent that interests forensic investigators. In the past Sloan had been called to testify in court on the subject of forensic biology and DNA analysis dozens of times, including one appearance in the Bermuda Supreme Court. (Not a bad place to testify, particularly in December, she reported.)

She confirmed that it was indeed blood that had been found on the TV in the master bedroom. The bad news was, the blood on the TV was a poor sample for a DNA profile, the quantity of DNA just wasn't there. So far, they were getting only partial results. The fact is, 99 percent of a blood stain is not suitable for DNA analysis. Parts of the blood like the platelets, red blood cells—they don't have a nucleus. It's only that one percent that matters, that is a white blood cell, with a nucleus for a DNA profile. Sometimes a negative test result comes back when blood is submitted, but it's rare.

Lahaie fumed. All that blood, and no DNA? He knew the forensic guys did good work. But it was not their ass on the line, he brooded.

"At the end of the day, the homicide detectives have to justify the case. We can't fall back on science, probability of this and that," Lahaie said. "My evidence has to show interconnected facts to prove murder beyond a reasonable doubt. Because when this whole thing goes to court, I am the one sitting beside the Assistant Crown attorney."

The DNA was there, all right—they just had to find it. Lahaie thought back to his first big file in the Major Crime Unit, the Stoney Creek rapist case. They had been trying to get DNA left by the perp but had not found it in enough volume. One witness had said the rapist wore a black ski mask of some kind, but police never found one. What they had found was a black and white sweater in a park. One day during the investigation, Lahaie had finished a jog and workout, was taking off his shirt in the Central Station locker room, and it hit him. Maybe the rapist hadn't been wearing a ski mask at all. Maybe he wrapped a shirt, or sweater, around his head. To a distraught victim, it just seemed like a ski mask. Check the sweater for DNA. Lahaie's hunch paid off. There was enough of it on the sweater, from where it had wrapped around the face of the rapist, to develop a DNA profile, which matched the profile of James (Ted) Wren, the suspect.

No, the rapist case had nothing to do with blood found on a TV set. But it had everything to do with wringing all you can out of the evidence, never stop revisiting it, peeling back layers. Lahaie put in a call to forensics at Peel Region. If hair from the bloodied victim pressed against the speaker portion of the TV, maybe some of the blood seeped into the tiny speaker holes there.

"Rip it apart," he said. "Rip the whole TV apart and send the pieces in."

On Monday, July 16, Lahaie received another call from Monica Sloan. She told him there had been no blood detected on a tire iron the detectives had submitted, or on a rubber bathtub mat in the shape of a foot that had come from the house. And the DNA profiles from the blood found in the Intrepid and on the mattress? The CFS had not yet developed DNA profile results for those samples, but at least it appeared they would have sufficient blood volume and quality to make the attempt.

The fact was, however, no matter what happened with the blood samples from the house, there was still no comparison DNA profile from Yvette Budram's remains. Without Yvette's DNA profile, even if DNA was developed from the mattress and car samples, it would be meaningless to the investigation. Lahaie had talked to Sloan about samples from Yvette's body that might yield a profile. Pulp from the teeth was one option. Also, scalp tissue, and what was thought to be heart tissue. The samples had been delivered, and Sloan had gone to work on them. A DNA profile developed in a lab will not indicate what your hair or eye color is, how tall you are. What the profile does indicate is how long a particular piece of DNA is, how many units long it is, in a particular location. And this is the part that will vary person to person, except in the case of identical twins.

In order to develop a DNA profile for Yvette Budram, Sloan isolated cells in the tissue samples submitted by the police. Chemicals are applied to break down cellular components. The process is called extraction—getting rid of everything else in the cells to isolate only the DNA. A minimum volume of DNA is necessary to develop the profile. If there is sufficient DNA, Sloan could move on to the amplification process—making copies of nine locations in the DNA that will form the profile. A tenth location gives the gender. In lab speak, these locations are called short tandem repeat (STR) *loci*—Latin for locations. The quality of the DNA must also be sufficient for the amplification process to work. If these locations could be charted in the DNA from the tissue samples submitted by police, then Sloan would have a DNA profile suitable for comparing to another profile—like from the blood found in the Intrepid or the mattress.

Monica Sloan had worked on the extraction process on the tissue samples from Yvette's remains, in order to move to amplification. And? It didn't work. Pulp from two of Yvette's teeth and tissue from the heart and elsewhere in the body were in such an advanced stage of decomposition, they were poor samples from which to develop a DNA profile. But might there be another sample from the remains that would work? Sloan suggested that perhaps the marrow from a larger bone would work—like the femur. Lahaie said they'd deliver the bone.

CHAPTER 16 ~ GET HAPPY

On Wednesday, July 18, Lahaie and Peel detective Jamie Davis visited Queensway Machine Products Ltd. in Etobicoke to execute a search warrant. Mohan was there that day, working in the lathe department. Lahaie combed through employment records to see when he had been at work around the time Yvette went missing. A company official told him that the normal vacation period for employees is the last two weeks of July and the first two weeks of August.

On the 2000 vacation schedule, Mohan had not requested any vacation days during those periods. Instead, he took his vacation in September. Lahaie saw that Mohan had been away from work between Tuesday, September 5, and Monday, September 18. In addition to taking five vacation days during that period, he had taken an authorized leave of absence from Tuesday, September 12 to September 18—an unpaid leave. Mohan had also taken an unauthorized leave of absence on June 14, 2001—the day he had been arrested at Pearson Airport.

The detectives spoke to Mohan. Davis asked him if he would take a lie-detector test.

"If you're not involved in the death of your wife, then you'll have no problem," Davis said.

"Exactly," Mohan said.

"Well, then—"

"Exactly—no problem."

Mohan lamented that he had not felt like himself the past few weeks.

"It's hard, especially if you lost someone you love, it's not easy for me," Mohan said. "I cry every night. Every night ... I know that my wife, look what she did to me, and look how she ended up today. I offered her everything in life."

"It's a tragic set of circumstances," Davis said. "And Mohan, we're trying to ascertain what the truth is."

"I will appreciate that."

Mohan told the detectives he was planning to go on vacation to Albany, N.Y. Planned on leaving next Monday.

"Do you intend to return?" Lahaie asked.

"Oh yeah, go every year."

But Mohan Ramkissoon did not drive to the border on that Monday, July 23. Instead, he headed with his two kids for the Rainbow Bridge in Niagara Falls three days prior. He packed for a long trip. The phone rang in Detective Sergeant Mike Thomas's office in the Major Crime Unit. Thomas had taken the precaution of flagging Mohan's name for border guards. A U.S. Immigration contact told him they had Mohan stopped at the border. "And his car is absolutely jammed with stuff."

The official turned Mohan away at the border as an undesirable. And then, the next day, Mohan showed up with his kids at the Queenston–Lewiston Bridge to the United States. Again he was turned away. Thomas briefed Lahaie and others about the attempted border crossings on Monday morning. They had to arrest him, Lahaie thought. These attempts to flee the country, the blood evidence found in the house. Thomas pointed out that they still had to eliminate Harjeet Singh as a suspect. But so far they'd had no luck in locating him.

"How are we going to find this guy?" Lahaie said to Detective Terry Hill, a veteran of 30-plus years with the police. When the pair had worked together, Hill got the nickname Bear, and the eager Lahaie was dubbed Cubby.

"What about the Canadian Embassy?" Hill suggested.

Harjeet's traffic ticket had been levied in Wyoming, but he was driving a car with New York plates. On July 19, Lahaie sent an email to the RCMP in Washington for assistance. The RCMP contacted the NYPD. It wasn't long before Lahaie got a call back from an intelligence officer in New York. They had found Harjeet, working days at a delicatessen in Queens called Deli Plus at 159 West 46th St. NYPD sergeant Justin McCaffery told Lahaie that Harjeet had been working at the deli six or seven months, after answering a want ad in a newspaper. Harjeet was living with a man named Sanjay Khanchawdani. The pair had recently gone on a vacation to California for two weeks. Sanjay worked as a cabbie. The deli owner had told police that Harjeet—who was using the name Harminder—was a good employee but sometimes didn't show for work, without explanation. Lahaie was stoked by the news, the process, the wonderment he often felt about the job welling up once again.

"Those guys are bloodhounds down there!"

He didn't high-five anyone, though. Lahaie had stayed clear of that kind of celebration ever since the day he found key evidence in the Stoney Creek rapist case and high-fived partner Larry Moore so hard he broke Larry's finger. It was part of Lahaie's wiring that, even though he was now a veteran detective, he still got juiced about new experiences on the job, forever a kid in a candy store. He loved telling the story of the time he went down to Daytona Beach with his partner, vice and drugs veteran Wayne (Benny) Bennett, to interview a "person of interest" in the murder of Damian Dymitraszczuk. So one night, off duty, they go to a legendary biker bar called Boot Hill Saloon. Benny had to see the place. With his undercover look—Bennett had once posed as a hit man biker—the scruffy long hair, he fit right in. Lahaie, though, clean-cut, could not hide his wide-eyed amazement at seeing this slice of life.

"Don't talk," growled Bennett as they walked in.

"Excuse me, what kind of beer do you have?" Lahaie asked the bartender. Might as well have been wearing a formal police uniform with a flashing light on his head.

"Ninja," said Benny, "you'd be lousy undercover."

* * *

On Wednesday, July 25, Mohan's financial adviser, Lori-Anne Davis, paged Lahaie. He phoned her back, and she told him that Mohan had called her the day before, asking her to liquidate Yvette's account. She had told Mohan he first needed to produce a will and death certificate. Mohan said he didn't have a death certificate. Davis told him there was nothing she could do for him without it.

"He said he's going to take a lie-detector test," she told Lahaie. "He said he wants to do anything to assist to prove his innocence, and start over."

That night, Lahaie called Monica Sloan at the Centre of Forensic Sciences. The femur bone had paid off. The marrow had produced a DNA profile for Yvette. They had now completely brought her identity to life from the mummified remains, first with a fingerprint, and now with DNA verification. But what about the blood samples found on the TV, mattress, and car? Sloan said there was still no conclusive DNA profile from the stain on the TV, but they would continue to work on it.

And the blood on the rubber molding around the trunk, and the trunk carpet? Bingo. They had a profile from all those samples. The DNA matched a female profile. Yvette Budram's profile. The blood on the bedroom mattress? Some of the DNA matched a male profile—and some of it also matched with Yvette. Sloan sent Lahaie her report the next morning. She wrote, "The probability that a randomly selected individual unrelated to Yvette Budram would coincidentally share the observed DNA profile is estimated to be 1 in 190 billion."

Lahaie was pumped. This was huge. In the absence of a witness or a confession, the murder of Yvette Budram was by definition a circumstantial case. DNA on the mattress, and in the car trunk, now made it a strong circumstantial case. But they still needed to eliminate Harjeet (Happy) Singh as a suspect. He made the pitch to his bosses to find and question Happy.

"Fine, go to New York—and don't come back unless you get him." That was the final direction from a senior officer on July 30, when he was approved to go to New York City.

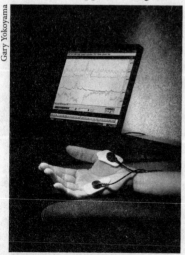
Gary Yokoyama

That same day, Mohan Ramkissoon voluntarily took a lie-detector test. No one is compelled by law to take a polygraph test, and the results of the tests are not admissible in court. Police use it as an investigative tool. The test measures the stress level of the interview subject, reflected in such things as the heart rate and blood pressure during questioning. The polygraph is considered to be accurate 95 percent of the time, but it can be beaten. In the United States,

A polygraph test.

serial murder suspect Gary Ridgway (known as the Green River Killer) once passed a lie-detector test and went on to kill 40 more people. Infamous CIA double agent Aldrich Ames passed numerous polygraph tests even as he continued to betray agents to the KGB.

Mohan's friend Avian gave him a ride to the station. She had urged him to take the test, clear his name. Mohan had initially resisted, said that his lawyer advised against it.

"What the hell's wrong with you?" said Avian. "You didn't kill your wife, you've told me that, you swear you didn't do it, why don't you want to take the test? You're going to take that test and prove you're not guilty."

Mohan failed the test. Jamie Davis met with Lahaie and Terry Hill, told them that the official result was "deception on all the issues." And Mohan had also refused to answer more questions after the polygraph. He was told the test result was "inconclusive."

That night Lahaie and Hill caught the 8:05 flight out of Buffalo for LaGuardia Airport. Lahaie had never been to New York City before. He was instantly taken aback by the size of the place. Empire State Building, World Trade Center Twin Towers, everything larger than life, like walking into a movie, this massive living, breathing entity. New York, New York, a world unto its own.

"You think Toronto is big—Toronto's Regina, baby!" he exclaimed.

As Lahaie and Terry Hill walked through the LaGuardia airport terminal, four NYPD intelligence officers were waiting for them. "You Detective Lahaie?" asked one of the plainclothes in a Bronx accent. "We're gonna take care of you. You hungry?"

They checked into a Sheraton, then dropped in at NYPD intelligence headquarters before swinging by Deli Plus where Harjeet worked. It was closed. The NYPD officers took the detectives to a deli boasting the best Reuben in the city. It was great, all right, but for the record, Lahaie thought to himself, the world's best corned beef sandwich remained the one served at Reardon's Deli Counter on King William in Hamilton.

"We just need to find this guy, Harjeet," Lahaie said, grateful for the hospitality, but slightly on edge about making the trip worthwhile. "If we find him, interview him, we'll buy drinks for everyone at the NYPD."

They returned to Deli Plus the next day. Harminder—Harjeet—Singh indeed worked there, said the manager. But he had not seen him in almost a week. "He says he drives a cab part-time out of Long Island," the manager added. "And he owes me $30."

The manager had a cellphone number for Harjeet, and left him a message to call, added that the police were looking for him. The cellphone number was enough information for the NYPD to locate the apartment where Harjeet had been living, 4249 Colden St., Apt. 6G. Single bedroom apartment, three beds. A seedy part of the city. When they arrived, it looked to be too late, Harjeet had blown town.

Why was he running? He was aware the police were asking after him, but would not have known why. Did he run because of his illegal immigration status? Or did it have to do with the murder of Yvette Budram?

Lahaie and Hill were at least able to meet Harjeet's roommate, Sanjay Khanchawdani. Sanjay had placed an ad in the paper for a roommate, Harjeet had responded. Sanjay said the cellphone Harjeet had been using was in fact his.

"He owes me $1,000," he said.

Later, with the roommate's approval, Lahaie searched the apartment, went through Harjeet's belongings, clothes, a leather bag. Noticed a suit jacket he had seen on Harjeet in a photograph with Yvette. Checked the pockets and found a cassette tape and a microcassette tape. Lahaie took them away. He found a photocopy of a driver's license belonging to a Doris Makkar, from Tupelo, Miss. He found a copy of a social security card in the name of Harpreet Singh Makkar, an international driver's license in the name of Harjeet Singh. Lahaie placed a phone call to Doris Makkar.

Lahaie also left a new message at Harjeet's cellphone number. They had left a couple of generic messages for him already, but now Lahaie made the pitch: The police are here to interview you as a potential witness, regarding the timeline involving the murder of a woman named Yvette Budram. That night at 10:30 p.m., the detectives received a return call from Doris. She was an African-American woman, and Harjeet's wife. She had taken his last name. Hadn't seen him since Christmas 2000, when he had just showed up unannounced. They had a daughter. Her husband was worried about his illegal immigration status, that he would be deported back to India. And he knew the police were looking for him.

"He wants to speak with you but he's afraid of his status," Doris said.

"We only seek him as a witness, we're not worried about his immigration status."

The next day, Thursday, August 2, Lahaie left three messages on Harjeet's cellphone, repeating their request to meet with him regarding the Budram murder. He did not get a call back. The trip seemed to have yielded little so far. Harjeet knew police wanted to speak with him, but that was about it, apart from the two tapes Lahaie had found in Harjeet's jacket. When Lahaie played the first tape, he heard conversations on the phone between Yvette and Harjeet. Why had he taped that? And on the second tape? Sounds of Harjeet and Yvette making love.

There was nothing left to do in New York. Harjeet had clearly left. And the trip had done nothing to clarify the case against Mohan Ramkissoon. Harjeet remained the potential suspect he had been before they arrived in New York. They had nothing clearer on the murder timeline. And, indeed, with the tapes, his status as a suspect was even murkier. Before their flight home, Lahaie met with some of the NYPD's tactical team members. They knew he was an ex-tac guy, that made him part of that brotherhood. They showed him their latest equipment, talked about the terrorist attack in 1993, when a truck packed with 1,100 pounds of explosives blew up in the basement parking garage of the World Trade Center. The tac guys told Lahaie that everyone feared that the next big attack might be a poison gas assault in the subway system.

Before Lahaie and Terry Hill flew home, the NYPD detectives took them on a whirlwind tour of the waterfront, Wall Street, the Twin Towers, anxious to treat their Canadian guests to a good time, took photos of them standing in front of the Statue of Liberty. Lahaie appreciated the gesture, but he could not really enjoy it the way he would have liked. He was still lamenting their failure to talk to Harjeet. At 10 p.m., Lahaie wrote a terse message in his Homicide Case Book.

Left JFK for Canada.

Back at Hamilton's Central Station Friday morning, Lahaie took heat for making the big trip to New York City and coming home seemingly empty-handed. One day the following week, though, when Lahaie checked his messages, there was one from Harjeet Singh. Lahaie tried to reach him, but failed.

The week after that, Harjeet phoned Lahaie, got him in the office. Harjeet was in Memphis this time. He was willing to meet Lahaie there. The trip to New York had not been a waste after all. If they don't track Harjeet to New York, they don't find his contact numbers, don't talk to his wife, and don't get the message to him about why they needed to speak with him. Harjeet told Lahaie that he was worried about his status, that he would be deported. He suggested that Lahaie meet him in person at the Memphis airport so he could give him a statement. Lahaie asked his supervisors if he could fly to Memphis. He was turned down. Lahaie was bitter. A tactical error, he thought. A big mistake. Much better to meet Harjeet in person, get a read on his credibility, get a DNA sample.

The next best thing was to tape a phone interview with Harjeet. In an interview that lasted over an hour, Harjeet admitted that he had been having a relationship with Yvette. Said he was shocked when he heard on the police phone message that Yvette had been murdered. He had been aware that Yvette had been arrested for the domestic fight with Mohan, though.

The key point for the investigation was, did Harjeet have the opportunity to kill Yvette Budram before leaving for the States? Where had Harjeet (Happy) Singh been in the days leading up to, and after, Yvette Budram's disappearance in September 2000? Through Harjeet's accounts of his movements, a picture emerged about his last days in Canada.

CHAPTER 17 ~ A RED DRESS

As the end of the summer neared in 2000, Harjeet Singh was still living in Mississauga. But he would tell others that he had decided it was time to leave the city, and Yvette, return to his life back in the United States. His claim for refugee status in Canada had been refused. He had 30 days to appeal, but would need $2,000 more to appeal it, plus lawyer fees. He wasn't working and was out of money. At least back in the U.S., he figured, there are plenty of illegals living there. And his wife and child lived there, too. His U.S. immigration case was pending, perhaps he'd even win that one. He had a friend in New York City, in Queens. That's where he'd go. But first, in early August, he left Mississauga for Montreal.

He knew a couple there named Ranjit and Prem Saini, who had moved to Canada from India about a year earlier. They let him stay in their one-bedroom apartment. While in Montreal, Harjeet continued to talk to Yvette on the phone on occasion, told her how much he cared about her, said it was breaking his heart but he had to leave her, and Canada. He agreed to see Yvette one more time, however. On Labour Day weekend at the end of the month he returned to Mississauga, courtesy of a ride from Ranjit Saini. Harjeet knew he wasn't welcome to stay at his onetime landlady's place, Yvette's neighbor, Maria Raposa. Maria was no fan of Harjeet's. Instead he bunked at the local Sikh temple. Harjeet saw Yvette on Friday night. They met at the Mississauga Gate motel.

"I'm leaving tomorrow morning, back to Montreal," Harjeet told her. Later that night he returned to the temple, and Yvette returned to her home. On Saturday, an Indian friend named Montu showed up at the temple to see Harjeet—and he had brought Yvette with him. Harjeet was furious. Why was he bringing Yvette to see him? Harjeet owed her money—$2,700. Was she coming for her money? Harjeet and Yvette argued.

She was upset with him because he was leaving. The money was just adding to her aggravation. He told her that Montu, in turn, owed him money, and when he got that, he'd pay her. Just after noon that day, while Ranjit and Montu went to Maria Raposa's house to retrieve clothes Harjeet had left there, Harjeet drove Yvette home. They talked in the car.

"Don't worry about the money," Yvette said. "Just give it to me later on. Your life is not going anywhere. Just go back."

"If that's what God wants for me, that's what I'll do," he said.

He dropped her off at 2382 Benedet. Then he went farther along the street and picked up Ranjit, and his clothes. He drove once more past 2382 before heading to the highway. Yvette was out in front of the house. It was the last vision he had of her, standing there, wearing a red dress.

Harjeet left for Montreal and, he maintained, never returned to Mississauga. It was the next night, Sunday, that Mohan Ramkissoon and Yvette Budram had the big fight in the house, Mohan called 911, the police came and arrested her. In Montreal, meanwhile, Harjeet heard about the arrest through the grapevine. And Yvette left him a couple of phone messages after her release from custody. She asked him to phone her at a Holiday Inn in Mississauga where she was staying temporarily. He tried to call her back at the hotel on Friday, September 8—the day she was released from custody—and Saturday, September 9, but was unsuccessful. He used a friend's calling card. Harjeet had memorized the friend's PIN for his own use. But Yvette was never there when he called.

Harjeet prepared to leave the country. He started talking on the phone more frequently with his wife, Doris, who was living in Mississippi. And he made contact with a smuggling pipeline near Cornwall, just over an hour southwest of Montreal, that helped illegals cross the border. Sometimes they mixed you in with a family—parents, five or six kids, everyone just says they are Canadian citizens crossing the border for shopping, and away you go. For Harjeet, they would go by water, take a boat across the St. Lawrence River into New York State. It would be Harjeet, the smuggler and another man hopping the border, a man of Pakistani origin.

He left the apartment in Montreal for Cornwall late Sunday afternoon, September 17. He paid the smuggler $800 U.S. to get him across. Harjeet had hopped the border smoothly before, but this time it was different. When their boat was in the middle of the river, they spotted another boat. Was it an immigration patrol? The other illegal with Harjeet started to panic. This was it, they were caught. He started to cry. Harjeet thought about jumping off the boat, swimming for a small island nearby. Instead their host managed to maneuver the boat in close to the island, use it as cover, hide. The other boat passed, and they resumed their voyage.

The next stop, on the other side of the river, was a native reservation near the town of Massena, N.Y. It was about 8 p.m. when they completed the crossing. The host said it was too dangerous to drive them to Massena as planned. Too much checking going on in the area by police. "What are we supposed to do?" Harjeet asked. "We can't stay on the reservation."

The smuggler decided they should bypass Massena, travel farther east, to Plattsburgh. From there they could take a cab to Albany. They made the trip, stopping at a hotel. "They're checking the hotels, the immigration people at night sometimes," the smuggler warned as he dropped the two men off. "Good luck."

"If we get caught, we get caught," Harjeet replied.

Harjeet was instructed to call a specific number for a cab company that would take him the rest of the way. That was part of the deal he had paid for. Except the number didn't work when he tried it the next morning, Monday. Harjeet called another cab. The driver agreed to take him to a train station in Albany, where he could connect into New York City. In Albany, Harjeet bought a ticket for the 2:05 p.m. train. He was in New York City by suppertime and did not return to Canada.

* * *

Did Harjeet's story add up? Was he in Montreal when he said he was, at the very time that Yvette Budram had gone missing? Did he have any window of opportunity in September to return to Mississauga and murder Yvette? Paul Lahaie had not met Harjeet, but now he had made contact with him, and Harjeet seemed more than willing to cooperate with him. He even started sending Lahaie receipts from his car rentals, phone bills to account for his whereabouts during the critical period.

Did his alibi of being in Montreal during the critical time period ring true? Detectives Dave Place and Jamie Davis were dispatched to interview Ranjit and Prem Saini in Montreal to see if his story made sense. Place and Davis showed up at their apartment accompanied by two uniformed Montreal police officers. They took the Sainis to a police station to get their statements under oath and on videotape. Prem was worried, seeing the police just show up like that unannounced. And she was embarrassed. They had only arrived in Canada in 1999 from India. In her culture, if police come to your house it is cause for shame.

The police officers told the couple they wanted to talk to her about the man named Harjeet Singh, better known to them as Happy. Prem wondered what it was all about. She knew that Happy and his friend Montu had a dispute over money—Happy had left some menacing messages at the apartment to be passed on to Montu if he called. Was that why the police wanted to question them? Ranjit and Prem had family back in India, four young kids, elderly parents. They knew that harm would come to them if they said the wrong thing about the wrong person. It happens back home.

At the station, Prem refused to take an oath before giving her statement. She knew she could not answer the questions truthfully, and could not lie to God. But Ranjit agreed to take the oath—and denied that Happy had stayed with them in August and September 2000. He said that Happy had not stayed at their apartment since June 1999. After refusing to take the oath, Prem simply said she didn't know anybody named Happy. The next morning, feeling guilty, Prem phoned Dave Place, who had returned to Hamilton. She told him she lied to police. Yes, she knew Happy, she said. He had lived with them. Later, Paul Lahaie spoke on the phone with Harjeet about his friends the Sainis.

"Why won't Ranjit corroborate that you stayed there?" Lahaie asked.

"Ranjit has his own immigration problems," Harjeet replied. He added that there was a tenant on the third floor of the residence and Harjeet helped him move. He'd verify he was there.

Clearly the Sainis were not going to be the most effective witnesses on Harjeet's behalf. Far from being an alibi, they had muddied the waters considerably. They had either outright contradicted Happy's account, or had lied under oath about it. Lahaie spoke on the phone with Harjeet's wife, Doris. She said she would give a written statement asserting that she and Harjeet had talked

on the phone almost every day at a Montreal number in the days
leading up to his arrival in the U.S. on September 17.

Lahaie studied phone bills from the Saini residence in Montreal. It showed frequent calls to the U.S. in August and September,
presumably made by Harjeet. There was a gap on September 1–2,
the Labour Day weekend. That made sense, Harjeet would not have
been using the number because he had been visiting Mississauga
for the last time. And then, on September 2 at 9:11 p.m., he appears
to have made another call from the Sainis' line—presumably upon
his return from Mississauga. The records suggested that, during
the next two weeks, Harjeet made numerous calls from Montreal,
including calls on September 15–16, and then again early in the
morning September 17, and that afternoon at 3:34 p.m. After that,
there were no calls made from Montreal. He had made his break
for the border and crossed into New York State. Hadn't he?

Lahaie followed up Harjeet's border-hopping story. One of the
receipts he got from Harjeet was for the Plattsburgh Quality Inn.
Lahaie phoned the hotel. Did they have any record of a man staying
there named Harjeet Singh? The answer was yes, he had checked in
on September 17 at 11:30 p.m. and checked out the next morning
at eight-thirty. Stayed in Room 105. He had paid cash. Lahaie asked
the manager to fax him a copy of the driver's license Harjeet had
used as ID. And he phoned police in Plattsburgh and requested that
they seize the registration information. Phone records and other
receipts suggested that, after his stay in Plattsburgh, Harjeet had
remained in the U.S. through the fall, first in Queens, N.Y., then,
after taking a Northwest Airlines flight south, in Missouri. A few
weeks later, he rented a car in Pennsylvania. He had continued to
make phone calls on his friend's calling card.

Harjeet was not a straight shooter, certainly. He had a criminal
record, had been convicted of food stamp fraud at a business he
owned. (Food stamps are coupons issued by the U.S. government to
people with low incomes that can be redeemed for food at stores.)
That conviction had precipitated a deportation order against him.
He traveled and worked under aliases to avoid being sent back
to India. He abused his friends' phone cards, owed them money.
And Harjeet had, as Lahaie discovered from the tapes he found in
New York, bizarrely taped intimate conversations and moments

with Yvette. Why? He told Lahaie he did it to document that it was a two-sided relationship, in case Yvette ever tried to deny her role someday, for any reason.

"That's her nature, she'll tell you today that she loves you and tomorrow she would be, you know, will start arguing very strongly like she don't know you," Harjeet said. "So I just thought I would tape something—I can show she was calling me, too. It wasn't just me running to her house, it was something from both sides."

With all of Harjeet's issues, it did appear that Lahaie had not only Harjeet's statement on where he had been on the likely date of Yvette's murder, but he also had documents that seemed to back up the story. To Lahaie, that was the final hurdle that needed to be cleared to seal the case against Mohan Ramkissoon.

"We gotta arrest this guy," Lahaie told Mike Thomas.

But that call was Thomas's to make. At 8 a.m. Thursday, August 16, 2001, he told Lahaie to obtain a Feeney warrant. Police cannot simply show up at a house and make an arrest at will. Not any more, not since a 1997 Supreme Court of Canada decision in *R. v. Feeney*. The court said police must, as a general rule, obtain a warrant before they enter a private dwelling to make an arrest or apprehend someone. The decision came following the case of a man in British Columbia who appealed his conviction for murdering an 85-year-old man on the grounds that police entered his trailer and arrested him, and confiscated bloodstained clothing, without having first obtained a warrant to arrest. The intent of the new statute was to protect privacy rights, although critics said it also had the potential to prevent police from acting swiftly.

At 9 a.m. Lahaie met with a justice of the peace. By 10 a.m., he had his warrant. Police had the green light to go to Mississauga and make the arrest. Just before noon, Thomas, Lahaie, and Dave Place met in the Major Crime Unit. They usually met each day to discuss the latest in the case. But this was a special meeting. Dave Place did not feel comfortable with what he was about to say. Wasn't his nature to be contrarian. But he had to call it the way he saw it. It's not uncommon for detectives to disagree on strategy in a big case. This was one of those times. He had been involved in the case from the first day, just like Thomas and Lahaie, knew the evidence they had so far accumulated. Place had watched Mohan

Ramkissoon under questioning twice, and he was not entirely convinced of his guilt. Yes, Mohan had failed a polygraph test, but for Place that was not overwhelming proof. He knew there are varying reasons why people fail polygraphs. They might be lying. On the other hand, the pressure of the situation, or their intimacy with the victim, might skew their response. But, more important than the optics on Mohan, Place felt they had not yet gathered enough evidence about the other possible suspect, Harjeet. They had a timeline on Harjeet's whereabouts around the period Yvette had gone missing in September 2000. But when had Yvette died? They didn't know that, not yet, not until the Bug Lady finished her work. Did Harjeet have even a small window of opportunity? Phone records, and Harjeet's statements, suggested that he had been in Montreal. But his landlords in Montreal were not corroborating it. Could it be proved that he really made those calls? The detectives needed to have their case in order before taking it to the Crown prosecutor, and before taking it to court. Place told Lahaie and Thomas that he didn't think they should be arresting Mohan, at least not yet.

"I think more needs to be done to eliminate Happy," Place said. "We've got to get this guy out of the picture."

Place thought they were jumping the gun but at the same time, knew that there are times when you can't wait until you have all the answers before making an arrest, because you might never get to that point. Place knew the meeting wasn't a forum for debate; he had said his piece, that was all he wanted to do. Like everyone, Mike Thomas respected Dave, and he expected his men to speak their minds.

At 12:45 p.m. the three detectives went downstairs to the car pool and, instead of the usual unmarked vehicle, checked out a white police cruiser.

CHAPTER 18 ~ "I HAVEN'T DONE ANYTHING"

Benedet Drive, Mississauga, Ontario
Thursday, August 16, 2001

The afternoon was gray and hot, the air thick. It started to rain. Detective Paul Lahaie knocked on the door at 2382 Benedet Drive. A woman answered. Likely someone helping out with the kids. Lahaie could see Mohan Ramkissoon standing in the hallway.

"Could you please step outside?" Lahaie said.

Mike Thomas and Dave Place waited on the front step. Mohan slipped on a pair of shoes and came out on the porch. Lahaie and Thomas put the cuffs on Mohan.

"I am arresting you—" Lahaie began.

"For what?" Mohan said. "I haven't done anything."

"I am arresting you for the murder of Yvette Budram. It is my duty to inform you that you have the right to retain and instruct counsel without delay. You are not obliged to say anything unless you wish to do so, but whatever you say may be given in evidence. Do you understand?"

"I understand," Mohan said. "Can I talk to my kids?"

Dave Place, despite his misgivings about making the arrest, did not feel bad that Mohan was being taken in. The issue was more about timing. Mohan Ramkissoon was clearly the No. 1 suspect. Mohan was escorted to the police car.

The ride through the rain back to Hamilton on Highway 403 was dead quiet. They passed a sign advertising the exit for the African Lion Safari. Lahaie wondered if Mohan would show something, some kind of recognition in his body language or face. But the man showed nothing.

Before being locked in one of the holding cells off the Major Crime Unit at Central Station, Mohan was searched. His wallet contained $460 in American cash and $335 Canadian.

"When can I call a lawyer?" he asked.

"You'll have that opportunity before speaking with me," Lahaie replied.

A veteran Mississauga defense lawyer named Tom Carey had been referred the case. When Mohan called, Carey was not in. He spoke with an associate of Carey's. Mohan told the associate that he did not want to answer questions, and he was told his rights that he was under no obligation to do so. Later in the evening, just before eight, he was led to an interview room.

Mohan had dealt with the police several times before in connection with Yvette's failure to appear in court. He had been interviewed once by Peel detective Jamie Davis. Had taken a lie-detector test. Had been interrogated for over nine hours after being arrested at the airport. And yet this time, Lahaie thought Mohan came across as very nervous. He was shaking. Mohan finally knew that his future, his life, was in jeopardy, Lahaie thought.

"Okay," Lahaie began. "Inside this room is Detective Paul Lahaie, I'm a detective in the Major Crime Unit, and also there's Detective Mike Thomas. And your name is, sir?"

"Mohan Ramkissoon."

"You understand that today I'm the officer that arrested you?"

"Yeah."

"I've arrested you for the murder involving Lilawattee Yvette Budram, who is your wife."

Lahaie took him back to the night in 2000 when Mohan called police and reported an assault against him by Yvette.

Mike Thomas (left) and Paul Lahaie.

"All right. One of the things—you helped Yvette, because, all through this, I always believed that you really love your wife Yvette. Is that correct?"

"Of course."

"I mean, even today I know that you love her very much. I've gone through your wallet. I still see there's a picture of Yvette among other things ... Prior to that, prior to that assault, there's never been any problems between you and Yvette?"

"No."

"Like you haven't hit her?"

"Never."

"You never punched her, never hit her with anything?"

"No."

"I understand, being a married man, and I do have my ring on, like every married couple, they have problems, is that correct?"

"That's correct."

"You said … you never had, never fought against each other, right?"

"No."

"No physical confrontation?"

"No."

"So there shouldn't be any blood anywhere in your house involving you or Yvette, is that correct?"

"One time I remember, one time she hit me. Yeah, you're right. One day she hit me and cut me here."

Mohan pointed to a spot underneath his right eye. He said he didn't remember when it happened, but it was years ago. Lahaie asked if there was blood in that incident. Mohan said yes.

"And the blood-letting was in which room?"

"The master bedroom."

"Is there any explanation for any blood anywhere in the house?"

"From me?"

"From anyone."

"No."

"Would there be any explanation for any blood being any-where in either vehicle that your family owns? The truck or your Chrysler?"

"No."

"OK. Now do you know where Yvette was found, sir?"

"No."

"If I said to you that the place where Yvette was found was near the African Lion Safari, are you familiar with that area, sir?"

"I've been there twice before."

"I saw a picture of your kids riding an elephant."

"That's correct."

Mohan said the last time he had been there was August 2000. Yvette was there with him and the kids. The time before that was in 1996.

"And is there any other reason you can think of that you may know that area?"

"No."

Lahaie asked about the day that Jamie Davis called him at work and Mohan panicked. "What hours were you working that day?"

"Six-thirty to four."

"So there was really no reason for you to leave your work, was there?"

"No."

Lahaie took him through the day—he flees work, doesn't tell his boss, picks up the kids from the sitter and school, he has no vacation days booked but heads to a travel agency.

"And out of the blue you buy three one-way tickets to Guyana."

"That's true but like I explained, I wasn't running." The airline was on strike, he said, offering a deal, it was cheaper to fly one way than two way. "So I use one way and after my two weeks if the price of the other airline ... I'll take it and get a cheaper price and come back."

"Oh, I understand that, that sounds pretty reasonable to me. But what seems unreasonable to me is that you're at work and all of a sudden you get a phone call from the police, you go from work, you don't tell your employer that you're taking a vacation. You don't tell your nanny what you're doing." And, added Lahaie, the next morning, he takes a taxi, and rather than have it come to his house, grabs one ten minutes from his house. "Like, myself, if I wanted to go to Guyana that day and I have small children and I'm a single parent, I'd have the taxi come to my front door. Was there any reason why you were afraid to have a taxi come to your front door, sir?"

"No."

And then, Lahaie continued, Mohan takes the cab to work. He takes the kids in the front door of work and exits out the back, through a field. "Was there any reason why you had to go out the back door at the place of employment, sir?"

"Like I said I'll answer a question when my lawyer's here. I'm not going to answer any more question."

"Well that's fine and you don't have to answer any more questions, sir. But I'll just continue on—"

"But I—"

"—with what I know, so that you know what I know. Now you don't go back home, you go to the Fort York Motel. It's ten minutes from your house. That doesn't make any sense that you would pay $65 to stay at a motel when you can go to your house. Does that make any sense to you, sir?"

"As I said I'll answer the question when my lawyer's here."

"That's fine, sir. You know what? And you don't have to. Now just so I know further, that you make a phone call to your financial adviser, and instruct her that you're going away and you want the money liquidated from your accounts that you hold and have the money sent to New York. Now for somebody who is just going on vacation that doesn't make any sense."

"Like I said I can't answer your questions."

"Sir, I'm not asking you to comment on anything. But I want you to know the conclusion police have come to here. I want you to know why you're sitting in that chair...Now you've already explained to me that there's no explanation that you can come up with why there's blood. But there's blood on your TV. A whole lot of blood. Thirty square inches. Is there an explanation for that?"

"I don't know."

"We look at the mattress and we find an irregular part of it cut out. Is there any reason for that, sir?"

"I said when my lawyer's here I will tell you."

"Then we look in your car, and we find blood in the trunk. And you know where all that blood is matching up, sir? Guess who?"

"I don't know."

"It's your wife's, sir. Is there any explanation for the blood in the car?"

"I don't know. I don't know."

Lahaie tried to ease Mohan into a position to confess.

"I believe in God, sir. I am a Catholic. One thing I know is that people like you. They think you're a great guy. What I see is an individual who was very upset by his wife who committed an affair, extremely upset. You are a very patient man. But you lost your control just once. You lost it just for a second. It wasn't long. It was a reaction."

"I never—I never lost my patience."

Lahaie stood up.

"Well, I'm done, sir. Detective Thomas, do you have any questions you want to ask?"

Mike Thomas looked into Mohan's eyes. "What was the result of the polygraph test?" Thomas asked.

"They told me it was inconclusive."

"Do you want me to tell you what the truth is?"

"I don't know. They never tell me, I don't know."

"Do you want me to tell you?"

"Whatever you say, I don't know."

"What do you think the truth is? What do you think the truth is?"

"I don't know."

"The truth is you failed."

"I don't know."

"No, you did. That is the truth."

"I don't know."

"You failed by a great margin, a huge margin. And you know the two main questions where you completely were lying? When they asked you, 'Did you kill your wife?' And 'Did you dispose of the body?'"

"I no answer the question the way I answer all the questions."

"Mohan, we're giving you the opportunity right now. I know there's an explanation for why this happened. And we would like to hear that from you."

"I don't know."

"We have accumulated six or seven bankers' boxes full of information right now. And there is absolutely no doubt that you are responsible for Yvette's death."

"I don't know nothing."

"But there's got to be a reason it happened."

"I don't know. I don't know anything about it. Like I said the last time I seen her was Sunday evening. I never see her back."

"You don't want to give us an explanation?"

"It's not that I don't want to. I don't know anything, sir. I don't know anything."

"You know, I find that a really interesting choice of words. 'Cause usually I find that innocent people are saying, 'I didn't do it.' And you're just telling me you don't know anything."

"Well, the same thing is that I don't do—I don't know anything, I didn't do anything. I don't know anything about her death. I don't know."

"You've said that about 15 times since we started here. All we're looking for is an explanation, Mohan. We know what's happened, OK? This is an opportunity for you to give your side of the story."

"I don't have no side of the story. I don't know anything."

Thomas suggested that perhaps Mohan blacked out when she was killed. Or maybe he was sick or was drinking. No, Mohan said, he has never blacked out, does not smoke or drink. "I don't know anything about her death."

"Do you know how shocked we were when we saw those photos from African Lion Safari? It was a big coincidence, wasn't it?"

"Yeah, probably because that's the only picture I have. I have pictures of Wonderland here and there. And Marineland. Wherever we go, I take pictures."

"Yeah, but the ones you took with you were the ones from the African Lion Safari. So that's just an interesting choice of pictures that you took. Because that just happens to be within, you know, 1,500 feet of the front doors of the African Lion Safari where Yvette was found. Just think about everything, Mohan. Just think about it."

"I have nothing to think about, sir."

"No?"

"Nothing to think because I don't know anything, I haven't done anything."

As the interrogation came to a close, Lahaie stepped back in to the conversation, his voice soft, eyes earnest. "I went through the case with you, sir. I want you to know that I am a very fair person."

"That's correct, I agree."

"That's why I'm sitting here looking you in the eye and telling you what I have and what I'm willing to go to court with. And I'll be sitting in there. But you know what? I really thought that you would come up with some sort of explanation. I really did. And I think the reason there isn't an explanation forthcoming is, this is totally out of character for you. Totally. I know you're a peaceful man. And what you have to overcome is your children. I know that your children mean everything to you. I know that the risk in losing them, losing their standard of living, the risk of sharing them, that meant more to you than everything else. I know that. And I feel your pain that way. Otherwise sir, I know just that one moment you panicked. Just that one moment."

"No."

"And you're still fighting for your children right now in that chair."

"No."

"I know you are."

"Never."

"We're just going to go over the same thing over and over and let the court decide. I'm going to bring them all into court, the biologists, the police that found blood, the hotel people, the school people, the nannies, the financial planner, the travel agent. They're all gonna come in. I'm bringing your boss Lou in, I'm bringing Szabo in. And the taxi driver. Do you see where it's going?"

"I know where it's going, but like I said, I haven't done anything. I got nothing to do with it."

"What made you go back to work that day? Why'd you go back with your kids?"

"Like I said, I'll answer questions when my lawyer's here, Paul. I've been very polite. I've been cooperative from the beginning."

"The only thing you're hiding, Mohan, is the truth."

"I'm not hiding the truth."

"We'll see in court then."

Mohan was delivered and booked into the Hamilton–Wentworth Detention Centre, better known as Barton Street jail. Lahaie was disappointed. At one point he thought he could see the man cracking, emotionally, felt like he might be pushing him to the edge. What did the detective see when he stared into Mohan Ramkissoon's dark eyes? He had once looked into the eyes of a serial rapist and saw a sociopath. And Mohan? Not in that category. Mohan seemed relatively bright. And calculating.

Knows the system. Skirted the law in the past, came to Canada under an alias. Has felt all along he could handle the police. Lahaie had watched the taped interview from Mohan's first arrest at the airport. Even then, here was this man, arrested for murder, caught by surprise at the airport, surely terrified, and presented with the news that police had found the body of his slain wife, yet he has the presence of mind to keep hammering on the Harjeet Singh angle, presenting Happy as the alternative suspect—just as he had with several people over the past year, backing up his story. A good strategy for him, Lahaie thought.

Into September Lahaie focused on organizing statements and marshaling a narrative of the investigation for the upcoming bail hearing for Mohan, while also gathering more information from Harjeet Singh. He met with Mike Thomas to talk about the case. They knew the defense was sure to present Harjeet to the jury as an alternative suspect. There was the affair, he owed Yvette money, he leaves Canada right around the time she goes missing. The defense would try to hang it all on him. They had to get more on Harjeet.

CHAPTER 19 ~ BLOWFLY

As Lahaie worked cataloguing disclosure evidence for the case on the morning of September 11, he heard, along with the rest of the world, about the collapse of the Twin Towers in New York City. He had just been there a few weeks earlier looking for Harjeet. He thought back to his conversations with the NYPD tactical guys. They had been wrong; gassing the subway was not the mode of attack chosen by the terrorists. Lahaie, who had fallen in love with New York, kept picturing the waterfront as he had seen it from his cruise around the harbor, the Twin Towers that stretched seemingly to the clouds. Gone. He phoned down to the NYPD, couldn't get through, kept trying, eventually talked with one of the officers he had befriended on the trip. The good news was, he was alive. But others the officer knew were dead. Just like that.

Mohan Ramkissoon's bail hearing was scheduled for October 30 in Hamilton. Lahaie called the assistant Crown attorney who had been chosen to prosecute the case and argue before a judge that Mohan should be kept in jail until his trial. The prosecutor's name was Kevin McKenna. Lahaie sent more than a dozen boxes filled with documents—photos, witness statements, forensic reports, polygraph test results, detectives' notes—to McKenna for him to review in advance of the hearing.

Gary Yokoyama

McKenna was intrigued by the assignment, all the forensic evidence involved. He was 44 years old, had joined the Crown attorney's office in 1992 after working in private practice for seven years. He had an easygoing manner, a dry sense of humor. Lahaie and McKenna hit it off immediately. The detective figured that if McKenna had grown up in his old Hamilton neighborhood, in Saltfleet, they would have been buddies for sure. Good guy, Kevin. And that voice,

Assistant Crown Attorney
Kevin McKenna.

Lahaie thought, that radio-style baritone McKenna had, perfect
for the courtroom.

Kevin McKenna had always known that law might end up
being his career. His father, Ted McKenna, had been a highly
respected civil litigator in Hamilton for years. But he died young,
after a heart attack in 1968, when Kevin was just 11. And seven
years after that, his mother, Yvonne, died from cancer. They were
tough times, to say the least. How does that kind of pain, at that
age, shape someone? One thing it did not do was deter Kevin
McKenna from ultimately pursuing a career in which he would
routinely be called upon to immerse himself in the details of the
worst kinds of crime and tragedy, cases involving wife beaters,
child molesters, child killers, drunk drivers, a child-molesting
priest. As an assistant Crown attorney, he would have the weight
of expectation placed squarely upon his shoulders by the shat-
tered loved ones of victims. They looked to him to deliver justice,
closure, revenge. Often all three.

He felt that the death of his parents was never far below the
surface for him and, in McKenna's line of work, that was a good
thing. Gave him a balanced perspective. Forced him to see the big
picture all the time. Be honest, work hard, try to be a good person
and parent, just like his mom and dad had been. Understand that
in the end, little things don't matter, save your energy for the big
problems. On those occasions when he lost a case, McKenna
could sense the anguish in the gallery from a victim's family when
an accused was found not guilty. Emotionally, though, he found
some measure of comfort in the role of the assistant Crown attorney in the Canadian justice system. In theory, the Crown is
not out solely to win a conviction. Rather, the legal tradition is
that he is to bring the case forward on behalf of the State, present
all the evidence in the case firmly but fairly. He is not paid by the
conviction. The test of the evidence is whether the case is proved
beyond a reasonable doubt. Either you can meet that test, or you
can't. That is the system. And yet there are times when it is difficult
to remain dispassionate about it.

There was one case that stayed with him: Kuzyk. It had been
two years earlier, 1999. A 26-year-old woman was charged with
killing her 15-month-old godson. The child had two skull fractures,

bleeding behind the eyes, bruising. Experts testified that there was no way the toddler could have died by accident. It was blunt force trauma. Could McKenna convince the jury of the godmother's guilt? The godmother, Shelly Kuzyk, said the boy had fallen off a bed. Her defense lawyer offered her boyfriend as a possible alternative suspect. After an 11-day trial, the jury deliberated on Kuzyk's fate. It is always the worst part—the waiting. Not knowing how it will end. Rips your heart. One hour of deliberation passed. Two. Three. Four. Five. Six. Seven. And then the ringing of the phone, the adrenalin rush, the verdict is in, this is it. Back in court, the jury foreman stood and announced the verdict. Not guilty. The dead toddler's parents and family gasped in disbelief, the accused godmother burst into tears and hugged her lawyer. No one would ever do any time for that boy's death.

At times like that, McKenna did his best to call upon his intellect, to rationalize, focus on process. Next steps? Are there grounds for appeal? No. He knew there were not. It was over. In the future, when Kevin McKenna was asked to name one of the cases in his career that stuck out in his mind, he would not cite a great victory. No. It was Kuzyk. A child was dead. It had been a homicide. And no one would be brought to justice for the crime.

* * *

At noon on Tuesday, October 30, Kevin McKenna sat at a table at the front of a courtroom for Mohan Ramkissoon's bail hearing, a stack of boxes beside him full of documents. Could the Crown prove to the court that the suspect should be denied bail? That would largely depend on the evidence presented by Paul Lahaie. As the lead investigator, Lahaie would be the prime witness called by McKenna to the stand to answer questions for the court about the case. He entered the court and sat beside McKenna at the table.

McKenna looked over at the detective. The Crown lawyer was shocked. The detective didn't have so much as a notebook with him, much less a briefcase. I've got 15 boxes of material with me, thought McKenna. This is a murder bail hearing. Is he not prepared? McKenna leaned over to Lahaie before the hearing began.

"Ready?" McKenna asked.

"Yup."

"You've got nothing?"

"Just ask me the questions," Lahaie said.

Lahaie entered the witness box looking reserved on the outside but buzzing with energy inside, as always. This is what it's all about, he thought. McKenna stood and began asking questions about the case. Lahaie launched into the case narrative without notes, quoting documents verbatim without missing a beat. He was so wired, so prepared, the case was a part of him now. McKenna had Lahaie in the witness box for most of the day until they broke at 5 p.m. Then it was time for Mohan's lawyer, Tom Carey, to take his turn. At a bail hearing, defense lawyers want to hear as much as possible, to educate themselves on the case, and build a transcript of quotes from witnesses for future use in the preliminary hearing and, if it happens, the trial itself.

Mohan's lawer, Tom Carey.

Even after all his years on the job, Paul Lahaie was still something of a fan, appreciative of the drama in which he was fortunate enough to be a player. He enjoyed the process, admired the skill of the lawyers. Here was Tom Carey soaking up all this information, which he would be able to quote from memory down the road. Brilliant. Lahaie thought Carey came across as something like the classic southern gentleman lawyer. He just had that way about him. What was the name of the senator who presided over the Watergate investigation hearings, Lahaie wondered? Ervin. Sam Ervin. North Carolina. That's who came to mind.

Carey questioned Lahaie over the course of two and a half days. Lahaie handled it all smoothly. Kevin McKenna was astounded. Not only could the detective describe details of the case without notes, but he was up there citing tabs in binders by number. *Yes, in volume 6, tab 13, you'll find the witness statement....* When McKenna stood to leave the courtroom, he was left wondering if the detective had a photographic memory.

The judge made his decision. Bail for Mohan Ramkissoon was denied. Tom Carey filed an appeal, but that was not going to be heard for several months. Mohan's new home, for now, would continue to be on Barton Street. The next step was the preliminary hearing, which would not take place until the spring of 2002. Then, if the prelim went smoothly, the murder trial itself would follow. The detectives and the lawyers knew that bail was one thing, but the burden at trial would be higher. The case remained a circumstantial one against a man who had steadfastly maintained his innocence.

Was the evidence strong enough to convince a jury of Mohan Ramkissoon's guilt beyond a reasonable doubt? He had motive. His wife had not treated him well, they had had intense fights. He was aware of an affair she had been having with another man, an affair she seemed to rub in his face. The most compelling evidence so far was conduct after the offense that suggested a guilty mind. Buying the one-way airline tickets for himself and his kids to Guyana, pulling the kids out of school when the police called him, skulking around in advance of the flight—it did not look good on him. Mohan had been telling people that Yvette had run off with Harjeet. He even cancelled Yvette's gym membership, and in the space for the reason for canceling, he wrote, "Wife left me."

In addition, police had an interesting statement from a neighbor of Mohan and Yvette's, a man named Agostino (Gus) Lobianco. Shortly after Yvette had gone missing in the fall of 2000, Gus said that Mohan had told him he suspected the police were watching him. But police didn't find the body for another five months. So why was Mohan paranoid about police following him? As far as Mohan knew, she was alive and well, perhaps had run away with

Harjeet, just as he had told others. Why would he think police would suspect him of foul play? And how to explain Mohan telling two people—his financial adviser Lori-Anne Davis and Yvette's eldest son Leonard—that the pandit had predicted that Yvette would be found after the snow melted in a wooded area? The pandit, his spiritual adviser, had in fact said Mohan might "hear from the police in May or June." Did all of it not suggest that Mohan knew Yvette was dead, and that he knew exactly where her body was?

In preparation for the preliminary hearing, the detectives continued gathering evidence. Paul Lahaie interviewed a boarder from 2382 Benedet Drive, a man named Seth who had known Yvette and Mohan. Seth worked at a Sunoco full-service gas station. He had been at the house on the night of September 3, 2000, had heard the big fight between the husband and wife.

"When Yvette was arrested," Seth said, "she told Mohan that she'd pay him back. Something like that." At one point, he said, he heard Yvette tell a friend that she wanted to divorce Mohan, sell the house, and that she had "someone in California."

Lahaie also interviewed Dr. Mughal, Mohan and Yvette's family doctor, and executed a search warrant on their medical records. In Dr. Mughal's notes dated May 26, 2000, which was three months before the big argument between Mohan and Yvette, Mohan was talking about marital problems with Yvette. Another entry, from January 25, 2001, quoted Mohan talking about Yvette, who was now missing. He told the doctor she was murdered, and that his pandit said they'd find the body in May. At a visit on March 9, 2001, along with his daughter, Preet, Mohan had told the doctor that his wife's whereabouts were still unknown.

"I couldn't believe it when he told me," the doctor told Lahaie. "He showed no emotion, we were just standing here and he continued to talk in the corridor."

There were two areas where the detectives continued to focus: one, track down Harjeet Singh for a face-to-face interview; two, fill in the blanks on the timeline of death. A critical question remained unanswered: When was Yvette Budram murdered? Soon they got word that the Bug Lady had come up with an answer.

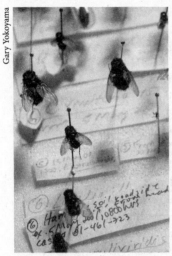

Gary Yokoyama

Blowflies collected from the scene.

* * *

October 2001
Entomology Report Submitted to the Ontario Provincial Coroner's Office
Re. Hamilton-Wentworth Case No. 01-461-723
By Dael E. Morris
Insect Investigations
"The timing of emergence of adult flies in conjunction with climatological and bionomics data were examined using the degree hour method of quantitative analysis to determine when blowflies first colonized remains."

The forensic entomologist had spent nearly six months researching the blowfly samples taken from the remains of Yvette Budram to determine when she died. Technically, her mission was not to determine a specific time of death, but rather the time when the blowfly colonization process had begun—which is approximately consistent with the time of death. It can begin minutes, or hours, after a death, depending on the temperature and environment.

In April she had gathered specimens from the remains during the autopsy at Hamilton General Hospital and at the scene where the body had been found. Out on the 8th Concession West in Flamborough, Morris programmed outdoor smart data readers to log the temperature and relative humidity every 30 minutes. The readers were in place for seven days, from April 19 to April 26, 2001. She requested climate data from Environment Canada for the area from September 2000, when Yvette had last been seen, to April 2001, when the body was found: wind speed, wind direction, precipitation. Morris placed some of the blowflies she had caught in formalin or a 70 percent isopropyl alcohol solution to freeze them at that moment in their development. And she studied the larvae she collected in the insectarium in the basement of her Toronto home, placing them on raw beef liver in aerated clear plastic bags, rearing them to adulthood so she could identify their species. Temperature and light exposure were monitored in the insectarium, consistent with conditions of the outdoor environment from which they had come.

She observed the blowflies go through a complete generation from egg to adult under controllable conditions, watching the flies that had colonized the remains go through their life cycle, but was unable to culture some of the blowflies through to the next generation. There might have been a sterility problem, perhaps caused by the presence of drugs in the dead woman's system, such as methamphetamine, or the antidepressant amitriptyline, which can produce sterile flies and high pupae mortality. For those larvae that did survive through to the next generation, Morris used a series of mathematical formulae, applied to models, to compare their life cycle to the specimens she had collected in various stages of development from the remains. She entered climate data into the equation, then counted backwards in time to determine when the blowflies first colonized the remains.

Morris concluded that there were two waves of blowflies. In the second wave, three types of blowflies colonized the remains— *Calliphora vomitoria, Lucilia illustris*, and *Phaenicia caeruleiviridis. Calliphora vomitoria* first laid its eggs on October 3 or 4, 2000. In the first, earlier wave, only black blowflies—*Phormia regina*—had laid their eggs, colonizing only the head of the body. It was a curious finding. The black blowflies should have colonized everywhere, they should have been present in other parts of the body. But they were not. In addition, other species of blowfly should have also colonized the body at about the same time, but that did not happen until later. It was as though the body had been colonized in two different environments, or that the rest of the body had been covered for some period of time. The black flies had been there long enough to develop to the pupa stage, but something happened to them to kill them or do damage to them, and then came new waves of blowflies later.

It might have simply been that the body had been moved from its first location, retarding the development of the *Phormia regina*. It might have been because the body was moved far from the place where it had first been wounded, to a new environment.

If the body had initially been inside a house, the blowflies would have found the corpse. They always do, unless, Morris reflected, the building is hermetically sealed.

She officially concluded that the first wave of colonization had most likely occurred on September 20, give or take five days—sometime between September 15 and September 25. This was the time frame in which Yvette Budram died, in the moments after she was beaten and strangled, before her body was left in the brush along the 8th Concession.

Meanwhile, Paul Lahaie received big news from DNA expert Monica Sloan at CFS. Her latest report on the case included an update on the search for Yvette's DNA in the bedroom. The chunk of the TV in the bedroom had been sent in for analysis at Lahaie's urging. And now Sloan confirmed that the lab had indeed found more blood on that larger sample and, after further study, had produced a DNA profile from it. It matched Yvette's profile. Her DNA could now be proven in court to have been contained in blood evidence found on the mattress, in Mohan Ramkissoon's car, and on the TV.

CHAPTER 20 ~ MURDER TIMELINE

As the preliminary hearing scheduled to begin in the spring moved closer, Lahaie and Thomas continued to gather evidence towards establishing a timeline for Yvette's death and the whereabouts of both Mohan and Harjeet Singh during the relevant times. The later in Dael Morris's September timeline that it could be proven Yvette was alive, the more likely it was that the finger pointed to Mohan as the killer and not Harjeet Singh, who had left the country.

Thomas obtained school attendance records for Mohan and Yvette's daughter, Preet, for September 2001. Preet had been in school Thursday, September 14. She had been absent Friday, September 15, a PD day. She was in school Monday, September 18, Tuesday the 19th and Wednesday the 20th.

Lahaie interviewed a woman named Janice Luckese, the owner of a child care company called Kiddie Kare, Yvette's former employer. Luckese recalled that she received a call from Yvette on September 15, 2000. Yvette was phoning from her Benedet Drive home—Luckese remembered seeing the number and "Budram" on her call display. The call came sometime after 10 a.m. Luckese recalled that in that phone call, Yvette had apologized to her for the trouble with the law she had gotten herself into.

"Yvette was talking to me about an abusive situation," she told Lahaie. "She apologized to me, and she said that Mohan had hit her first, but he charged her first. She told me, 'He's at fault, and you can ask him. He's right here.' She offered to put him on the phone but I didn't want to go there."

"Did you hear Mohan's voice in the background?" Lahaie asked.

"I don't recall hearing his voice, I can't be 100 percent sure on that."

Luckese said that she received a phone call from Mohan in the fall. He told her that Yvette ran off. She's having an affair. It was odd, Luckese thought. Why was he telling her that? She barely knew Mohan. She told him Yvette didn't work for the agency any more. And Mohan didn't ask her if she had heard from Yvette.

On December 6, Lahaie interviewed Maria Raposa, who lived down the street from Yvette and Mohan and had taken in Harjeet as a boarder.

"When was the last time you saw Harjeet Singh?" Lahaie asked.

She said it was Labour Day weekend, 2000. "Since September 2, 2000, until today we don't see Happy any more."

"Do you know Yvette Budram?"

"Yes, she lived down the street. She used to come here and see Happy all the time. This guy never worked. She would stay here overnight and not go home to her husband. Happy told me the truth, that he was having an affair with her. I said, 'Not in my house any more.' I told him she's not allowed to come to my house any more. Kicked him out of the house in June."

Lahaie asked when she had last seen Yvette.

"I saw Yvette when she got out of jail. That was a Friday in the afternoon [September 8.] I saw her the next week. I came from Benedet walking with the kids I take care of and she drives up from her house towards me. She was in the passenger side. I don't know who was driving. She rolls the window down and swears at me. I go home with the kids and call the police."

She said soon after the police arrived and she told them what had happened. Paul Lahaie later learned that the police officer had listened to Raposa, and then proceeded to knock on the door at 2382 Benedet. There were two cars in the driveway. Mohan Ramkissoon answered the door. All was quiet inside, the blinds drawn. He said that Yvette wasn't home. Agostino Lobianco, the neighbor whom Mohan considered a friend, related to Lahaie a conversation in which Mohan had said he convinced Yvette to move back into the family home after the domestic charge.

"I know she could get in trouble," Mohan had said. "But I've convinced her to to come back to the house with me."

As the preliminary hearing got underway, the established timeline so far could account for Yvette's whereabouts up until Friday, September 15, 2000. But that was about to change.

* * *

John Sopinka Courthouse
Hamilton, Ontario
May 1, 2002

The preliminary hearing had begun, and Paul Lahaie was in court listening to evidence being presented. Agostino Lobianco had been in the witness box that afternoon. Lahaie noticed a woman in the gallery on hand to watch. Out in the hallway, just before 2 p.m., Lahaie approached her and introduced himself. The woman was Agostino's wife, Mayela. The police had not interviewed her. Might he have a word? They chatted.

When was the last time she had seen her friend Yvette? She told him that Mohan and Yvette had visited her home not long before Yvette had gone missing. It had been on September 17, the Sunday. Mohan, she said, had just come back that day with the kids after spending the weekend across the border in New York State. Lahaie perked up. *September 17?* That was the latest date yet any witness had suggested Yvette had been alive.

"Can I get a statement from you?" Lahaie asked. She agreed. He took out his notebook. "You said to me that Mohan Ramkissoon and Yvette Budram had shown up at your residence on a Sunday in September 2000," Lahaie said. "Would you explain that to me again?"

"I know it was a Sunday because Agostino was at work, and worked eleven to seven-thirty. At about 5:30 p.m. I saw both of them. Yvette was with the two kids in a truck and Mohan was in a small burgundy car that he had." She said both Yvette and Mohan had asked if Agostino was home. He was something of a confidant to both of them. "And I said no, he was working," Mayela continued, "and that he would be back at seven-thirty if they wanted to wait."

Yvette then chatted with Mayela, told her about the September 3 incident in which she had been charged, that Mohan had called the police on her. She added that she wanted out of the marriage, to live on her own with the kids in an apartment. "Mohan was standing there in the kitchen as well while we're talking together," Mayela recalled. "I said my concern was for the kids. I asked if she had talked about it with him and she said yes. And Mohan said, 'Don't worry, honey, we could work it out.'"

Then Yvette told Mayela that she was going, was tired of waiting for Agostino, but she would come back another time to talk to him. Yvette left with the two children, and Mohan followed alone in his car. And there was something else, Mayela told Lahaie. She recalled that Mohan told her Yvette was due in court on the Wednesday coming up, September 20.

"Mohan said that he was going to decide on Wednesday whether or not to release the charges."

Back at the police station, Lahaie called a contact, an intelligence officer with Canada Customs. Had either of Mohan's vehicles crossed the border in September 2000? The officer checked plates AFLJ 779 and 512 XKO. The Infiniti and the Chrysler. The Infiniti had returned to Canada via the Peace Bridge on Sunday, September 17, at 11 a.m. There were three Canadian passengers. They had been away 48 hours. They had spent the weekend away, leaving sometime on Friday the fifteenth.

Lahaie could now see the death timeline:

- *Sunday, September 3, 2000*: The big fight at 2382 Benedet between Mohan and Yvette, the knife pulled, the death threat. Yvette arrested, taken into custody. From the night of the arrest to September 8, Yvette is in police custody for the assault charge filed by her husband.

- *Friday, September 8*: Yvette is released on bail. That same day, she returns to the family home on Benedet Drive, violating her court conditions to keep away from the house.

- *Saturday, September 9*: Yvette is at the family home when relatives from upstate New York visit. Mohan claims to others that he forgives her, that he wants her back. But Yvette continues to talk of divorcing him. After the relatives leave the house, a boarder overhears an argument between Yvette and Mohan. "I don't want you to stay," Yvette says. "We can work it out," Mohan replies.

- *Monday, September 11*: The day Yvette is seen driving on Benedet, the day she swears at neighbor Maria Raposa.

- *Friday, September 15*: Yvette phones her employer, the day-care provider. All signs suggest Yvette is spending time in the house in the days leading up to, and including, September 15—the front end of Dael Morris's projected murder timeline between September 15 and 25. That same day, a PD day for his daughter Preet, Mohan takes the two kids across the border.
- *Sunday, September 17*: Mohan and his daughters return to Canada at 11 a.m. At about 5:30 p.m. that day, Yvette, who now has the two kids, drops in at Mayela Lobianco's house. Mohan, alone, shows as well. She leaves the house before 7:30 p.m., and Mohan follows. It is the last time Yvette is seen alive.
- *Monday, September 18*: Employment records show that Mohan Ramkissoon does not go to work on this day. He has been on vacation days from September 5 to September 11, and then, from Monday, September 11, to Monday, September 18, he is on a leave of absence.
- *Tuesday, September 19*: Mohan returns to work that morning.
- *Wednesday, September 20*: Yvette's court date was to have been on this day. Mohan tells at least two people that he will attend the hearing—so he can ask that the charges against his wife be dropped. He felt he had made a mistake calling the police, despite her threatening him. It was serving only to drive her away from him. He wants her back. But Mohan does not show for the court date. And neither does Yvette.

* * *

After testimony from witnesses and the police and forensic experts involved, the preliminary hearing concluded in May 2002. The prelim is the Crown's opportunity to present evidence for the court to determine if a trial is warranted. The judge determined that the Crown's case had proven strong enough that Mohan Ramkissoon should indeed be committed to stand trial for second-degree murder in the death of his wife. But Detective Paul Lahaie knew there was still a shadow over the case that would haunt the investigators. Harjeet (Happy) Singh.

Even though he was convinced of Mohan's guilt, at the prelim Lahaie felt the heat building on the Harjeet factor, could see how Mohan's lawyer was going to target the man as having had opportunity within the death timeline to kill Yvette. Who was this mystery man who had an affair with Yvette then disappears across the border into the United States around the moment she went missing and was murdered? The evidence from statements so far suggested that Harjeet left Mississauga for Montreal on the Labour Day weekend, September 2, and that he stayed with the couple named Ranjit and Prem Saini in that city. The question was, did Harjeet in fact stay in Montreal from that point until September 17, when he claimed to have crossed the border? The hotel records showed that he stayed at a Plattsburgh hotel that night. But did he ever see Yvette again? How did he feel about Yvette? Did he have motive to kill her?

Lahaie felt Harjeet had been very cooperative with him so far, talking on the phone, providing him with receipts. But to a different set of eyes, Harjeet had kept himself pretty mobile since Yvette's death, hadn't he? He had not ventured back into Canada. Was he on the run? Might a jury view his actions through that prism? Lahaie was bitter. He knew his bosses at Hamilton Police should have sent him to Memphis months ago like he requested to get a statement from Harjeet in person, add credibility to the man's words, get a DNA sample from him. It was a mistake and it was coming back to bite them. He had to push hard to get to the U.S. again to interview Harjeet in person.

On June 17, 2002, he spoke with Harjeet on the phone. Harjeet was in San Jose this time. He agreed once again to give a statement in person.

"Do you want to meet in L.A. or San Jose?" Harjeet asked.

"You know what? I've got relatives in San Jose," Lahaie said. "That works for me."

That afternoon at 3 p.m., Lahaie spoke to senior Major Crime officer Warren Korol about hitting the road again. "I have to find Harjeet Singh," Lahaie said.

"So where is he?"

"California. San Jose."

Korol listened. Ever since he had reviewed the case file the previous fall, he had known that the Harjeet angle would need to be explored further. Korol had trekked across the globe to India five years earlier to chase the Sukhwinder Dhillon serial poisoning case.

"I'll contact the Crown to arrange to fly you and Mike down there," Korol said.

In addition to getting a statement and DNA sample from Harjeet, they had to try to get a commitment from him to come up to Canada to testify in person when the murder trial began. That would be a tall order, given his illegal immigration status in both Canada and the United States. He would surely be hesitant to come back. What if he came up for the trial and was then arrested for being an illegal when he tried to return to the States? Or what if he comes up for the trial just in time for the defense to finger him for Yvette's murder?

"Whatever you have to do, you gotta get this guy," Korol said. "You gotta bring him back up here to testify."

On Wednesday, June 19, Lahaie and Mike Thomas drove the 45 minutes to the U.S. border into New York State en route to the Buffalo Niagara International Airport. Lahaie was even more wired than usual for the assignment. First, there was the matter of the border. Even as a police officer, Lahaie was paranoid about crossing the border and getting through security at airports, especially in light of 9/11, because of the darker hue to his skin. He already had once been taken behind a partition to get a full body search while traveling and, another time, at the Las Vegas airport, he was searched for explosives. Lahaie started up on the issue with Thomas in the car.

"Michael, I'm worried, I'm gonna get searched," he said.

"Aw, don't worry about it," Thomas replied. "I'll do all the talking at the border. We'll be fine."

"I fit the profile."

"We'll be fine."

The border went smoothly.

"See? I told you," Thomas said. "No problem."

The airport was another matter. They both got searched in

separate cubicles. After the search, they were in line showing boarding passes to get on the aircraft, when an official pulled them out of the line. They were searched a second time.

"Paul, I'm never traveling to the U.S. with you again," Thomas cracked.

When they landed in San Jose, Lahaie was still worried. He had chased Harjeet to the U.S. once before and hadn't found him. What if he missed him again? The arrangement was all based on trust. The man had every reason to avoid the police, and was under no legal obligation to help them. The detectives retrieved their bags in the airport and waited outside on the curb. Sure enough, Harjeet drove up and parked beside them. He drove them to a coffee shop. It was the first time either detective had talked with him in person. He was not what Lahaie had expected. He was a personable guy, came across as thoughtful.

"What are you looking for?" Harjeet asked.

The detectives explained they needed a DNA sample, a statement—and his testimony in person. Harjeet had a decision to make. Whether he attended court or not, the defense was likely to raise his name as an alternative suspect. That could very well lead to Mohan Ramkissoon being acquitted in Yvette's murder, they said. They drove to a police station in San Jose, where officers provided a room in the homicide section to get his statement, and facilities to get his fingerprints and DNA sample. The detectives asked him outright: Did he kill Yvette Budram?

"I didn't do it," he said.

During all of their conversations, and questioning, Thomas studied Harjeet, was convinced he was telling the truth. Harjeet agreed to come up to Canada to testify if necessary.

"Somebody's got to speak for Yvette," Harjeet said.

Later that day the detectives said goodbye to him. Harjeet turned to Thomas.

"Mr. Mike, here's my cell number," he said. "When you need me, just call. Anything you need."

The detectives headed back to their hotel. Thomas phoned the Major Crime office in Hamilton with an update. They had the next day free before they had to fly back to Canada. Lahaie convinced Thomas to swing by and meet some of his relatives in San Jose.

They got to the house, met an aunt, and before they knew it, other cars started pulling up—cousins, aunts, and uncles. The full Lahaie experience. As usual, he regaled Thomas with detail.

"Here's cousin Ernie, guy's a prince, once owned a bar and his claim to fame is hooking up the first TV in a bar in the state so locals could watch the baseball Giants play. True story, Michael!"

After that visit, Lahaie made another pitch to Thomas to pop up north to San Francisco. Thomas had never been there before, and in keeping with his low-key personality, wasn't a fan of big cities, period. But Lahaie would not leave it alone and Thomas let himself get talked into it. And he loved San Francisco. A gorgeous spot. Lahaie had been there before, gave his partner the whirlwind tour: Fisherman's Wharf, where they saw the hundreds of seals stacked on top of one another barking away, took photos at the Golden Gate Bridge. Lahaie had last been in the city in 1999, and now, post-9/11, the former tactical officer noticed, underneath the famous bridge, were soldiers toting automatic weapons.

"You got your picture taken in front of the Statue of Liberty, now the Golden Gate. You're doin' all right on this case," Thomas said.

The detectives caught the early flight back to Buffalo the next morning. Mohan Ramkissoon's trial would not begin for another 17 months. The detectives felt good. They had started with next to nothing—an unidentified skeleton. And now they had Yvette's blood in the bedroom, in Mohan's car, Mohan trying to flee the country. All that blood and DNA evidence, Mohan's post-offense conduct, and now Harjeet's statement and his apparent willingness to return to Canada to testify, it was all good. How would it all look in a court of law, to a jury? What might the defense call as evidence? Would Mohan take the stand? The detectives thought the man was a professional liar. Would deny everything. The case looked solid. Mike Thomas knew from personal experience, though, that nothing is a sure thing.

CHAPTER 21 ~ POETIC JUSTICE

There had been six other cases on Mike Thomas's plate when he took over supervision of the Yvette Budram homicide. Persons were ultimately charged and convicted in four of those. A trial in the fifth was still pending. And the sixth? That was the one-armed-man case. He had a *Hamilton Spectator* article mounted on his office wall to remind him of that case, and the lesson he could not afford to forget. Forced himself to look at it every day.

Who was that man in the large photo, and why was he laughing? The accused was a man named Nikola Golubic, who had a prosthetic limb and was charged with second-degree murder and attempted murder. He claimed self-defense. Not a chance, thought Thomas. It seemed to everyone like a slam-dunk conviction. Overwhelming evidence. So after court was dismissed, and after an hour into jury deliberations, Thomas is having lunch at Sundried Tomatoes across the street from the courthouse and gets paged. The verdict is in. Even the accused man's lawyer thought the instant verdict was extraordinary. Why so quick? Not guilty. Thomas was shocked. Cool-headed, as always, even at a time like that, he said all the right things to the media. I'm disappointed, he said, but we must accept the jury's decision.

He actually wasn't making that part up. He had to believe in the system, even when he thought someone guilty walked free. Still, it ate him up. He felt so sorry for the family of the victim, that the system had not supported them. Was there something in the case he had missed, something he didn't realize would have a significant impact on the jury? Lesson: when you have accumulated all your evidence, collect some more. Don't stop gathering. And think about how the jury is going to see it, what will be magnified to their eyes. It's about what the jury sees, not what the detective sees or believes.

Anyway, Thomas got ribbed pretty good for that one around the Major Crime Unit. Teasing, dark humor, one-upmanship, it's all part of the cop culture. Thomas put a newspaper article about the trial up on his wall, where he'd be sure to see it, especially the big photo of Golubic looking down at him, every day, the one-armed man not just smiling—cripes, he's actually laughing after the verdict. It was Mike Thomas's daily reminder that there are no slam dunks. And few clean endings. Almost a year to the day of his acquittal, the one-armed man died suddenly in his apartment.

Gary Yokoyama

Mike Thomas hung a photo of the one-armed man on his wall.

Don't stop gathering: There was one angle in the Budram case that Paul La-haie and Thomas had tried to advance, long shot though it seemed. It involved just a few lines Lahaie had jotted in his white homicide notebook. Prior to Mohan's arrest, La-haie had interviewed Avian Kalliecharan, the outspoken family friend whom Mohan and Yvette's kids called Auntie Avian.

"I became aware that Yvette was missing in December 2000, near Christmas," she said. "I saw Mohan at the store. Preet told me that

she had never seen her leave, and that 'Mommy never said good-bye.'"

And then, without provocation from Lahaie, Avian brought up a point she felt the detective needed to hear. She said there was a story floating around that Mohan had come to Canada from the U.S. because he was on the run from police. The last city he had lived in before moving to Canada was Miami, but he had lived in New York before that, in the Bronx, where his brother lived. Mohan had a girlfriend, or at least was pursuing a young woman there, but something terrible happened to the girlfriend's mother. She was murdered. Avian heard that's why he headed for the Canadian border.

Had the NYPD charged Mohan? Suspected him? Without a charge having been laid against Mohan, Lahaie and Thomas knew it was highly unlikely they could use anything from a previous case against him as "similar fact evidence" in the murder of his wife. (Similar fact evidence may be admitted by a judge when prior actions by the accused show a nexus between the prior behavior and the offense for which he has been charged.) But what the detectives did hope was that evidence, even without a charge, that Mohan had run from the law in the past—guilty or not—would mean he would be kept in jail until trial, and not released on bail. He was clearly a flight risk, they could argue. Lahaie contacted the NYPD. Had Mohan been on their radar with respect to a murder in the Bronx in the late 1980s? Officials with Bronx Homicide told Lahaie they would look into it. Then 9/11 happened. After that, the Hamilton detectives knew the NYPD, strapped for resources already, wouldn't be motivated to devote manpower to investigate a 15-year-old cold case.

With Mohan in custody and the Yvette Budram murder trial looming, the New York angle may have seemed of little conse-quence. But then, 12 months before the trial was to begin, Lahaie received news via a phone call from an official at the Ontario Court of Appeal in Toronto. He couldn't believe what he was hearing. Mohan Ramkissoon was being released. He had been in the Barton Street jail in Hamilton for 14 months, denied his application for bail. But now, Lahaie learned, Mohan had successfully appealed. The Ontario Court of Appeal had overturned the Hamilton court's decision to keep him behind bars until trial.

He was released Wednesday, February 5. He was a free man. The court felt Mohan was not a flight risk. Paul Lahaie was furi-ous. He tried to rationalize it: due process, yes; the courts need to be the vanguard of democracy, yes; make sure all citizens are protected. Yes, yes, he agreed with all that.

"But this is *murder*," he said. "The stakes are high. The guy is obviously a flight risk, he tried to leave the country three times already—once to Guyana, two other times packing his car full of luggage and belongings and trying to get across the U.S. bor-der."

And, Lahaie lamented, what about the witnesses who had already talked freely to the detectives about Mohan, people the accused knew well? Could they be in danger? Lahaie worked the phone, calling witnesses to let them know Mohan was out. If they encountered any problems, he said, call him.

Still burning, he phoned Mike Thomas with the news.

"He's out, Michael," he said. "The idiots let him out."

Thomas, cool customer though he was, could not help but join in the venting.

"If he makes a run for it," added Lahaie, "I'll chase him myself."

* * *

In the fall of 2003, with the trial a few months away, Thomas and Lahaie continued to shore up the case. Mohan's favorable treatment by the courts—his release from custody—once again highlighted the potential case-breaker that was Harjeet Singh. "Happy" had agreed to return to Canada to testify, but it was still an open question if he would show—they couldn't force him to do so. Could the prosecution lead evidence in court proving that Harjeet was either in Montreal, or in transit to upstate New York, when Yvette had been killed—most likely between September 17 and September 20?

If the jury accepted Harjeet's statements, and the pattern of phone records, suggesting that he had been in Montreal right up until September 17, when he hopped the border, his potential status as a murder suspect would evaporate. If the detectives' timeline was accepted, in order for Harjeet to have murdered Yvette on September 17, he would have had to drive from Montreal to Mississauga, kill her, take the time to clean up the scene, dump her all the way out in Flamborough, then drive back to Montreal before crossing the border from eastern Ontario into New York state en route to Plattsburgh—all in one day. It made little sense. But what about those phone calls in Montreal?

To date, Harjeet's landlords in Montreal, Ranjit and Prem Saini, had not corroborated his account. Had Harjeet really made those phone calls? What about the couple's contradictory statements and evasions, and Prem's refusal to take the oath? Thomas and Lahaie left Hamilton for Montreal at 5 a.m. on Wednesday, October 1. Six and a half hours later they exited off the Trans-Canada Highway into old East Montreal, the Jarry Park area of town, where immigrants had flocked after the war.

The detectives met Ranjit and Prem at noon. Prem expressed her discomfort with giving a statement at the police station previously, for Peel detective Jamie Davis and Hamilton's Dave Place. Having to attend to the police station had brought shame to the family, she said. This time, the detectives said the interview would be in their home. Prem added that she feared that whatever she had to say about Harjeet, the phone bills he left them holding to pay, or whatever else the police wanted to know about him, might endanger family they still had living in India—Harjeet's home country.

"I respect Canadian law," she said, "but in India, money and status buy influence. Our family could get hurt. Happy comes from a wealthy family."

"Have you or your family received any threats from Happy?" Lahaie asked.

"No."

She told the detectives how bad they had felt about not giving Davis and Place straight answers the last time around.

"I want to make it perfectly clear to you, Prem," Lahaie said. "We only want the truth. That's it."

Prem agreed to take the oath, and offered a statement, with Ranjit out of the room. Then Prem made tea in the kitchen while her husband gave his statement. In their new accounts, they both said that Harjeet had in fact lived at their place in the days leading up to, and including, September 17, as reflected by the phone records. Happy had constantly used their phone, they said. In the one-bedroom apartment, you could hear him talking every day. Prem made the meals, Happy was there for dinner every night until he left for good. He was a pain in the neck, left town with just the clothes on his back, owing them money for running up their phone bill. After the interviews were complete, the four of them sat and chatted some more in the apartment and drank their tea. Lahaie handed them subpoenas to appear in court. The detectives hit the highway and were back in Hamilton by 10 p.m.

The detectives knew Mohan's defense lawyer would try to make hay with the new statements. *So, Prem and Ranjit suddenly change their tune?* But they also knew it was far better than leaving their previous ambiguous statements on the record.

Less positive was news the detectives heard prior to trial. Thomas and Lahaie had been watching anxiously as another big case they had worked came to its conclusion. They didn't know it at the time, but it had implications for the Yvette Budram case. It was the case of a gang-style revenge killing at a house on Sherman Avenue North in lower Hamilton the previous year. Two men had been caught and charged with the second-degree murder of a 20-year-old man named Desmond Mingo, who was shot while trying to negotiate the sale of counterfeit money. One was a man named Jahmar Welsh, the other Adrian Roy Baptiste—a member of a Toronto street gang called the Bloods. When Baptiste had been on the run from police the year before, Mike Thomas had sent messages out to him through the media. "The smart thing to do is just turn yourself in," Thomas was quoted in the *Hamilton Spectator*. "If he wants to tell me his side of the story, I'm willing to listen. But if he thinks things will die down and go away, he's mistaken."

The judge presiding over the trial was Justice Nick Borkovich. Thomas and Lahaie lamented how the trial had progressed. They felt Borkovich had leaned against the Crown's case from the get-go. They thought the judge seemed intent on chipping away at their case at every turn, through his handling of legal arguments, his comments, even his body language before the jury. Every judge has a style, an orientation. Borkovich had a reputation, among detectives and lawyers, for being among those judges who are relatively defense-friendly. But the detectives were still taken aback by it. Borkovich hammered on the reliability of the Crown's witnesses, some of whom were—unavoidably—gang members. Mike Thomas stewed.

"You can't pick and choose your witnesses," Thomas said. "We had sworn statements from them, the court should have allowed them. But Borkovich did not let the jury hear them."

And then, in the judge's charge to the jury—the final words the jurors would hear before going into deliberations—Borkovich said the Crown's witnesses had lied under oath before and during the trial. It was dangerous for the jury to rely on them, he said. Thomas and Lahaie were in court on December 19 for the jury's decision. Baptiste and Welsh were found not guilty. The detectives were bitter. It wasn't just about losing their case. One of the implications of the case had been that the shooting was done in self-defense. But once you start down that road, you're just asking for more shootings, Thomas thought.

"It's about the safety of the community, we live here, too," he said.

Six days after the verdict, on Christmas Day, a family member of victim Desmond Mingo found a card left on his grave. It read: "Yo Desmond. We beat the rap."

After the smoke had cleared, Thomas and Lahaie sat back in the Major Crime office, reflected on the case—and made a prediction.

"The thing is," Thomas said, "either Baptiste or Welsh—or both of them—will be dead or arrested within two years."

Jahmar Welsh would, a year and a half later, be charged with first-degree murder in the shooting of a Woodbridge man named Youhan Oraha. And, on December 27, eight days after the acquittal in the Mingo killing, five rounds from a semiautomatic weapon tore through Adrian Roy Baptiste as he sat behind the wheel of his silver Lexus in a parking lot in northwest Toronto.

Lahaie thought about the ending to that story a lot. Baptiste was a killer and had himself been murdered. Poetic justice? Not

in Lahaie's book, not at all. Only God should make that kind of call. The thing was, if Baptiste had been convicted, he would have been in custody. And still alive. Who knows, Lahaie thought, had Baptiste lived, he might have had an epiphany, changed his life. As it happened, he had been given a gift verdict by the jury. Could have used that gift to become a better man. Such a waste.

Mike Thomas, Paul Lahaie and the Budram case evidence boxes.

As the trial for Mohan Ramkissoon approached, the detectives wondered who would be appointed to preside over it behind the bench. Then they heard the news. The judge for their case would be Justice Nicholas Borkovich. The detectives were aghast. *Oh, no.* Of all the judges in this town, thought Thomas, they get the same one who didn't like their witnesses in Mingo. The other Major Crime detectives got wind of the news.

"My condolences on Borkovich," one detective teased Lahaie.

They would be playing catchup, right from the start.

CHAPTER 22 ~ EDGE OF SANITY

Tom Carey thought the case was fascinating, and Mohan Ramkissoon's lawyer also well knew there were points in the Crown's case open for attack. Beyond the specifics of the case, Carey had the defender's advantage of not carrying the burden of proving how Yvette Budram died, or who, in fact, killed her. Carey was not there to, as he put it, "play Lieutenant Columbo" for the jury, play a whodunit game. As in any murder case in Canada, the onus was on the Crown, the prosecution, to prove to the court beyond a reasonable doubt that the accused, Mohan Ramkissoon, had caused Yvette's death. Carey's job in defending his client was to simply cast a single doubt on the Crown's case.

Carey, a 20-year-plus veteran of the courtroom, had defended about a half-dozen homicide cases in the past. Defenders are not obligated to believe in the innocence of their client. It is unethical, however, to point the finger at an alternative suspect if your client has in fact privately admitted his guilt to you. Tom Carey had no reason to disbelieve Mohan Ramkissoon's innocence. The case was circumstantial and Mohan had steadfastly maintained his position—to Carey, and to the police.

Carey had been a studious boy growing up in Toronto, took an early interest in history. While other kids dragged their parents to the movies, he and his brother dragged their mom and dad to museums. He held a variety of summer jobs growing up, including delivery boy by bicycle for a local pharmacy. Early on he had wanted to be a journalist, like his sister. But in the end he calculated that law was his best bet. He came to love his work. It was real life, he felt; court cases offered snapshots of people's lives, the human drama, tragedy, comedy, pathos. All quite compelling if you have any interest in the human condition. Carey did not belong to the school of thought that believes you are born either a prosecutor or a defender. His passion for the law was broader. Over the course of his career, in addition to defending clients, he did work for the Crown, doing Superior Court duty in Brampton on cases that involved importing narcotics. And he did part-time work as a Small Claims Court judge for 14 years. Even police detectives who had worked on the other side of a case from Carey felt he was a pro. Away from court, he was involved in his Catholic church, the local historical society, had a passion for Norman Jewison movies.

He had a reputation away from the courtroom as an entertaining conversationalist, a storyteller, a raconteur. He himself didn't act, but Carey had directed *Witness for the Prosecution* in his senior year of high school. And he could frequently be heard doing his best Al Pacino-losing-it imitation from Jewison's 1979 movie *And Justice for All* ("I'm outta order? You're outta order! This whole damn court's out of order!"). The movie had an over-the-top quality, Carey thought, characters literally breaking down, but there was a core of truth. And the film did capture the edge-of-sanity feeling that can often pervade the criminal courts.

As in all murder cases, the Crown would set the agenda in the trial of Mohan Ramkissoon. It was the Crown bringing the case against him. It had the resources of the State to gather forensic evidence, to tap the resources and authority of the police for witness statements. But then the bar the Crown had to clear in order to win—proving its case beyond a reasonable doubt—was high. The Crown's case must be utterly transparent. Everything assistant Crown attorney Kevin McKenna knew about the case, Tom Carey would know—but the reverse was not true. A defense team can gather its own information, keep its cards close to the vest, can be cagey, unpredictable.

As trial approached, Carey received stacks of disclosure documents from the Crown. Carey was able to read through every page of notes taken by the detectives who chased the case, and all the forensic reports. The defense has the option of calling evidence or not at trial, and either way, the defense needn't disclose anything to the Crown. There were big decisions for Tom Carey to make. He had already contemplated where the trial should be held and in what format. Carey looked into having it moved from Hamilton to Peel Region, where Mohan and Yvette had lived. His client was a member of a visible minority and, while Hamilton is a diverse community, Peel would probably provide a more diverse jury pool. But the Peel Crown attorney's office had declined to try the case, and Carey pursued the issue no further.

As for the format, nearly all murder cases in Ontario are tried before a judge and jury. Rarely is it judge only. It happens on occasion in a province like Alberta, for example, but not in Ontario. Carey asked Kevin McKenna if he'd consent to judge only. It is the Crown's prerogative to refuse. McKenna said no. Carey's biggest call, though, was deciding whether or not to call his own evidence. The defense is free to call no witnesses. Presenting no evidence can work against you, but it gives the defense the advantage of addressing the jury in closing remarks last, after the Crown speaks. Would Carey call any witnesses? And would Mohan Ramkissoon take the stand? McKenna would need to wait until the end of the trial to find out if the accused would speak for himself.

One piece of evidence that Mohan was certain would help his case was a document he had signed in December 2000, to petition for divorce from Yvette. In the document he mentioned the affair she had been having with Happy.

"If I know my wife is dead," Mohan said, "then why is it I go and pay $1,800 for a divorce? Why would I do that?"

Carey would certainly use it. Here is Mohan, this man, by the Crown's account so devious, who also tries to divorce a woman he purportedly knows to be dead? Carey needed to poke holes like that in the narrative the Crown would present, that Mohan Ramkissoon was the only person who conceivably could have killed Yvette. He knew that perhaps the biggest potential fault line in the Crown's case was Harjeet Singh. He needed to reveal Happy's role in the case to the jury. The police were concerned enough about him as a potential suspect to chase him down to New York, then San Jose, weren't they? Carey knew he looked like a pretty good suspect in the murder: Yvette's lover who wanted monogamy from her. Owed her money. And is it mere coincidence that this man disappears at the same time as the deceased, and that he hops the border on September 17 and never returns? As for credibility, thought Carey, Harjeet was disreputable. The aliases, the criminal record, the border hopping. All the Crown had to go on was his word, and that didn't amount to much.

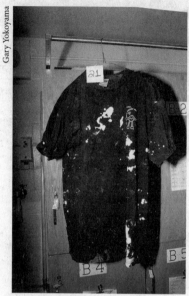

Gary Yokoyama

Oh, and there was the matter of the "Happy Massager." Carey noted that among the items in the recovered items from refuse strewn in the ditch along the 8th Concession near where Yvette's body was found, was a black T-shirt that had a logo reading, "It's me ... the Happy Massager." Happy? That was Harjeet's nickname. A stretch to think that there was a connection between Harjeet, the T-shirt, and Yvette's murder. Wasn't it? Perhaps not, to just one juror.

The "Happy Massager" t-shirt.

As the trial approached, Harjeet's wife, Doris, received a call at her home in Tupelo, Miss. She didn't recognize the man's voice on the other end. He started asking her questions about Harjeet.

"Has Happy ever been known as a fitness instructor?" the man asked. "Or known as the Happy Massager?"

Doris figured the man was probably gathering information for the trial. She was correct. The man identified himself as a private investigator, working for the defense team.

"Don't you have all your information already?" she asked.

Later Doris laughed at the notion of her husband as a fitness instructor.

"I wish I had the looks to marry a fitness instructor," she said.

Tom Carey requested that the Crown submit the Happy Massager T-shirt for DNA testing in order to compare it to the sample given by Harjeet Singh.

As for Paul Lahaie, he did not let up on the eve of the trial. On January 6, 2004, just 13 days before the trial began, he continued to review case documents and notes. He had written down scores of phone numbers taken from billing records, receipts; had followed up on most of them, made cold calls to numbers used by Yvette and Mohan. Lahaie now noticed there was one call he had not followed up. On September 25, 2000, at 9:10 a.m., Mohan had dialed 416-947-2000 on his cell. Lahaie dialed the number. It was a number for the *Toronto Sun* newspaper classifieds section. It turned out that Mohan Ramkissoon had placed an ad to sell a car—Yvette's SUV. He had placed the ad to run from September 26 to October 2, 2000: Infiniti SUV fully loaded. Lahaie tracked down and interviewed a woman who had answered the ad and gone to 2382 Benedet in Mississauga to look at buying the vehicle.

"I have a difficult time getting rid of the car, selling it," Mohan had told her when he showed off the SUV. "Bought it for my wife, it meant so much to her. Was her pride and joy."

Interesting, Lahaie thought: "Here is the supposedly grieving husband; loves his wife so much. A week after she disappears, he doesn't know where she is—and he's *selling her car*? And why is that? Because he knows that she's never coming back, because she's dead."

Lahaie updated his notes with the new information to pass along to Kevin McKenna. It was a nice bit of evidence to add to the case. Lahaie was pleased. But then, at 5 p.m. that same day, Lahaie heard bad news. He spoke on the phone with Harjeet Singh in San Jose, Calif., about his availability to testify. It was still up in the air. In fact, it was not looking good at all. Happy said he was on his last immigration hearing in the United States. Coming back to Canada now was not a good idea. Also, a 9/11 Code Orange terrorist security alert had just been ordered in the States. In that climate, Harjeet might never make it back there after the trial. The border would be a nightmare.

Lahaie knew they needed Harjeet there in person for the jury to hear, to assess his credibility. If he could not make it to testify, it could mean losing the case. The next day, January 7, Lahaie spoke with Harjeet again. Happy repeated his position. He was reluctant to make the trip north of the border. Meanwhile, Tom Carey had brought forward a formal motion to Justice Nick Borkovich. Carey could not simply raise Harjeet in court as a suspect out of the blue. By law he needed Borkovich to accept his submission that Harjeet be officially declared an "alternative suspect." Kevin McKenna argued against the submission. Borkovich sided with the defense. Harjeet Singh would be presented to the jury as an alternative suspect in the murder of Yvette Budram.

* * *

John Sopinka Courthouse
Hamilton, Ontario
Monday afternoon, January 19, 2004

"Mr. McKenna," intoned Justice Nick Borkovich.

Assistant Crown attorney Kevin McKenna rose, wearing the customary black robe, following the British tradition where both defender and prosecutor wear precisely the same uniform in court—no style points for dress shall be accorded by the jury. He stood from his chair at the front of the court, turned to face the jury for his opening address. It was his opportunity to outline the narrative of the case for the jurors.

"Ladies and gentlemen, good afternoon," McKenna said in his radio baritone voice.

Mohan Ramkissoon sat in the prisoner's dock, but he was still a free man, having been released on bail, and so was allowed to come and go freely from court each day. He wore a shirt and tie. Tom Carey sat up at the front across from McKenna. The defense does not give an opening address. It is the Crown that presents the state's case.

Paul Lahaie sat at the table next to McKenna, his heart pounding. It's all or nothing time, Lahaie thought. There had been plea bargain discussions between the defense and the Crown, as there often are in murder cases. But Mohan refused to plead anything other than not guilty. He had never claimed responsibility for Yvette's death to anyone. Hypothetically, if Mohan had pled guilty to hitting Yvette in anger, but not meaning to kill her, the jury might have been called to decide whether he was guilty of murder or a lesser charge like manslaughter. Instead, the charge remained second-degree murder. (The charge was not first-degree murder because there was no evidence being presented that Mohan had planned in advance to murder his wife.) And so the jury was going to be left with a stark choice: freedom for Mohan Ramkissoon or Millhaven Institution, the maximum security federal prison near Kingston, Ontario.

Jury selection had been finalized that morning; Mohan watched members of the jury panel file in for McKenna and Carey to vet. There were not enough faces of color, Mohan thought. There were several potential jurors who appeared to share Mohan's ethnic origins, but as it happened, they had asked to be excused from jury duty. The jury agreed upon by McKenna and Carey was white, with one juror of Asian heritage. Mohan was not pleased. The jurors will look at him and see dark black skin, much darker skin than Yvette had, or Happy, he thought, and they will hold it against him. They will see a "Paki," he said.

"My name is Kevin McKenna," the prosecutor continued before the jury. "Beside me is Detective Paul Lahaie, one of the investigating officers, who is going to assist me throughout this trial. The accused, Mohan Ramkissoon, is charged with murder in the second degree—that is, that he caused the death of a person. In this case, the Crown's evidence will attempt to prove that he caused the death of his wife, Lilawattee Budram, who also went by the name of Yvette. The evidence begins with the finding of the decomposed body of Yvette Budram on April 17, 2001, near the intersection of Concession 8 and Cooper Road, in the former town of Flamborough, which is now part of Hamilton. It was a very short distance from the African Lion Safari."

Multiple skull fractures. A ligature found around the neck. Official cause of death, blunt force trauma to the head and probable ligature strangulation. "Because of the advanced state of decomposition of the body it took some time for the police identification officers to match her fingerprints and identify who the deceased was. This was done on June 7, 2001."

He said that Yvette died sometime between September 15 and September 25, 2000. "We do not have an eyewitness to the crime, but rather the evidence provides a story or a picture from which, at the end, I suggest, there is only one inescapable conclusion, and that is that the accused killed his wife, Yvette Budram."

The key for McKenna was to tell a story through the evidence that did not allow for alternative theories that the defense could exploit. Consider the weight of the evidence. Use common sense. He made sure to mention Harjeet. McKenna knew that Tom Carey would be playing that card eventually. Don't play games with the jury, get it out there now.

"You will hear that Yvette Budram was having a relationship with a Mr. Harjeet Singh. He had a nickname of Happy. You will hear evidence that the accused found out about the relationship before the death of Yvette."

McKenna concluded: "I would like to make one comment about juries generally. You bring to this trial the life experience of 12 different individuals and, as well, 12 different perspectives of common sense. When you are watching and listening to each witness, and at the end when you are considering all of the evidence, I ask you to please apply your common sense to reaching your verdict."

He began calling witnesses to retell the investigation into Yvette's death. Tom Carey had the option of cross-examining each one. The first witness was Steve Dmytrus, the off-duty firefighter who discovered the remains and phoned police. Later came forensic investigator Al Yates, who recounted how he identified Yvette from fingerprints taken from the severed fingers. When court adjourned for the day, the jury left the room, then Mohan Ramkissoon stepped down from the dock and walked out through the door into the hallway. Mike Thomas burned every time he watched Mohan leave freely, in his regular clothes. Sometimes, by coincidence, they both ended up among the same group of people on the courthouse elevator. What would the other people think, Thomas reflected, if they knew a murderer was riding the elevator with them? They would not be impressed. Thomas wasn't. He hated it.

CHAPTER 23 ~ ALTERNATIVE SUSPECT

The next day, forensic pathologist Dr. David King took the stand. He had testified about 600 times in the past. King took the jury through his attendance at the scene when the remains were found, the decomposition of the body, the autopsy, the skull fracture caused by several blows with a blunt instrument.

"I think it would have been a severe amount of force, depending on the object that caused it," he said. "But it would take quite a bit of force to produce these fractures."

"And the object that may have caused it, are you able to comment on that at all?" McKenna asked.

"It could have been something fairly large and heavy. I am not saying it was. If it was one impact, something in the order of the head of a baseball bat. But I certainly couldn't be certain of that."

The jury was shown photos of the ligature that had been wrapped around Yvette's neck, photos of the skull itself. King had said that the skull fracture suggested that she had been lying on a soft surface.

"Now, the soft surface, in your opinion would a mattress constitute a soft surface?"

"Yes."

"Thank you, Doctor. Those are my questions."

Tom Carey stood to cross-examine. Blood had been found in the master bedroom at 2382 Benedet. Yvette's blood. That meant Yvette had been murdered there. Or did it? Only a small amount of blood was detected. How could that be? Maybe she was murdered somewhere else. By someone else.

"You have talked about internal bleeding," Carey said. "Does it go without saying that there would be significant external bleeding expected with these injuries?"

"Yes," King said.

Would that, Carey pressed, have caused blood spatter?

"If there was more than one blow or impact I would expect blood to be forced out, yes. I think we are getting to the edge of my expertise."

If the bedroom was not necessarily the murder scene, the optics on Mohan Ramkissoon as the prime suspect changed significantly. Was it possible, Carey asked, that Yvette could have been killed at the scene where she was dumped? That was possible, King replied.

"Is it also possible that this victim was struck by more than one assailant?"

"I suppose I couldn't completely rule it out, no."

King had noted in his post-mortem report that the body had been thrown into the brush at the roadside.

"If I suggested to you a scenario with two or more people," continued Tom Carey, "I am going to suggest that two people, one with the arms and one with the legs, removing a body from a vehicle and potentially flinging that body—was it consistent with two or more people flinging her in that manner?"

"I suppose I can't rule that out," King said.

When a defense lawyer cross-examines, he cannot introduce his own evidence. Technically he must only cross-examine on points and themes brought out by the Crown's examination. But Carey was able to float a couple of points that would mean little to jurors at this early point in the trial, but might be referenced later. Carey asked King if he had found any eyeball tissue on the remains. There had been none, said the forensic pathologist.

"You would have to bear with me on this," said Carey, "but have you ever heard of any science that might be called retinal imaging, with a suggestion that somebody who had died, if you examined their eyes you could see the last image under the microscope, the last thing they saw—have you ever heard of that?"

It was a veiled reference to the police interrogation of Mohan Ramkissoon, in which the concept of retinal imaging had been mentioned in an effort to trick Mohan, or at least to see how he would react to the suggestion that Yvette's eyeball tissue would reveal her killer. Why was Carey bringing it up? So that he could raise it to criticize police investigation methods?

"Is it make-believe," Carey asked, "or is there some science to it?"

"I think at the present time it is thought to be make-believe," King replied. Carey pursued the theme no further. Near the end of his questions, Carey presented a photo of a T-shirt to King.

"I don't know whether you have seen this T-shirt?"

"No."

Carey told him it was found near the ditch on Concession 8. The logo on the T-shirt said "It's Me ... The Happy Massager."

"I guess just curiosity led us to find out what the 'Happy Massager' is," Carey said. Next he held up a small wooden massage tool. It had a round head with three pegs, with smaller round heads attached. This, said Carey, was a device in fact called the Happy Massager. "Is that a type of thing that could be used to inflict the kind of injuries you have seen?"

"I think it would be highly unlikely," King said. "I don't think it is robust enough to cause that area of fracturing and I don't think it matches the anterior area of fracturing either." It would be difficult, he added, for someone to hold it in such a way as to deliver a powerful blow. If you were holding it by one of the legs, it would break apart.

"It is not suggested this was the weapon," Carey said. "This was sent to us, but this is just an example of what—you felt it would quickly break and wouldn't be capable of delivering another blow, is that right?"

"That's my own feeling, yes."

Carey held up a ruler to measure the diameter of the Happy Massager. Carey passed the device to a juror, who passed it along to the others to handle. "It is somewhat of a coincidence, perhaps, that the T-shirt with this emblazoned on it is at the scene," he said. "But we will leave it at that for the time being."

* * *

"Mr. McKenna, next witness," said Justice Nick Borkovich.

It was the next day, Tuesday, January 20.

"Yes, Your Honor, it is the request of the Crown that this witness, Dael Morris, be qualified as an expert in the area of forensic entomology."

Dael Morris.

The Bug Lady took the stand. Her qualifications were reviewed, and then McKenna asked his questions. Morris reviewed her findings, the colonization of the remains by the blowflies, her discovery that the body had been moved from the point of death to the spot in Flamborough. While Morris had personally felt the death had been three days on either side of September 20, maximum, she had broadened that timeline in her official report.

In her testimony, she said that the time frame for Yvette's time of death had been between September 15 and 25, 2000. Her testimony spilled into the next day, Wednesday, and Tom Carey's cross-examination. Carey took her through her methodology, said that forensic entomology was "not an exact science," but he did not make any suggestion that her findings were not accurate. "You have a fair amount of confidence in your results?"

"Yes, I do."

Morris stepped down from the stand. She had thought she might get a rougher ride. The next witness for the Crown was Sonny Uppal, the clerk from the Mississauga Gate Inn, who had seen Yvette Budram and Harjeet Singh check in back in July 2000. It was part of McKenna's narrative that Mohan Ramkissoon knew all about his wife's affair with Harjeet, that Yvette had even used one of his credit cards to pay for the room. Mohan had reason to feel intense anger towards his wife. On the stand Uppal told McKenna that Mohan had come to see him at the hotel asking about a $30 charge on his credit card. He told Mohan it had been for a four-hour short stay at the motel.

"He wanted to know if I knew anything about the day the transaction happened." At the time, Mohan appeared worried and under stress, Uppal added. Carey cross-examined briefly.

The short stay, Uppal said, was for travelers needing a shower before going on their way.

"Do you get a lot of people coming in to use the shower?" Carey asked. "You get a lot of couples coming in for the shower special?"

"Yeah, I guess," Uppal replied sheepishly.

The parade of witnesses continued over several days. Among them was Glenn MacDonald, one of the boarders at 2382 Benedet Drive who had heard Mohan and Yvette fight in the past. But had MacDonald heard anything when Yvette had been murdered? In fact, while there were two boarders living in the backsplit house at the time of the murder—MacDonald, who lived in the basement, and a man named Seelan, who lived upstairs—nobody heard anything unusual during the critical time frame.

* * *

On Thursday morning, January 29, a bearded man wearing a turban entered the courtroom. He was, to all appearances, a practising Sikh. He entered the witness box and swore to tell the truth. Kevin McKenna stood.

"Mr. Singh, good morning," he said.

"Good morning."

It was Happy—Harjeet Singh. He had made it from San Jose after all.

When Paul Lahaie and Mike Thomas had seen him in San Jose 19 months earlier, he had not sported the turban or the beard, the attributes of orthodox Sikhism. Had Happy found religion? Or was it a more calculated move? Happy was something of a con, wasn't he? Tom Carey noticed the change. He would have to point it out to the jury. Lahaie didn't think it was a put-on. You can't grow a full beard like that in a couple of weeks, and Lahaie knew that, until just before the trial, Harjeet wasn't even sure he would attend. Maybe, Lahaie thought, after all Happy had gone through, and learning of Yvette's death, he had returned to his faith. Mostly Lahaie was just glad Harjeet had shown up. They needed his testimony, the jury deserved to hear him.

How had Happy gotten there? It had been on January 8—the day after Harjeet told Lahaie he wouldn't attend because of the Code Orange alert in the U.S.—that he relented, told Lahaie that he was willing to come to Canada even with the danger of his immigration status. And the next day, the Code Orange had been lifted. Two days before Harjeet was to appear in court, Lahaie and Thomas drove to the Buffalo airport to meet him. Lahaie worried about bringing a guy across the border whom they knew to be an illegal alien. They brought him back without a hitch, checked him in at the creaky Royal Connaught Hotel downtown by 11:30 p.m. The next day, Lahaie had taken Harjeet to meet with Kevin McKenna for two hours. And now, on Thursday morning, Harjeet Singh was, finally, in the witness box.

"Can you tell me where you currently live?" McKenna asked him.

"I live in California. San Jose."

There were two main lines of inquiry that McKenna needed to take Harjeet through. One was establishing Harjeet's relationship with Yvette. The second was that he was not in the Mississauga area at the time she had been murdered. Harjeet told the jury about his past, his arrival in Canada in 1999, how he came to know and love Yvette Budram. Early in their relationship she started inviting him to her home for breakfast from where he was boarding down the street. They started to meet at hotels.

"I take it when you say you went to a motel it was to have some kind of intimate relationship?" McKenna asked.

"Right."

"Can you recall how many times in total you would have gone to the Mississauga Gate motel with Yvette?"

"I'm not sure, like I said, I cannot recall, it was too long time, maybe 10 or 12 times. It could be more, it could be less."

McKenna took Harjeet through a timeline of his whereabouts in the time leading up to, and after, Yvette's likely time of death. Yvette had been alive, according to police witness statements, as of the early evening of September 17, 2000. The last time Harjeet had seen her, he said, was Labour Day weekend, September 2–3. After he saw her the final time, on the front step of her house in Mississauga, he returned to Montreal, where he had been staying with Ranjit and Prem Saini. He stayed in Montreal until September 17, when he left Canada for good across the border near Cornwall, for Plattsburgh, N.Y., and ultimately New York City.

McKenna painstakingly took Harjeet through a Bell phone bill listing calls made from the Montreal number he had been using at the Sainis' each day up to and including September 17. Most of his calls were to his wife, Doris, in Mississippi.

"And why is it we don't see that number any more after September 17?"

"Because we left that evening. We were supposed to cross the border at two-thirty, three o'clock, so we left from there, and after that I'm not calling any more."

"Now, item Number 17, that is a call to Jackson, Mississippi? Whose number is that?"

"That's my wife's number."

"Did you make that call on September 18?"

"No, I was not there. I didn't make that call. Actually, Prem also talked to Doris and she must have called and told her, 'He left from here.' Yeah, she must have called her."

McKenna completed his questions, and when court resumed in the afternoon, Carey started his cross-examination. The Crown had the phone billing records, but the veracity of Harjeet's whereabouts at the time of Yvette's murder rested, in part, on his own word. Carey immediately attacked Happy's credibility.

"Sir, you've told us your name," Carey said. "When is your date of birth?"

"It is 4/15/1970," Harjeet said.

"Sorry, can you just give me the month and the day and the year?"

"Yes, sir. 4/15/1970."

"So that is April 15, 1970?" Carey asked.

"Yes, sir."

"And have you used another birth date?"

"Yes, I did."

"What is that other birth date?"

"2/9/1968."

"So that is February 9, 1968?"

"Yes, sir. No, sorry, it is September, 9/2/68."

"September 2, 1968?"

"Yes, sir."

"And what is your full name? What is your legal name?"

"Legal name is Harpreet."

"Harpreet?"

"Yes, sir."

"Harpreet?" Carey repeated.

"Makkar. M-A-K-K-A-R."

"You swore in today as Harjeet Singh?"

"Because I use this name in Canada. That is the name, when I apply for immigration that is the name I change it to."

"It's an alias. You didn't legally change your name, did you?"

"No."

"And does that made-up name come with a made-up birth date?"

"Yes, sir."

"So Harjeet Singh has a birthdate of September 2, 1968?"

"Right."

"But Harpreet Makkar—and that is really you?"

"Yep."

"Has a birth date of April 15, 1970?"

"Right."

"Are there any other names you use?"

"No."

Carey asked him about the tapes Paul Lahaie found in New York, in the pocket of Harjeet's jacket. "Apparently there were some tapes found in the jacket. Do you know what I'm talking about? It was a microcassette. What were those tapes of?"

"I recorded her messages from my answering machine."

"Well, there was a little more than that, sir. Didn't you record actual conversations that you had with Yvette Budram—"

"I don't recall. I recorded some of her messages from the machine into the cassettes."

"And there is another recording that I am going to suggest, it is pretty clear if you listen to you, it is of yourself and Yvette in a hotel and it continues to the point where it records you and her apparently having sex. Am I right?"

"Yes."

"Why on earth would you record that?"

"Because I never trusted her ... I thought if something happened, she just might say, 'He was raping me,' or 'He was forcing me.' But I had the proof that it is both people involved in it."

Later Carey returned to Harjeet's immigration fraud, his aliases.

"You lied?" Carey asked.

"Yes, I did."

"You had no problem with that.... That doesn't bother you, I take it?"

"We come from where economically we are not OK. We don't have freedom. So, when you try to come to these countries and try to live here, and try to get better economically, you want to have freedom."

"Come on, sir, you are just scamming.... I am going to suggest to you, sir, that this court has no way of knowing when you are telling a story and when you are telling the truth, because you don't really feel bound by an oath, do you?"

"I don't understand the question."

"You took an oath today under a fictitious name."

"Yes."

Carey talked about Harjeet's record. There was an incident in 1999, in Tupelo, Miss., at a gas station store Harjeet owned. "I have in front of me a police department offense form," Carey said. The report said Harjeet had sworn at a customer who was asking for change for $40—then kicked his car, reached in the window, and grabbed the customer by the shirt.

"Is that a fair report of what happened?" Carey asked.

"No, sir.... He didn't ask for change for $40, he asked for change for hundred dollar. And the store is the baddest area of the town. I called the police department, the [customer] spit on my face because I did not have the hundred dollar change."

"So that man was lying and you are telling the truth?"

Harjeet admitted that he was charged in the incident.

"You admitted essentially the case for the prosecutor and you were fined?"

"I cannot recall. It is too long time."

"You've had pretty good recall for events in the year 2000 and this is 1999. When does your memory begin to fade, is it between 1999 and 2000?"

Carey asked about the Happy Massager T-shirt. He showed it to Harjeet.

"Are you familiar with that T-shirt?"

"No, I have never seen it."

"Apparently they come from California."

Carey moved on to Harjeet's stay at the hotel in Plattsburgh soon after he hopped the border on September 17, 2000. Carey said Harjeet had not used his own signature to pay for the hotel.

"It is my handwriting, but it is not my signature," Harjeet said.

"You are afraid of signing your own signature immediately after crossing into the United States?"

"Yeah, I was afraid of getting caught."

"You were afraid of getting caught, all right."

"Yes."

CHAPTER 24 ~ CAPACITY FOR VIOLENCE

Tom Carey kept Harjeet in the witness box the rest of the afternoon, and into the next day, focusing on the phone records, his relationship with Yvette, his border hopping. He was showing Harjeet to be someone with contacts everywhere, who used aliases, was a scammer, even had a violent streak. Carey said that Ranjit and Prem Saini, whom Harjeet had stayed with in Montreal, claimed that Harjeet had made threats against their families in India.

"Your family is well connected enough that the Sainis were fearful of what you might do to them? You made some threats against the Sainis, didn't you, Ranjit and Prem?"

"No, I did not. We were very good friends."

Carey questioned Harjeet's turn towards orthodox Sikhism—growing his beard and wearing a turban in time for the trial. Harjeet answered that at 21 years old, he was saved, embraced the religion, the beard, the turban. And then, after having broken with the traditions of his faith for a time, he was recently saved again, living in San Jose.

"I see," Carey said. "You are telling us that you now have been re-saved?"

"Yes, that is why I have the beard and the turban."

Near the end of the questioning, Harjeet recounted how he offered to help Paul Lahaie and Mike Thomas all he could in the case.

"So you have become a model citizen, have you?" Carey asked.

Finally, he introduced the notion that someone may have cut the material out of Mohan and Yvette's mattress simply to hide sexual activity from an affair—someone like Harjeet. "This [affair] wasn't something you wanted Mohan to know about?" Carey asked.

"Obviously, no. Who wants that?"

"And this wasn't something you thought was right?"

"It's not. It is 1,000 percent not right to have relations with somebody's wife."

Carey suggested that Harjeet or Yvette would have hidden evidence of the affair, such as dirty sheets from their sexual encounters.

"There was no evidence to hide," Harjeet replied. "If I had sex in her house I am not going to tell her to hide this and that."

Carey asked about the white satin nightie that Yvette had been wearing when her remains were found. "She had a white nightgown, kind of a baby doll nightgown. Are you familiar with that?"

"No ... I don't remember."

"You know when she was found she was wearing the baby doll nightgown?"

"I have not been told anything about those things."

Carey moved to Harjeet's crossing of the border on September 17.

"You were traveling with one suitcase?"

"One big suitcase."

"You are taking the things that are important to you ... and what you include in this stuff you are taking across the border is the tapes that you made of Yvette?"

"Yes, that was in my possession."

"You're leaving the country, you're not coming back, and you take—you make sure you take these tapes of Yvette with no need to worry about anybody suggesting to you that you assaulted her at that point, was there?"

"I got all of it, but didn't get the end of what you said. I took the tapes with me, yes."

"You took the tapes with you. At that point you had no need to worry about Yvette again?"

"I didn't have to worry about her, but I still wanted to keep it. Tomorrow somebody know where I am, they said you was the only one pushing this relationship, I have the proof with me."

"Thank you, sir."

"Thank you."

"No re-examination, Your Honor," added Kevin McKenna.

"Thank you, Mr. Singh," said the judge.

"Thank you," Happy replied.

* * *

A liar, fraud, adulterer, perhaps something of a sexual deviant, and a capacity for violence. Were these the messages the jurors were now receiving about Harjeet Singh, the other suspect? Paul Lahaie tried to put himself in the shoes of the jurors. What were they thinking? Harjeet was clearly not a model citizen. Would they be able to distinguish between the man's shaky character and the capacity to murder his lover? At least Happy freely admitted to his sins. And there is a big difference between skirting the law, not paying your friends back money, and murdering someone in cold blood. He had come to Canada, all the way up here to testify in a murder trial in which he knew the finger would be pointed at him. Wasn't that the most important character point of all, Lahaie wondered? Wouldn't jurors at least give him marks for showing up, for testifying? Didn't that mean something?

Lahaie received good news during a break in Harjeet's testimony when he returned a message from Monica Sloan with the Centre of Forensic Sciences in Toronto. She had news for him about the DNA test requested by Tom Carey for the Happy Massager T-shirt. Sloan told Lahaie there was no DNA found on the shirt for comparison. She'd fax him her technical report. There was no forensics, apparently, to back up the theory Carey was floating that connected Harjeet with the T-shirt found at the scene. But would Carey need the forensics to plant a seed of doubt?

Kevin McKenna resumed calling witnesses. He called a total of 41 to the stand for the Crown's case over 14 days. Mohan's financial adviser, Lori-Anne Davis, testified. So did Peel detective Jamie Davis. Yvette's eldest daughter, Lisa, appeared. McKenna called Harmeet (Montu) Singh, a friend of Happy's, a long-haul trucker, who testified that Happy had been back in Mississauga on Labour Day weekend, and that Happy had owed Yvette $3,000. Montu recalled in court that he had told Yvette to ask Happy about the money. When Yvette showed up at the Sikh temple where Happy was staying in Mississauga and asked about her money, Happy grabbed his friend Montu by the collar and asked why he brought her to see him.

McKenna called Mayela Lobianco, who testified that Mohan and Yvette had visited her home on September 17. She recalled Yvette mentioning a court date coming up in three days. But then, Mayela's husband, Gus, testified, he said he was certain Yvette and Mohan had actually dropped by on September 10, which contradicted his wife's account. It was a point for Carey. The earlier in the timeline Yvette had been murdered, the more likely the hypothesis that Harjeet was still in Canada at the time Yvette was murdered.

Mohan Ramkissoon's boss at Queensway Machine Products, a man named Lou Cela, entered the witness box. McKenna asked Cela if Mohan had been a better than average employee.

"I would not characterize him as better than average, no," Cela said. "There were some problems now and then. There were issues that were left unresolved."

"Did you talk to him about those issues?"

"On a number of occasions, yes."

"And did they get resolved satisfactorily?"

"No, not really."

McKenna reviewed the timeline with Cela. Mohan had been away from work September 12, 13, 14, and also on Monday September 18. It was an authorized leave. "So, an authorized absence, do you know whether or not a person gets paid for that?" McKenna asked.

"They don't get paid."

McKenna asked Cela about June 14, 2001, the morning Mohan had come to work with his kids and left work by 10 a.m. out the back door.

"It was surprising that he came to work with his children," Cela said. "The guys in the shop said he was here in the shop with his children, which was strange in itself because we normally don't bring our children to work."

Carey cross-examined.

"As I understood your evidence, you concluded that Mohan had not come to work to actually work, but that he had come to speak to you?"

"That is how I perceived it, yes," Cela said.

"And if there was a problem with day care or having to get the day off work for something involving the children, you could understand why the kids might be in tow to a brief meeting with you?"

"Yes. Just generally, I guess people would call ahead of time, not show up at the doorstep."

"And in this particular case, if he had called ahead of time you wouldn't have been there, is that right?"

"I wouldn't have been, but he could have left a message."

A Peel police officer named James Laing was called. As warrants officer for Peel Region, Laing was responsible for exploring the whereabouts of Yvette when she had missed court. In the course of his duty, Laing kept a regular watch on Mohan's house, also spoke to Mohan. Laing said Mohan had appeared cooperative, they kept in touch at least twice a week at first, and he continued to call Mohan through that winter and into spring 2001. Under cross-examination from Carey, Laing agreed that Mohan did seem genuinely concerned about his missing wife. Carey scored a point for his client when he suggested that Laing had personally advised Mohan not to file a missing person report, because a warrant for her was sufficient. Laing agreed.

"I had a conversation with him about should there be a missing person report and I said, 'You know, we don't need it.'"

So perhaps Mohan had not, in fact, been negligent in failing to file a missing person report? That had been one of the pieces of guilty-mind evidence against him. But now a police officer testified that he had advised Yvette's husband not to file the MPR.

Ranjit and Prem Saini from Montreal each took the stand to account for Harjeet's whereabouts during the crucial timeline. A Punjabi translator worked during the questioning. They were crucial witnesses for the Crown in terms of accounting for Happy's whereabouts during the time Yvette was murdered—but also key witnesses for the defense, given their inconsistent statements to police.

"When did Happy come to live with you in Montreal?" Kevin McKenna asked.

Prem replied that it was in August of 2000.

"And how long did he stay with you?"

"Almost one month."

"When did he leave, do you know?"

"Seventeenth of September."

"And do you know where he went?"

"He said he was going to New York."

McKenna pointed to a phone number projected up on a video screen for the jurors. "Now I am showing you a number, a call in to Jackson, Mississippi, at 7:07 in the morning. Can you tell us anything about that call?"

"I made that call," Prem Saini said. "Because Doris called in the midnight saying, 'Where is Happy?' And I said Happy left already. She said, 'Where is he?' I said I don't know."

McKenna continued. Prem confirmed that her husband and Happy had driven to Ontario in late August, as Happy had testified.

"Forgetting about the time your husband was away, was Happy ever away from your home overnight between the time he first got to your house and September 17?"

"No, sir. Every evening he used to be in our house—our one-bedroom apartment. I used to cook every meal, every evening he used to be with us."

"Now at some point you were contacted by the police. And when you were first contacted you gave a statement?"

"Yes. We lied."

Prem recounted how they were taken to the police station, how they felt fear about the process. "Why did you refuse to take an oath?"

"Because I'm not going to say the truth."

Prem explained that they were scared, and ashamed, to have the police at their door with Indian neighbors watching in their building. And Happy and his friend, Montu, had a dispute over money owed. The Sainis did not want to get caught in the middle of it, not when they had family back home in India that could be in danger if they rubbed someone the wrong way.

"In India there is no law and order," she said. "One day you see a person and the next day the person is gone."

She said police questioned them that first time until 2 a.m. They couldn't sleep that night, she rose, her conscience aching, but also feeling that God was looking over her. She phoned Hamilton Police detective Dave Place and told him she had lied. And then Paul Lahaie and Mike Thomas came calling to re-interview them.

"And did you tell them the truth?" Carey asked.

"Yes, sir, everything true."

"Now you have mentioned Happy and threatening messages to Montu and I believe you said it was about money. Did Happy ever threaten you?"

"Not us, but our answering machine he used to leave messages for Montu."

"How was he with you?"

"He was a pain in the ass, sorry for my language, please. Excuse my language."

Prem said she cooked and cleaned for the men, bought Happy his beer and liquor, their bills mounted and Happy didn't pay his share.

"But did he ever threaten you?"

"No, he was OK with us, he was living there, all the time on the money or busy watching Hindi movies or English movies."

Tom Carey cross-examined. Prem feared telling the truth to police initially?

"I'm going to suggest to you that you told Detective Place you were frightened because Happy threatened you?"

"I don't remember, sir."

"You don't remember."

"He didn't threaten us. He used to leave threatening messages for Montu on our answering machine."

Carey suggested that Happy had left them with a threat when he left their place in Montreal, not just for Montu for owing him money, but for the Sainis as well.

"You told Detective Place that Happy is very short-tempered and that he said to you, 'You guys have given my information to the police. I'm going to do this and that in India.'"

"No, he didn't say that."

"You don't know why Detective Place would have written down, 'You guys have given my information to police. I'm going to do this and that in India.'"

"I have no idea."

Carey moved on to suggest that Prem's husband, Ranjit, had helped smuggle Happy across the border. Prem denied it, Carey persisted. McKenna objected to the line of questioning. Judge Borkovich ruled in Carey's favor.

Later, Carey returned to the theme of Harjeet as having the capacity for violence. "You have told us today that while you are not acknowledging that Happy threatened you directly, you were frightened of him?"

"Yes, sir."

Carey wrapped up his cross-examination. The next day, Ranjit took the stand, with the Punjabi interpreter again translating. In his second interview with police, with Lahaie and Mike Thomas, Ranjit had corroborated his wife's account of the Happy timeline. But now Carey pounced on Ranjit lying under oath to police at the first interview. Prem refused to swear to tell the truth. Ranjit had sworn an oath and lied anyway.

"You understood it was a criminal offense to lie under oath to police?"

"At that time I didn't know that."

"You are a person of faith? You are religious?"

"Yes."

"And you swore an oath today using the Bible?"

"Yes."

In that first interview with police, Ranjit had said that in fact he had not stayed at their place in Montreal since June 1999, and that he had not seen Happy in Montreal since June or July 2000 when Happy was dropping off a load driving a truck.

"At that time whatever I told the police it was not true," he told Carey on the stand. "It was a lie.... But today what I am saying is the whole truth."

Carey bore on, taking Ranjit through his statement, even as Ranjit continued to remind him that he had not told the truth. "You were scared of what Happy could do to your family in India?" Carey asked.

"Yes, I was."

Carey asked Ranjit about the man's revised statement, that the last time he saw Happy was in Montreal, leaving their home on September 17, 2000. But had Happy said where he was going? The U.S.? Mississauga?

"And he told you he was leaving?"

"Yes."

"He told you nothing?"

"No, he said I am going to America."

"I am going to suggest he told you nothing, he just told you he was leaving?"

"Yes."

"Is that right? So he didn't even tell you he was going to America?"

"Yes, I did say to you that he told me I am going to America. I don't speak good English, please don't twist my words."

Carey reminded Ranjit that a private investigator who phoned Ranjit on behalf of the defense asked him about what Happy had said. "And your answer to him was 'No he no tell me nothing, sir.'"

"Maybe I didn't understand the question or something."

When Carey finished his questions, Kevin McKenna stood up.

"Mr. Saini, the conversation you had with the investigator, was that in English or Punjabi?"

"Yes, on the phone, in English."

"Thank you."

CHAPTER 25 ~ TACTICAL ERROR

The final Crown witnesses were the stars of the case for the prosecution—the forensic experts. The Crown could not put a murder weapon in Mohan Ramkissoon's hand, or place him at the scene out in the country where her body was discarded. The case rested on science putting the murder in the house, thus pointing the finger at her husband as the likely killer. In this, Bernie Webber was key. The Peel Police detective and blood spatter specialist took the stand.

Webber had appeared in court many times as a forensic expert and, as with everything in his work, he meticulously studied how to best testify from every angle. He explored the topic on the internet. What do juries find convincing when watching and listening to expert witnesses, when it comes to manner and appearance? In the U.S. they poll juries on such things; experts are considered credible who speak in plain language. Dress smartly but conservatively. Do not behave like a jerk to the defense lawyer, no matter how rough a ride you get. Webber always spoke metric, carried his metric converter calculator whenever he appeared in court. He figured you sound more scientific when you talk metric —even if some judges and jurors might not even understand it. Webber even reflected on his look, and that included whether his shaved head was an advantage or not. He had shaved it bald a couple of years before the case, and it suited him. For a police officer, it was a good look. Intense. But as an expert witness before a jury talking forensic science? He didn't want jurors to see him as a tough-guy cop—one who might even have it out for the accused. He wanted to look like an objective, credible forensics expert. Court is theater, he reflected, obviously you need to know your stuff, but you also have to come off the right way, you need all the help you can get on the stand, have to stack the deck.

After taking Webber through his lengthy resumé for the jury, Kevin McKenna asked him about his bloodstain investigation, to recount how he detected blood on the TV, bedroom mattress, and on the inside of the trunk of the car. Strong evidence for the Crown, but then McKenna knew Tom Carey was going to pounce on what Webber did not find. And so he brought up the issue himself.

"Did you find any blood on the headboard in the master bedroom?" McKenna asked.

"I did not observe any sort of reaction with luminol, " Webber replied.

"If you had someone on this mattress, who was struck over the head with a hard object, would you expect to find—where would you expect to find blood depart from the head area? Would you expect to find blood on the headboard, or the walls?"

Webber replied that, if there are multiple blows, the existing pooled blood will cause medium-velocity spatter—which he did not detect. McKenna asked, what if something is used to suppress the blood projection, "let's say for instance something is pulled over the head area, like a sheet or a blanket, and then there are subsequent blows? What will happen to the blood spatter?"

"I am not going to obviously observe the spatter, because it is going to be contained within that suppression device."

McKenna thanked Webber and took his seat.

"Mr. Carey," Judge Borkovich said.

"Thank you, Your Honor," Carey said. "Good afternoon, Constable Webber—or Sergeant Webber. On your recent promotion, congratulations."

"Thank you, sir."

Carey began by focusing on whether Yvette had actually been murdered in the bedroom as the Crown alleged. First: luminol as an imperfect indicator for blood in all instances. "I understand from the literature that, especially in the United States, there has been some judicial questioning of the reliability of luminol that would indicate blood, as it does react with other products."

"That is correct," Webber said, adding that, in Ontario, analysts are directed to submit all blood findings to the Centre of Forensic Sciences to verify the luminol reaction is in fact blood.

"And am I right that a false positive is common with a number of different products, bleach perhaps is the most common, but also products that have iron and copper in them? And cobalt ions also give that reaction?"

"Yes, that is true."

"Are you familiar with the product potassium permanganate? It is found in some dyes."

"I don't know what you are referring to, but there are many things that will react with luminol."

"And in terms of reactions, some cleaning solutions, Tide, for example, will give you a reaction?"

"That's correct."

"How about peroxide? Has that been known to give false positives?"

"Occasionally."

Carey next asked why Webber had found no evidence of blood anywhere else in the house, despite the bludgeoning of Yvette's head, and the alleged subsequent movement of her bloodied body from the bedroom. All that blood, and Bernie Webber can find nothing more than that on the TV and mattress? Even though luminol can detect a droplet of blood even if it has been diluted a million times?

"Do you have any idea how many crime scenes you have attended where you found blood, been looking for blood?"

"As an analyst at scenes, I have been 160 times."

"Is it common at scenes you have investigated to locate blood traces on or between the cracks of floorboards?"

"Yes."

"And between the cracks of tiles, between the grouting in tiles?"

"That is correct."

"How many hours in total did you spent in the Benedet Drive house?"

"I was in for over five hours on the sixteenth of June, and another five to seven hours on the eighteenth."

"And in that time you prepared a very thorough and exacting examination?"

"Yes, that was my purpose."

"Am I right that you tested basically a pathway that would have led through the master bedroom out through the bedroom door downstairs to the kitchen, the garage?" Carey asked.

"Yes, I did."

"And your testing revealed no evidence whatsoever of any blood?"

"That is correct."

Had Webber not sprayed crevices in the headboard? In the laundry room? The washing machine? The sink and bathtub in the bathroom? Yes, he said, he had. No blood was detected.

"Did you examine inside the faucets in various bathrooms and laundry facilities to see if they came into contact with any bloodied objects?"

"I would spray, essentially, the area of the taps. The better area is the tub or the sink that is underneath. And that was negative."

"And again, that was negative."

Carey moved on to the evidence of Yvette's blood that Bernie Webber did find.

"You would agree with me that the significance of blood belonging to a resident of a house where a person frequently is—that is less significant than finding, for instance, than finding Yvette Budram's blood in, for instance, somebody else's house."

"Well, I don't believe that is up to me to provide that opinion," Webber said.

Justice Borkovich interjected: "I don't believe it is, either."

"Perhaps I can put it this way—it is not uncommon to find evidence of the occupant of a house having had a nosebleed or some other incident involving blood in their home, in your experience?"

Now Kevin McKenna objected.

"Your Honor, with respect, I don't think this expert has any better qualifications to give that opinion than the ladies and gentlemen of the jury, talking about people having nosebleeds in their own homes."

Borkovich supported the Crown.

"Mr. Carey," the judge said, "it sounds more like an argument rather than a question."

"Okay, thank you. And in going through the entire home you found absolutely no evidence of a bloodied object being dragged or pulled through the house to an exit?"

"I did not."

"And you examined the garage?"

"Yes."

"And is it fair to say there is absolutely no evidence of contact of a bloodied body with any of the surfaces in that area?"

"That's correct."

Carey pointed out that Yvette died from blunt force trauma to the skull.

"With your experience and training you would have expected that there would be a high amount of blood from those injuries?"

Judge Borkovich again intervened.

"I don't think he is an expert to say that."

Carey pressed on. What about crevices in the headboard? End tables in the bedroom? And no blood.

"You left no stone unturned—did you look at the phone?"

"Yes. That was included in the luminol examination. All surfaces in the master bedroom were sprayed with luminol."

"You can find positive reaction for blood that has been on a surface of an object for months or even years, is that right?"

"That is true," Webber said.

Carey touched on a hypothesis he had planned to float for the jury. Was it possible that Yvette's blood in the bedroom could have been menstrual blood? She stains the mattress, later cuts it out, embarrassed? Perhaps a piece of stained clothing brushes against the TV. Webber had anticipated the point and had studied up on it. Definitely a first in his research. He wanted to know what would be considered reasonable menstrual blood volumes. He learned that some women can lose two cups of blood overnight. A significant volume, he reflected.

"I understand at one time there may have been tests that could determine the difference between menstrual blood and blood from the veins, but those are no longer used?" Carey asked.

"It is my understanding that test is no longer done because of its possible inaccuracy."

"There have never been any tests that could determine whether blood came from a cut on the finger, a bleeding nose, or a hole in the head?"

Webber replied that there are times when other evidence at a crime scene can suggest the source of the blood—but there was no such evidence in this case.

"Is there anything about the mattress stain that allows you to exclude the possibility that this is simply a stain from the deceased woman experiencing her monthly cycle?"

"No, I cannot."

Carey asked Webber whether there were any signs of an attempted cleanup in the bedroom—of the luminol showing reactions suggesting that bleach or other cleaning chemicals had been used.

"You did not see any evidence of extensive cleaning of the mattress surface?"

"Not to the degree I was able to."

The washing machines—did he spray the washing machines looking for signs that bloody clothing had been deposited there? Webber said he had. No blood was found. Blood in the car?

"Is it fair to say," Carey said, "that the evidence of blood that you found in the trunk of the car would be equally consistent with the blood of a cut hand?"

"Yes … if it were a single cut finger that finger would have to be moved along the surface to cause that area of reaction."

Finally, Carey seemed to suggest, how was it possible that if the killer lived in that house, he would knowingly leave a bloodied TV set in the bedroom?

"Members of the jury might be asking themselves how can somebody use this house, use this bedroom night after night, looking at the television and not see there is blood on the television and not be aware that they were in the room with a bloody television. Would it surprise you that somebody could be in that room on a daily basis and be unaware of that?"

"I think that is a good question for the jury and not for me. I was told it was there and so I saw it. Could I have walked by it and not seen it if I had not known it was there? Yes, it is possible."

Kevin McKenna had one more witness to call. That would have to wait until after the weekend, on Monday. Borkovich excused the jury, then addressed the lawyers. When was Tom Carey going to reveal if he was calling his own evidence—and Mohan Ramkissoon—to the stand?

"Mr. Carey," the judge said, "when we finish with the Crown's case you can take it for a given that I will expect you to do something at that stage."

"I will do something," Carey said. "I may be bringing a motion. I may be calling evidence."

On Monday, February 9, Kevin McKenna called DNA expert Monica Sloan of the Centre of Forensic Sciences as his last witness. In the prosecution's narrative of the case, the DNA evidence was an end, of sorts, in the story, and the definitive proof. It was as though McKenna wanted to drop the DNA trump card to close the case on perhaps the central question—was that Yvette Budram's blood in her bedroom? For if that was true, who else but Mohan would have murdered Yvette in that bed? With all the circumstantial evidence in the case, here was an expert who would take the witness box and speak only in terms of mathematical certainty.

McKenna took Sloan through her findings, from the blood found on the TV, the rubber molding in Mohan's car and the bedroom mattress.

"The piece of plastic taken from the television did have blood on it, but you were able to determine that the swab taken did match the DNA profile of Yvette Budram?"

"Yes."

"The rubber molding and carpet from the trunk of the car matches the DNA profile of Yvette Budram?"

"Yes."

"The bloodstains on the mattress, the dominant profile matches the DNA profile of Yvette Budram?"

"That's correct."

"And you indicated that the accused Mohan Ramkissoon could not be excluded as a minor contributor to the bloodstains on the mattress?"

"Yes."

It was an impressive pool of physical evidence. On the other hand, as Carey was about to highlight in his cross-examination, not even Monica Sloan could prove that Mohan Ramkissoon was responsible for the blood being there. Carey stood before Sloan and raised questions about whether or not the blood had even come from violence to Yvette Budram.

"I understand that at one time it was possible to make a determination between a woman's menstrual blood and the blood from veins—venous blood, I believe is the term? Is that right?"

"There used to be a test for menstrual blood," Sloan said.

"However, one of the reasons it is no longer used forensically is that it is a very insensitive test. We can't detect very much and there are a lot of cases where the test would give us a false positive."

Sloan had no way of knowing if the blood came from a hand, the head, suggested Carey.

"No, I do not know where that blood came from in terms of its bodily source," she said.

Carey moved on to the blood in the trunk. "The difficulty with carpets in trunks of cars or other vehicles," he said, "is that they are often repositories for groceries, including raw meats. If you do your test, and the roast beef has left blood in the trunk of the car, you get a positive—"

"I would get a positive test. I certainly wouldn't get a DNA profile from it."

Carey asked if she would be able to determine if blood in the car, or anywhere else, could have even been present long before Yvette Budram died.

"The bloodstains could have been there for months or years?"

"That's possible, yes."

Carey asked about the Happy Massager T-shirt. There was white staining on the shirt. Did she know if the stains were bleach?

"I do not."

He asked Sloan about the DNA tests on the shirt. She said she found no blood on it. And she tested the neckline of the shirt for DNA from skin cells, and no DNA was detected, she added. After Carey finished his questions, Kevin McKenna stood.

"There will be no re-examination of this witness, Your Honor. I can indicate that is the case for the Crown."

McKenna was finished presenting evidence. Tom Carey now had the option of calling his own evidence and witnesses. Would he call Mohan Ramkissoon to the witness box? McKenna had his questions ready for Mohan's cross-examination just in case. Detectives Mike Thomas and Paul Lahaie figured it was a sure thing Mohan would testify. And they wanted to see it, wanted to see Mohan account for himself. How would he explain it all? How would he account for the fact that he told his stepdaughter, Lisa, that he had been in touch with Yvette—two months after her death? That would be a good one to hear, thought Thomas. On the other hand, though, Thomas had reservations about Mohan going into the witness box, too. He had seen him in action under intense questioning—seen him weep, explain away everything, seen him avoid cracking under pressure. He thought Mohan was a professional liar, who probably thought he had what it took to get up in front of the jury and convince them that there was no way he killed his wife.

Surely Mohan could sense the jury was hungry for his testimony, wanted to see him in the box to read him better, judge his sincerity, assess the alibis that Tom Carey had not been permitted to develop, given the parameters of cross-examination. What was Carey's opinion on Mohan testifying? Any good defense lawyer will explain the pros and cons to their client. In the end, after making their best argument on which way their client should go, the lawyer will leave it up to the accused to decide. It was Mohan's call to make. In a circumstantial murder case, it's often considered best for an accused to keep silent. O.J. Simpson famously did not take the stand and was acquitted. Don't let the prosecution make you twist up there. Let the evidence, and the potential holes in the evidence highlighted by the defense, do the work for you.

Do juries hold it against an accused who does not take the stand? Kevin McKenna, for one, figured that juries are sophisticated enough to know how the game is played. They know cross-examination can make most anyone look bad, and understand that just because an accused doesn't take the stand, it doesn't equate with guilt. But while testifying is risky, the potential benefits are obvious. An accused who stands and openly declares, "I didn't do it," would strike an emotional chord in most people. Police detectives place stock in heartfelt denials of guilt from a suspect, why wouldn't a juror? How can a juror muster any empathy for an accused who will not speak for himself?

Tom Carey stood before Justice Nick Borkovich and made his announcement. He was not calling evidence in the case. There would be no witnesses, and that included Mohan Ramkissoon. Lahaie was pleased. He was certain the jury wanted to hear the man defend himself, and he was denying them that. A tactical error, Lahaie thought.

Chapter 26 ~ Voice of Authority

Had Mohan wanted to testify, defend himself against the charge that he bludgeoned and dumped his wife? He told others that in fact he wanted to take the stand, proclaim his innocence, but that Carey had argued it was best that he not do so. Mohan agreed with Carey and decided against testifying. Was Mohan's story true, though? Others close to the case heard a different story, that Mohan had actually refused to testify from the start. He was frightened at the prospect of facing the Crown. As for Carey's account of what happened, he could never reveal the content of his private client conversations on the matter. In general, he allowed, taking the stand is often the toughest call for the defense to make—but it is, he said, the client's decision.

Carey's one advantage in presenting no evidence was that he would get to address the jury after the Crown. His would be the final words the jury heard, apart from the charge to the jury from Justice Borkovich. The closing arguments began on Thursday, February 12. Kevin McKenna took the jury through the narrative of the case he had been weaving over 14 days, how and when Yvette died, the timeline, the evidence. McKenna's deep baritone, the voice of authority and reason, washed over the room.

In Canadian criminal trials, there is more latitude in closing remarks allowed for a defense lawyer to perform. In keeping with the British tradition, however, the Crown is expected to retain the sober voice, present the case firmly, but fairly, see that justice is done dispassionately. McKenna's approach was to never sell the jury short. Don't play games with them. Be honest. Articulate your case for what it is, highlight the strengths, but don't avoid the weaknesses. The defense, if they're any good, will focus on those weaknesses. If McKenna avoided them, the jury would wonder why. And so he had to mention Harjeet in his own closing remarks.

"All the evidence says one thing: Happy was living in Montreal. There is not a hint of evidence that he was anywhere near Mississauga at the relevant times."

There was one thought he wanted to leave the jury with regarding Happy.

"He lives in California. He came here to testify. Does that sound like somebody who is culpable or responsible for any of this when he voluntarily comes back from California to testify? Of course not."

That the defense was presenting Happy as an alternative suspect, he said, was "classic smoke and mirrors with absolutely no evidence at all." Mohan had opportunity: Yvette was spending time in the house after her release from jail. Mohan had motive: Yvette flaunted her affair in front of him, treated him horribly, humiliated him, sometimes in front of relatives. Mohan displayed a guilty mind: as Paul Lahaie had learned late in the investigation, Mohan advertised in the newspaper to sell Yvette's car on September 26, six days after Yvette failed to show in court.

"Would you not think at that point he might be a little bit more concerned about her, her whereabouts, the personal items, the credit cards, not contacting her children? Do you think that might not be a little bit more important to him at that point in this short time period than 'I want to unload her car'?"

More signs of a guilty mind: Mohan told a friend that he felt he was being followed, and this was in the fall of 2000, before the police in fact had any knowledge of him. He ran from the police when they tried to get him to come in to answer questions. Pulled his daughter out of school, bought one-way plane tickets to Guyana.

"Why is he running?" McKenna asked. "Remember, no one has told him that Yvette had been found and identified."

As McKenna continued, Lahaie and Thomas listened and tried to block all they knew from their minds. A jury never knows the entire story, is never told everything the police uncovered. The system doesn't work that way. Can't dwell on it. No way they could get it included as evidence before the jury. But still, if only the jury knew another piece of the puzzle, if only they knew about the notation in Paul Lahaie's case book about the New York connection.

"Blood."

Kevin McKenna paused, wrapping up his remarks, closing with forensics. "I started off suggesting in any circumstantial case the evidence has to be looked at as a whole, in the big picture. Look at the little pieces of evidence in conjunction with the other evidence. Her blood in the bedroom. Her blood in the trunk of the car. Her blood on the television. A mattress with a great big huge hole cut out of it."

McKenna knew Tom Carey would probably float the notion again that the blood on the bed could be menstrual blood. "I would think that one would go through a lot of mattresses if every time there is a little staining from monthly bleeding, people are cutting a huge hole out of the mattress. That is ridiculous ... I don't think anyone is suggesting blood on the television is menstrual blood.... Don't just look at one piece of evidence. Just the mattress—well, you know, menstrual blood. Just the TV—well, I don't know, it could be a blanket when they are cleaning up a nosebleed. Trunk of the car—well, maybe she cut her finger. Is there any doubt she was killed in that bedroom? Absolutely not. Look at the big picture. Look at all the evidence. Apply your common sense."

McKenna expected Carey would allude to the forensic report, which said there was no sign of a cleanup in the car or the bedroom, no sign that someone had scrubbed away evidence. "Well, I don't know, it depends on how you define cleaning. Why use Tide when you can cut the stain right out of the mattress? Is that not evidence of cleaning?"

McKenna concluded. Think logically, he said, use common sense; just imagine a person, any person, make up a fictional character. "Who else is going to go into that bedroom, kill Yvette Budram on the bed, remove her body from the bed, take the sheets and blankets away, cut a hole out of the mattress, turn the mattress over, remake the bed—because you certainly couldn't let the accused know something untoward happened in the bedroom—remake the bed, find the keys to the car, put the body in the trunk, drive out to the African Lion Safari, dump the body and then we will return the car and we will return the keys? Who? Who conceivably could have done that other than the accused? There is nobody. It makes absolutely no sense that there is a person, that we have either heard from or fictional, that could conceivably have done that. Ladies and gentlemen, thank you for your attention."

* * *

Now Tom Carey had his opportunity. It had been the Crown's show so far, he had been constrained by cross-examining witnesses the Crown presented. And now, having elected to present no evidence, this was his moment, his chance to make the case for Mohan Ramkissoon, sow doubt in the minds of the jurors. Closing remarks are the defense lawyer's chance to freewheel, not constrained by rules that govern examination and cross-examination of witnesses, nor the staid traditions that must be observed by the Crown in terms of style. It was the perfect forum for an experienced counsel like Carey, a natural performer.

"Good morning, members of the jury," he began. "They used to say on Monty Python, 'And now for something completely different'—the defense side of the case."

Carey always endeavored to treat the jury with respect, respect their intelligence, and also lighten the mood whenever possible. Talk to them. Use humor when appropriate. The Crown, he said, has told its side of the story, but "the rules that govern jury cases allow me, on behalf of Mohan Ramkissoon, to have the last word."

He stressed that his client was innocent until proven guilty, beyond a reasonable doubt. The murder of Yvette Budram is a complicated case, he observed, there had been much technical evidence. "The question here is not 'whodunit?' It is, frankly, not your job to play detective and figure out what happened. You are here to decide if the Crown has proven beyond a reasonable doubt that Mohan Ramkissoon caused his wife Yvette's death."

And deciding whether or not to put a man in prison, he added, is a very serious matter.

"You will be called upon to make probably one of the most important decisions you will ever have to make in your entire life." The Crown's case was a circumstantial one, the narrative not as clean as it may have seemed in the trial—reflected in the actual criminal indictment against Mohan. "The indictment in this case is interesting, I suggest, because it is so vague. The Crown alleges that Yvette Budram was killed between September 15, 2000, and April 17, 2001. How she was killed, how the accused caused her death, is not specified."

Carey's mission was to unravel the story Kevin McKenna had told, point to weaknesses in the narrative, the pieces that do not fit so neatly. The Crown argued common sense. Well, Carey suggested, common sense surely also suggests that if Mohan had wanted to kill Yvette and cover his tracks, he would not have done so in the manner the Crown alleges. Does it make sense for Yvette's husband to kill her, then leave her by the side of that country road? Carey emphasized where the victim had lain. Was it, in fact, as the Crown said, in the brush—the suggestion being that it had been somewhat hidden from sight? Or rather, Carey said, was it more accurate to say the body was in relatively plain view, "at the side of the road," where a jogger could in fact see it? Why not dump the body, he said, in one of the many swamps in the area? Why not leave it in the African Lion Safari itself with "these flesh-eating animals, lions, tigers and bears?" Why not bury the body?

"This is not, I suggest, the way somebody would leave a body, if that somebody is her husband—the first person that anyone is going to suspect, a husband who had been in a fight with her not two weeks before." And why would he leave her wearing her jewelry, her watch, her nightgown? "All of this serves to identify her. Did whoever so callously left her body there want it to be found? Were they in a position not to be suspected?" Dr. David King had said the body was thrown into the brush, as evidenced by the position of the victim's limbs—and Mohan is a small man. "That is a two-person procedure. At least two people didn't care if she was found the next day or not.... How did this slight man get the body out there?"

The fingerprints had been the key in identifying Yvette's body, prints that existed on the RCMP database because of the charge against Yvette. "Not a lot of people would know that this woman had fingerprints on record," said Carey. "But I tell you one person who would know would be her husband.... Her fingerprints had only been put on record because her husband called the police two weeks before she went missing."

Carey criticized what he said was the Crown's "attack" on the victim, on Yvette, in suggesting she treated Mohan horribly. "I've been around for a while. I don't think I've ever been on a case where the victim was attacked by the Crown attorney.... The submission by my friend is in order to make you accept that 'Well, of course he killed her, who wouldn't?' Don't buy into the suggestion that this was a horrible woman and of course he was driven to the end of his rope. That's what the Crown wants you to think."

He countered the notion that Mohan's failure to file a missing person report was damning. On the contrary: Peel officer James Laing had said on the stand that he suggested to Mohan that he didn't need to file one. Carey turned to Harjeet Singh, the alternative suspect. Who was most likely to be with Yvette when she was wearing sexy lingerie when she was murdered?

"She certainly wasn't wearing it for her husband," Carey suggested.

Smoke and mirrors? The Crown talks about smoke and mirrors? It was the Crown that brought Happy up here to testify, said Carey. They considered him important enough to do that. Can you believe anything Happy says, though? As soon as he gets into the witness box, he lies. "You know if this was Pinocchio, you know what would be happening.... You saw his body language. He wanted you to believe he was a man of religion. He obviously changed his appearance from when he was in that picture you will have in the jury room. I suggest he showed absolutely no respect for women, especially Yvette Budram, that he was a hypocrite, he is an admitted liar who didn't really show any respect for an oath."

Happy flees the country around the time Yvette is killed, hops the border, doesn't even pack all his clothes from Montreal, but takes the tapes of him and Yvette being intimate. Why? Happy, Carey said, was a possessive man who demanded fidelity from Yvette. All of his friends are afraid of him. The Sainis in Montreal won't talk to the police about him because they fear him. They only talk when Paul Lahaie and Mike Thomas visit them on a followup trip.

"So the police come back to Montreal, what, two years later to get the real story. Happy ... is kind of a nuisance here for the Crown. We can't have Happy doing violent things when we know it is the husband." As for Mayela Lobianco, a key witness for the Crown's timeline on when Yvette was last seen—was it credible that she saw Yvette alive on September 17? She didn't even give evidence at the preliminary hearing, she just gives a statement to Paul Lahaie off the cuff when her husband, Gus, is testifying.

"Nice lady, Mayela, but English is not her first language. She is bad on dates—that was her evidence: 'I am not good on dates.'"

Forensics: Yvette's blood on the mattress, the TV, the trunk of the car. True, but perhaps it wasn't a murder that put blood and DNA in that bedroom. Perhaps the affair between Happy and Yvette did. "This isn't smoke and mirrors that the mattress could be something other than a murder scene. One of the owners of this mattress is having an affair with a guy and she doesn't want to be found out. That mattress has on there stains that have been left from the cutout. Could they be evidence of vaginal secretions? Yes. Could they be evidence of a sexual encounter at the wrong time of the month or something like that? Absolutely. There is no evidence that excludes that possibility."

Tom Carey concluded. Surely the main point was, whoever dumped Yvette's body obviously wasn't concerned that it would be found. No effort was made to bury the body, disguise the body, get rid of her jewelry or clothing. The Crown suggested she had been wrapped in a tarp to prevent blood from dripping in the bedroom or the car. So why was no tarp or bag found at the scene where the body was found?

"Why would you bother taking the time to take her out of the bag? So you think you would leave the bag. You would leave the covering that prevented the blood from being all over the house. Well, guess what, there is nothing there. She's got the nightgown, it looks like it might have blown up over her head and that's it."

It was an argument that neither the Crown, nor the detectives, could counter. Where was the tarp? Or, if there had been no covering on the body, how was it possible there were no further signs of blood in the house, or signs that blood had been cleaned up? The two pieces did not fit.

Chapter 27 ~ Admitted Perjurers

In his final words, Carey invoked, without saying their names, the falsely accused—those, like Guy Paul Morin and David Milgaard, who had been convicted of murder in the past in Canada and later found innocent and released. You, jurors, will live with this decision the rest of your lives, Carey was suggesting.

"Your final verdict ... has to be one that sits with your conscience. You have to be *sure*. The stain of wrongful conviction has marred the Canadian judicial system in recent years. That stain, the inquiries around those cases, are a warning about the frailties of certain kinds of evidence…. If you vote for conviction in this matter, you don't want to be tossing and turning in your bed a couple of nights from now, wondering whether you made the right decision. If you have a nagging doubt now on the evidence, you must render a verdict of acquittal. The death of Yvette Budram, no matter what other people have said about her, was a terrible tragedy. To convict Mohan Ramkissoon for her murder, I suggest, would only compound that tragedy."

Tom Carey took his seat.

Paul Lahaie and Mike Thomas still felt good about their case. Carey had performed well, but they also thought Kevin McKenna did a great job. Happy had testified, all that forensic evidence. They felt good, anyway, until the judge addressed the jury.

Judge Borkovich's charge to the jury would be the last words jurors would hear before deciding Mohan Ramkissoon's fate. It is the moment when a judge outlines legal points for the jury to consider before they deliberate, and also offers any comments and summarization of the case in general.

"The time has come when your most difficult duties begin in this case," Borkovich began. He explained points of law. "The sole issue for you to decide will be whether or not the accused caused the death of his wife." The accused enters these proceedings presumed to be innocent. That presumption of innocence remains throughout the case until such time as the Crown has used evidence to prove the accused is guilty beyond a reasonable doubt.

"A reasonable doubt is not an imaginary or frivolous doubt. It is based on reason and common sense. If you believe the accused is probably guilty or likely guilty, that is not sufficient. On the other hand, it is virtually impossible to prove anything to be an absolute certainty. If, based on the evidence, you are sure that the accused committed the offense, you should convict."

Next, he reminded the jury that two critical Crown witnesses— Harjeet Singh and Ranjit Saini—had at one point in the investigation lied under oath. "The fact they have lied under oath is a very serious matter. It seriously affects the credibility of their testimony. There is a great danger in accepting such evidence on its own."

The judge reviewed the Crown's case in brief, including the Crown's position that Harjeet (Happy) Singh was in Montreal when Yvette was murdered in Mississauga. "There is evidence establishing that Happy Singh was in Plattsburgh, N.Y., as of 11:58 p.m. on September 17, 2000. The evidence of him being in Montreal consists of his testimony, and that of Ranjit Saini, two admitted perjurers.... There is no other evidence that Happy was in Montreal."

He moved on to summarize the defense position. "It is the position of the defense that the evidence called by the Crown establishes that the lover Happy Singh had motive and opportunity. As triers of fact you cannot simply accept the evidence of Happy, Ranjit Saini, or Ranjit Saini's wife, Prem, that Happy was in Montreal and, therefore, could not have committed the crime. Happy and Ranjit are admitted perjurers."

Although Happy was in Plattsburgh at midnight on September 17, the judge continued, he had "plenty of opportunity" to be in Mississauga on September 15, 16, and 17, and then get to Montreal and Plattsburgh by midnight on the seventeenth. "As well, Happy had motive.... Why did Happy suddenly disappear after September 17, 2000?" The defense suggests that Happy's sudden disappearance after September 2000 is the action of a guilty man, Borkovich said.

At his seat, Mohan Ramkissoon was growing more confident as the judge's charge went on. As for Paul Lahaie, as he listened to the address, he was not pleased, but on the other hand he had prepared himself for it. Borkovich had given a defense-oriented address in the Mingo case, too. Lahaie just hoped the jury would see through it. All those TV shows, the CSI shows, they can hurt prosecutions because the bar for evidence is too high—but on the other hand, the shows help the public become more astute, they know how the court game is played, how to weigh evidence. Or so he hoped.

Was Borkovich allocating more time to refute the Crown's case in his address than he had spent reviewing it? The fact is, in criminal jury trials, most judges in the Canadian system consider it their obligation to ensure a strong defense for the accused is presented. It is thought that the Crown deserves no such assistance, since it represents the State and has more resources behind the case it is bringing forward.

Borkovich continued: If the accused drove the body to the African Lion Safari, he asked the jury, where were his kids all that time? Why were tenants in the house not aware of something, if the accused had killed and cleaned up a bloody mess after the fact? "It's reasonable to assume there were tenants in the house at the time of the murder. And the kids slept on a bunk bed adjacent to the bed in the master bedroom. Is it reasonable to infer that they were with their father? If so, they would have been in the residence at the time the Crown alleges the accused killed his wife."

Borkovich went through a play-by-play of what the accused would have had to do "to kill his wife without being seen or heard by anyone in the house": remove the body to the car; dispose of the evidence of bloody sheets; cut out the hole in the mattress; clean the place in a manner so as to erase any sign of a cleanup; transport the body and "single-handedly toss the body into the field ... and return home without being seen or heard." Not only that, he continued, but "under the circumstances is it reasonable to infer that there was no evidence of a cleanup because there was no cleanup? Dr. King testified there would be severe bleeding. Only traces of blood were found in the bedroom and the trunk of the car.... Is it reasonable to infer the accused was capable of throwing the body single-handedly to the spot in which it was found? Is it reasonable to infer she would wear the nightgown for the accused man when the evidence suggests that she did that for Happy?"

And then, finishing his comments on the evidence, the judge said: "Neither counsel mentioned to you the T-shirt found near the body. What is the significance, if any, of the logo Happy? That is for you to decide."

That was the concluding comment Borkovich made on the evidence—about the Happy Massager T-shirt. *Found near the body? A logo that says Happy?* The shirt was not found near the body. It was in the ditch with plenty of other litter. And the full logo said, "It's me: the Happy Massager." Wasn't the T-shirt, at best, merely a distraction in the case? Even Tom Carey had not mentioned the T-shirt in his closing remarks. And the judge was invoking it, in the last words on the evidence he leaves with the jury?

Lahaie couldn't believe it. He burned with anger. At his seat in the prisoner's dock, Mohan Ramkissoon was now more than optimistic. His lawyer had done an excellent job, he thought, and now, also, the judge. Reasonable doubts? No juror could hear that charge to the jury and not find him completely innocent, he thought.

* * *

The jury was dismissed just before noon on Thursday, February 12, 2004, and was out the rest of the morning and all afternoon. That the jury was not yet unanimous was perhaps a bad sign, thought Tom Carey. The longer they were out, the more he thought it was indicative that the jury would ultimately arrive at a guilty verdict.

Jury deliberation is as tense as it gets for all those connected with a trial. For the Crown and the defense, the case is out of your hands and there's nothing more you can do, you are a spectator to the fate of a case that has dominated your waking and sleeping hours for months. For Kevin McKenna, the loss of control was the toughest thing to handle. The Crown essentially frames the case. He had called all the witnesses, woven the narrative for the jury to consider. Now he was left to simply wonder how the jury would interpret his presentation. And he knew that when the jury did come back, it would render a verdict without giving one reason for it.

In the United States, jurors are interviewed by the media after high-profile cases. But not in Canada. Typically jurors declare a verdict and are never heard from again. (Under Canadian law, it's not illegal for jurors to talk to the media, or anyone else, about what they felt during jury deliberations, or their opinion about the case in general. But it is illegal for them to say anything specific about the nature or substance of the jury's deliberations.)

After nearly 10 hours of deliberation, the jury returned to the courtroom at 9:30 Thursday night. Still no verdict.

"I think it is time to send everybody home and the jury to the hotel," Judge Borkovich said. Court resumed the next morning. It was Friday the 13th, a frigid, windy day. At 10 a.m. the jury resumed meeting. Eleven o'clock. Noon. One. Two. Three. The detectives were anxious. Mike Thomas was concerned jurors might feel that, while Mohan may have killed Yvette, the potential penalty was too harsh, since there was evidence that she treated him so poorly. Maybe they'll feel sorry for him, lack the stomach for giving Mohan second-degree murder.

At just after 3 p.m., 15 hours into deliberations, the phone calls finally came to McKenna and Carey. A verdict was in. Everyone returned to court. McKenna took his seat at the front of the court, Paul Lahaie beside him, Mike Thomas in the gallery. Tom Carey sat at his table at the front, and Mohan Ramkissoon was in the dock, wearing a shirt and tie as he had throughout the trial. It was 3:20 p.m.

"Twelve members of the jury are present, Your Honor," said the court registrar.

"Thank you," said Borkovich.

"Members of the jury," the registrar continued, "have you agreed upon a verdict?"

The jurors in unison: "Yes, we have."

Thomas and Lahaie wore their best stoic faces but churned on the inside, the investigation, the case, playing back in their minds. What could they have done differently? It had been nearly three years of work for them.

"Would the foreperson please stand? Do you find the accused at the bar guilty, or not guilty of count Number 1 as charged?"

"Guilty."

Guilty? *Guilty?!* Mohan Ramkissoon was shocked. Guilty— how could the jury be that biased against him? How could anyone listen to the directions from the judge and still think he's guilty? Was it racism? How was it possible? The courtroom remained very quiet. Paul Lahaie felt short of breath. His eyes welled with emotion. The jury—he was so grateful to the jury. Keep it professional, he thought. Don't show anything. Mike Thomas exhaled. He looked across the room and exchanged a wordless stare with Lahaie.

Tom Carey stood.

"Could we have the jury polled, please?" he said. It is the last shot for a defense lawyer, a long one at that. Perhaps there will be one juror who will balk, break the critical unanimous vote when asked to stand and speak for themselves. The registrar called out each juror. Each of the 12 repeated, "Guilty." In the fourth homicide notebook Lahaie had filled on the case, he simply wrote:

15:20 Jury reaches a verdict.

The verdict final, Mike Thomas scanned the faces of the jurors. Jury duty on a homicide case is emotionally draining. Thomas had been at trials where, after a not-guilty verdict was read, one juror would look over at him and shrug apologetically. This time, Thomas wanted to make eye contact with anyone who needed it, let them know without speaking a word that they had made the right decision: *You don't know everything I do. There is more to the case than you heard. You did the right thing.* For one thing, the jury had not heard about a card the detectives had not been able to play. Perhaps it was not too late to still play it.

Uniformed court constables moved to escort Mohan Ramkissoon out of the dock. Crying, he dug into his pocket and handed the car keys of his Intrepid to Carey. This time Mohan walked not through the public court entrance, but the door off to the side, leading into the holding area for prisoners. He was not going home, he was not taking a vacation. He was heading to Barton Street jail.

Justice Borkovich still needed to decide his sentence at a later date. Mohan would automatically receive a life sentence for second-degree murder, but Borkovich had the flexibility to set the number for when he'd be eligible for parole at anywhere from 10 to 14 years. Mohan would need to return to court to learn his fate.

In the courthouse holding area, Mohan was searched before being taken to jail. He had entered the courthouse that day a free man. Had he planned to make a quick trip upon leaving the building? The court officers found $5,000 in American cash in his wallet.

Chapter 28 ~ Memory Keeper

Forensic anthropologist Shelley Saunders got calls from Hamilton Police with updates when Mohan Ramkissoon had been arrested, and again when he was convicted, although she was not called to testify. Saunders had faced a life or death challenge in recent years— cancer. She fought both colon and kidney cancer, and won. She continued to teach at McMaster University, set up a $20,000 scholarship program for anthropology graduate students, was the first anthropologist to be accepted into the Royal Society of Canada, an elite body of scientists, and established the McMaster Ancient DNA Centre for DNA research.

But then on May 14, 2008, Saunders could not survive a third bout with disease. She died in her home of pancreatic cancer, leaving a husband, Victor, and grown children, Barb and Robert. Near the end of her life, her daughter, Barb, had the chance to say her piece to her mother: "I told her that I wanted to be exactly like her in every way."

Saunders had been on kidney dialysis six days a week at home for five years, even as she worked a full schedule at school and rarely talked about what she was going through. And that included working cases for police. One night, she answered the door at her home. There was a police officer on the front step. He was holding a bag. Always happens come the fall and spring, people walking their dogs come across bones in forested areas. They bring them to the police. The police show them to Shelley. She watched the officer pull a skeletonized foot out of the bag. Five digits. Saunders tried to keep her black Labrador retriever, a hunting dog, at bay. He was leaping all over the place, smelling the bone. Saunders looked at the evidence. She knew right away. The calcaneum, a bone in the heel, was very narrow. Classic sign. Could only be one thing.

"Bear paw," she said.

* * *

After the Yvette Budram case, the Bug Lady, Dael Morris, played a role in the investigation into one of Ontario's most haunting cold cases, that of university student Lynda Shaw, who was abducted along Highway 401, the busiest road in Canada, murdered, and her remains burned. The case went nowhere for years. But blowfly eggs had been collected from Shaw's remains in 1990. The eggs were clustered on charred clothing. In 1991, the forensic entomologist had received a piece of fabric with the eggs attached, and she photographed the eggs before returning the evidence to the Centre of Forensic Sciences. But nobody pursued the entomology angle, and she was not asked for any further opinion.

But then, in 2004, a London OPP detective chasing the Shaw case called Morris after coming across her name in an old casebook. Of course Morris had kept her original photographs of the eggs. Might her study of the photos confirm the detective's working theory about the murder—that her body had been moved? Morris calculated that it had not been warm enough outdoors for flies to lay eggs between the time Shaw went missing and eyewitness accounts of the fire in the spring of 1990.

"One could only conclude," said Morris, "that Lynda's remains had lain in an environment warm enough to facilitate reproduction of blowflies before she was removed and set on fire."

The body had been moved.

The Bug Lady continued driving her black '87 Omni, kept busy with her work and other interests. Enjoys reading crime fiction in her leisure time, because of her interest in forensics, primarily. And, she reflects, because after a few bumps and bruises, in the novels, the hero usually comes through in the end.

* * *

Hamilton Ident man Al Yates studied the identifiable points on the fingerprint: seven, eight, nine. Ten. Ten points! He had the killer identified. Didn't he? Negative, came the response. No match. How could that be?

"What do you mean it's not him?" Yates said, playfully agitated. "What are you talking about?"

The forensic detective who unlocked the final lock in identifying Yvette Budram's remains was playing the new *CSI* home
computer game with a group of friends. Never ceased to be fascinated by forensics, even enjoyed catching the *CSI* TV shows on
occasion, overblown fiction though they usually are, he reflected.
The computer game was kind of fun, actually. But not realistic.
A forensics officer can make a positive fingerprint ID with six
or seven identifiable points, if you add other factors—unique
characteristics, pattern matches. And now, the computer game is
telling Yates there's no match, even with 10 points?

"That does not happen!" Yates lamented. "Nature does not
allow it to happen."

On the day after the Mohan Ramkissoon verdict, Yates read
the headline in the *Hamilton Spectator*. It was a good verdict, he
thought. Justice done. Yates felt—what was it exactly? A sense of
contentment, for Yvette. She did not end up as a Jane Doe in that
country field. And her killer did not end up free.

Yates retired from the police, officially on December 31, 2003,
after 30 years wearing a badge, the last 15 of those in forensics.
Why did he leave at that point? That was another story. After he
retired, Al came to miss the people he worked with, and the job.
There had been times in forensics when he hadn't wanted to take
holidays, he was so into his craft. Back when he had identified
Yvette for the investigation, Yates was presented with the Hamilton
Police Service Employee of the Month award for his work on the
case. Put the glass plaque on display in his den. Fellow forensic
investigator Gary Zwicker got teased relentlessly by the boys for
that one—it's the way cops are. Zwick had been out at the scene
on the 8th Concession West collecting evidence, attended the
autopsy, rehydrated the finger, worked for weeks getting a quality
print. Did great work. Then ol' Al comes in and gets the glory, the
lucky guy. But Zwicker was the first to acknowledge that Yates
had brought an experienced eye to the case, and it paid off. Luck
had nothing to do with it.

On the other hand, luck had everything to do with another
good day for Al Yates. It was the event that prompted his early
retirement. Yates was one of 13 Hamilton police officers who
went in on buying lottery tickets one day. They shared first prize:
$25 million.

* * *

Forensics framed the circumstantial murder case against Mohan Ramkissoon, but Harjeet (Happy) Singh had been the prosecution's essential card. If Happy hadn't shown in person to testify—warts and all—the case would have been shaky. The detectives knew it. If he doesn't testify, he remains a ghost out there for the defense to hang the murder on.

It had been soon after his testimony that Hamilton police arranged for him to fly out of Hamilton International Airport. The ticket purchased for Harjeet was for an open-ended date, because they didn't know when his cross-examination would finish. And at Harjeet's request, the ticket was purchased for Vancouver. Why Vancouver? Did he want to try to settle there? More likely he had contacts in the city who could get him across the border, so he could rejoin his wife, Doris, continue to try getting status in the United States. Or maybe he was destined to return to India, where he had well-off relatives. No one knew for sure. As time passed not even the detectives knew where he ended up.

On the day he finished testifying, Happy walked out of the courtroom for the last time. Paul Lahaie met him in the hallway to say goodbye. Much of what Harjeet had done—the infidelity, certainly, but also the immigration fraud—was wrong. But at the same time, reflected Lahaie, what about where the guy had come from, India? The Sainis had talked to them about that, the fear they had of police corruption over there. A difficult world to live in, even for people of means in the local context. If he, Lahaie, had a chance at a better life in Canada, would he have cut corners? Would he always respect domestic immigration laws?

Harjeet stuck out his hand, Lahaie took it, looked him in the eye, they shook.

"Good luck," Lahaie said.

He watched Happy leave, escorted by another officer. Lahaie had the feeling he'd never see the star witness again. Harjeet had come to Canada to testify when he could have avoided it. Took his shots on the stand. He admired him for it. The detective grinned. He'd never lend the guy money any time soon, though.

* * *

Paul Lahaie knew that so long as you're in Major Crime, you are a keeper of the memories, and you are never off the clock. The Damian cold case—the murder on east Hamilton Mountain of Damian Dymitraszczuk? Lahaie continued to work it, looking for new avenues to chase, even during the Yvette Budram case. What about other evidence in the Damian case locker that had not yet been tested for DNA? Worth a shot. No, there were no big leads to chase. But, he reflected, there were a lot of nervous guys out there.

And there was still the case of four-year-old Cindy Williams, the little blond girl abducted in 1974. Every time he glanced through the historic case file he'd see it. She stayed with him, not as an active open file, but almost like a symbol, of justice left undone, of limitations, and of Lahaie's belief that despite the little girl's end, she was in a better place.

He was an emotional guy, stuff like that got to him. And so too did the piece of art he received one day, one of those moments when the job inspires you. The framed crayon drawing hangs in the Major Crime Unit. On the back is Lahaie's name. In the Stoney Creek rapist case, Lahaie interviewed an eight-year-old girl who had been assaulted, degraded by the sociopath. It was delicate work, but the little girl talked to Lahaie, described her horror in detail. Some time after their conversations ended, she handed him a sheet of paper. She had done a crayon drawing.

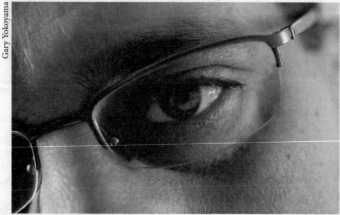

Gary Yokoyama

Paul Lahaie.

Sometimes you get hung up on promotion, ego, the job—everyone does. But times like that are reminders that you should just stay focused, anchored. She was just this little kid, and here she is, helping the detective gain perspective. Like a little guardian angel, he thought. The drawing, this card she made, was full of color. And the caption she had written said: "Police are kind. And cool. And good looking." Well, the first two out of three ain't bad, anyway, Lahaie mused. He got the drawing framed, hung it in a hallway in Central Station, saw it most every day. When he retires, he's taking it with him.

Retirement might come sooner rather than later. The shelf life of a homicide detective is not long. You don't realize how much Major Crime dominates your life until you move to a different branch of the police service. Lahaie had to put a wall between his working life and his personal life. There are guys out there who might like to see him dead. That's part of the job. He could handle himself. But what about those close to him? He professed not to have nightmares about the work. He could deal with it. Couldn't he? You can never tell what lies under the surface.

Guys like Lahaie and Mike Thomas, they seemed to be able to separate themselves from the work, keep it together. A rare few of their colleagues over the years did not, took extreme measures to find an escape, sought a final, sudden refuge in their own firearm, killed themselves. You can't get too close to the cases, you let yourself get too deep into the emotion pool, you might never get out of it, Lahaie reflected. That can be tormenting or even fatal. But, as with most of his Major Crime colleagues, exposure to crime scenes and autopsies and pornographic glimpses of the worst of the human condition had not led to a hardening of the heart.

In quiet moments, Lahaie could be prodded to tell the story of his father's battle with Alzheimer's. The son had been able to say goodbye to the father before he drifted off into a permanent sleep a few years back. "I'm pretty tired. I've got to go now, got to sleep," the father had told the son from his hospital bed at the end.

"I know, Dad," Paul replied. "That's good. You should do that."

"I'll see you tomorrow."

And the son reached over with his hand, brushed the father's hair back off his forehead. Knew he wouldn't wake up. Years later Lahaie would tell that story, remove his glasses, two tears leaving a trace down each cheek as he spoke. He did not pause to wipe them away, the drops or the trail they left. He just let them dry in their own time.

* * *

It was a repressively hot summer day in Hamilton, one of those days in the lower city when everyone is warned to stay inside, when the heat and humidity build and just sit there, as though trapped under an inverted cast iron bowl. Paul Lahaie had picked up the jogging bug years ago working for the RCMP out in Vancouver, where his partner on the service was into marathons. In the locker room in Central Station, he changed out of his dark suit, tie, and crisp white shirt, and into a pair of old shorts and plain white T-shirt. Down the stairs, out the back door. He started on his regular route, up York Boulevard, all the way up to Dundurn and back, went through a neighborhood. A good diversion, running. Or maybe not. His eyes stared straight ahead, but as he ran they registered a man and woman arguing over in front of that house. Domestic? There's another guy loading stuff into a car across the street. He belong there? That's why you have to hang it up before too long.

Lahaie never stopped thinking about the past, and not only the cases. He thought about the road traveled, about the Saltfleet neighborhood where he grew up. During his workday, Lahaie would sometimes drop by the old family home to visit Ma, who had long outlived his father. Ma was still sharp as a tack. Would take a look in his tiny old bedroom. That was where he used to peek around the corner after bedtime, sneak a golden few extra minutes of *Hockey Night in Canada* on the TV. And on summer nights, he talked through the screen of his window across the yard to his cousin who lived next door, maybe plan the road hockey game for the next day out front, where the shallow grass drainage ditch was always in bounds. It was a street where everyone knew one another, immigrant families pitched in, pooling their expertise to help build garages. Different times, different people.

It wasn't just hot, it was crazy hot, that day Lahaie set out on his daily run from Central Station. Not a good idea to be out doing anything, much less running. But he had struck out with typical enthusiasm on the baking sidewalk, without taking even a moment to stretch. He grinned.

"Got miles to stretch."

He was no sprinter, and his gait was hardly Olympian, he liked to joke. But the fact was, he moved at a deceptively good clip. More relentless than quick. When Lahaie finally returned to the station, strode through a wall of cool air, his face glistened, the white T-shirt gray with sweat.

A uniformed cop chided him.

"Bit hot for a run today?"

"Nah. Perfect."

* * *

John Sopinka Courthouse
Hamilton, Ontario
March 1, 2004

Mohan Ramkissoon was transported from Barton Street jail back to court for his sentencing hearing. Assistant Crown attorney Kevin McKenna stood before Justice Nick Borkovich and argued that Mohan serve the maximum time in jail before being up for parole—14 years. Tom Carey argued for the minimum, 10 years. He called a man named Milton Kong, and then his wife, Sheila Kong, to the witness box to speak positively of Mohan's character. Milton Kong said that Mohan was a quiet man and loving parent. He said although Mohan worked full-time outside the home, he also did most of the cooking, cleaning, and child rearing in the family. Mohan and Yvette had a "loving relationship, but there were times when they would have a spat and Mohan would try to quiet her down. Yvette was a more aggressive type of person."

McKenna did not cross-examine either witness.

"Mohan Ramkissoon," Borkovich said, "is there anything you wish to say before I pass sentence on you?"

Mohan stood. Now was his chance to speak, having not taken the opportunity during the trial. "Yes, Your Honor," he began. "I loved my wife more than anything else in the world. For all the years we were married, I had never ever lifted my hand to my wife. Today I am being accused of killing her. That is the most sick thing I have ever heard. We all know, those who heard the evidence from the beginning know, exactly who is the real perpetrator in this case. I am innocent of my charges. In 2002 I was offered way less than what the Crown is asking for, but I told my lawyer: 'I am not going to negotiate my innocence. Because I am innocent of my charges.' And I will maintain that."

He concluded, his voice cracking: "Today I will be separated ... most important, from my two little angels. Your Honor, I am innocent. I was released for over a year and I never did anything wrong, because I am innocent and I maintain that."

"Thank you, Mr. Ramkissoon," the judge said.

And then Borkovich made his decision. He announced that he was sentencing Mohan Ramkissoon to life with a chance for parole after the maximum 14 years. The penalty for taking Yvette's life and leaving her body in a field was hardly enough as far as Lahaie and Thomas were concerned, but at least it was the maximum allowed. Case closed—almost, anyway.

Soon after his conviction, Mohan Ramkissoon filed an appeal. Might an appeal court find a crack in the circumstantial case? And even if the appeal failed, Mohan still could see light at the end of the tunnel: a life sentence, yes, but a chance for parole after 14 years. What were his chances? For his part, Mohan felt he stood a good shot at being granted early parole.

Parole officials look for acceptance from convicts of their deeds, taking responsibility, and rehabilitating. What if Mohan continued to deny his guilt? Thomas and Lahaie talked about it over coffee.

"You watch," Lahaie said. "He'll get out. Will be a model citizen in prison, has kids, family man. And when it comes closer to this parole hearing, he'll fall on his sword. Show remorse, redemption, whatever it takes to get out. Then he can go buy a new SUV, God love him."

But the detectives still had one more card to play, one last chance to try to keep Mohan in jail for the rest of his life. Lahaie put in a call to the NYPD and turned to a notation he had made near the end of his fourth Homicide Case Book on the Budram case:

NYPD Case #3017
Offense date Dec 03/87
Vic: Chattergoon, Rampati
3073 Park Ave #4F
N.Y.

CHAPTER 29 ~ CONFESSIONS

Burlington, Ontario
October 2005

Mike Thomas and Paul Lahaie sat across the table from two other detectives at a bar called Emma's Back Porch, just outside Hamilton. They were all off duty that night. Had a few pops. Talked shop. Like all homicide detectives, the four shared a bond, even though the two across the table came from a much larger city than Hamilton—one where there was far more violent crime. Their names were Steve Kelly and Kevin Tracy.

Kelly, the son of a cop, had grayed hair, a mustache; Tracy looked like he could double as a pro wrestler—shorter, but tattooed, Popeye-sized forearms, and legs that swelled with muscle against his pant legs. Thomas ordered another round of Alexander Keith draught, the beer that hails from Canada's Maritimes. The visiting detectives had never heard of Keith's before. That was because they weren't from Canada. They were from New York City. Bronx Homicide.

A year and a half had passed since Mohan Ramkissoon's sentencing. Lahaie had called Bronx homicide about the information he heard through his investigation about Mohan's role in the murder of Rampati Chattergoon. The wheels still turned slowly in New York. But Thomas had also dropped a tip to a journalist with the *Hamilton Spectator* about the cold case in New York, a murder in which Mohan Ramkissoon had at one time been a suspect.

"You might want to make a call down there, see what's going on with the case," Thomas had told the journalist. And now, here were the Bronx detectives. Thomas figured Bronx homicide more vigorously pursued the file because of the *Spectator*'s pursuit of the story.

Steve Kelly had by now delved into the case, interviewing the family of Rampati Chattergoon, others who had been questioned at the time of her murder. He explored the forensics locker to review evidence. Eventually he developed a narrative of what he believed had happened back then.

The detectives finished their beers and Steve Kelly and Kevin Tracy returned to their hotel. They had an early morning coming up, were driving to eastern Ontario to Millhaven Institution, the maximum security federal prison in the tiny lakefront village called Bath, near Kingston, three hours southwest of Montreal. Time for the NYPD to make an unannounced, and long overdue, visit to Mohan Ramkissoon and take him back to his days in New York.

* * *

New York City
December 1987

Mohan Ramkissoon was 20 years old. After leaving his native Guyana, he had now lived in New York for a year, although he had no legal status in the United States. He lived in the Bronx with his older brother. The brother had married a Guyanese woman with the surname Chattergoon. The woman's family had also recently moved to New York, the Bronx. After the wedding, Mohan continued to live with his brother and now his new sister-in-law. And he set his sights on another young daughter of the Chattergoons, decided he wanted to marry her.

But the woman's parents weren't so sure about their daughter dating Mohan. The mother, 46-year-old Rampati Chattergoon, was very protective. Mohan became obsessed with Rampati's daughter, who was just in her late teens, 16 or 17, when Mohan first met her. The family didn't want the daughter to become involved with Mohan, much less marry him. For one thing, she was too young, they wanted her to complete her education first. And they believed it unseemly that a second girl in the family might marry another Ramkissoon.

There were other issues, too, when it came to Mohan himself. He grew increasingly aggressive about his desire to be with the young woman. Rampati told him to stay away from her daughter. They argued. He begged the daughter, cried, pleaded for her to meet him, phoned her repeatedly. She agreed on occasion to secretly meet him. With time, much later, the family saw Mohan's behavior in a different light. He had been a loose cannon, came off most of the time as quiet and unassuming but was prone to sudden rage.

The morning of December 3, 1987, Rampati Chattergoon was at home alone, her husband at work, the kids at school. Back then, New York City's crime rate had improved from the dark days of the 1970s, but the city was still six years away from the radical decline in street crime that marked the mayoral reign of law-and-order champion Rudy Giuliani. In the late 1980s there were about 2,000 homicides a year in New York, compared with a third that many by the end of the 1990s. Rampati was, by nature, and by necessity in that neighborhood on the west side of the Bronx, highly security conscious. If anyone rang at the door, she would always look out the window of the tenement building in which they lived to get a visual before opening the door. Even her own daughters had to ring the bell before she would open the door.

At 11 a.m. that day, one of her daughters came home from school. She found her dead mother on the kitchen floor, blood everywhere. NYPD crime scene investigators determined Rampati had been hit three times with a blunt object, a rolling pin, and stabbed 11 times. There was no sign of forced entry. Clearly the woman had known her killer, had willingly let the person in. Police interviewed family and acquaintances, including Mohan Ramkissoon. Apart from the poor relationship with Mohan, she had no enemies, no one who would want to do her harm. The investigation went nowhere. And it was one of 1,672 homicides that year in the city. The case sat cold. Shortly after that, Mohan Ramkissoon moved to Miami before returning to New York, and, ultimately, meeting Yvette Budram in Canada.

* * *

Millhaven Institution
Bath, Ontario
October 2005

Bronx Homicide detective Steve Kelly felt a chill, and it wasn't the temperature inside the federal prison. It was seeing Mohan

Ramkissoon for the first time, as he entered the interview room and walked towards him. He did it, Kelly thought. The evidence he had already reviewed, the interviews he had done to date, pointed to that conclusion, and now, seeing him in person, he just knew it.

Gary Yokoyama

The two detectives introduced themselves. Mohan seemed shaken at first. He had never met these cops with Bronx accents and NYPD badges. This wasn't the Hamilton or Peel police he was used to dealing with. Detective Kevin Tracy was an intimidating physical presence with his thick tattooed arms. Kelly decided to give Mohan a sense of what they knew, put some of it out there on the table—Mohan's pursuit of the daughter, the death of the mother, Rampati Chattergoon. But while Mohan's

Bronx Homicide detectives Kevin Tracy (left) and Steve Kelly.

body language showed fear, he did not crack. He just sat there, listened to the story, not interrupting, a blank look on his face.

Finally, Mohan said, "I have nothing to say."

He repeated that line several times. Denied everything. The guy's a piece of work, thought Kelly. Lies through his teeth, even about basic facts he had to know were true. Lies so automatically it's as though he believes what he's saying, too. Or he just refused to address the point, will not go there. At the end of the questioning, the detectives suggested Mohan take a polygraph test to clear his name. He refused. There was nothing more they could do with him that day. They figured, let him sleep on everything they had injected into his mind. Leave the door open for him to get in touch with them if he wants to tell the truth. After nearly three hours of questioning, the detectives said goodbye to Mohan Ramkissoon. They would not need to visit him again, they told him.

Kelly had no doubt in his mind that Mohan killed Rampati Chattergoon. But he had to build his case further back in New York before taking what he had to the district attorney to try to get it before a grand jury and obtain an indictment against Mohan. (In New York state, a grand jury is composed of 16 to 23 people who evaluate evidence against an individual charged with a crime to determine whether the accused should stand trial.) If they could charge him, get an indictment, there would be someone waiting at the door for him if he were ever released from the Canadian prison. He needed to further explore the evidence packed away in boxes in storage. The homicide was 18 years old, and they didn't collect forensic evidence nearly as well back then.

Was there DNA that could be amplified from the scene—Mohan Ramkissoon's DNA? Kelly kept in touch with the Chattergoon family in the Bronx. A sad, horrible story, he thought. Real nice people, too, a hard-working, tight-knit family. The family became engaged in the investigation. They read stories from the newspaper in Canada, the *Hamilton Spectator*, about Mohan's conviction in Ontario for murdering and dumping his wife's body. It placed his peculiar personality, and actions, from the past in an entirely new context when considering the murder of their loved one.

They told Kelly that Mohan had, in fact, attended the funeral and wake for Rampati. He outwardly seemed supportive of the family at the time, but that calmness about him, it was as though he was at peace with it all, as though he had a weight lifted off his shoulders. Nobody put it together back then, but in retrospect, it did seem odd. Most damning of all, the daughter, the one Mohan had loved in vain, revealed that in fact Mohan had returned to New York from Miami after the death of Rampati, and had tried to abduct the young woman on the street, even made innuendoes about having killed her mother. She got scared, yelled at some pedestrians that she feared for her life. Mohan took off in a car and disappeared, heading to Canada not long after that.

Steve Kelly's personal life, and the investigation, took a hit late in 2005 when he was in a bad car accident. Chain-reaction collision, he was rear-ended. Fractured his leg. Lucky to be alive. Went back to work early, earlier than he should have. He wanted to get back into the case. More forensics testing had been done on evidence, on the rolling pin, the knife, the blood. And then, in January 2006, Kelly and Kevin Tracy made a surprise return to see Mohan in Millhaven Penitentiary. Catch him off guard, see if he'll have more clarity of mind this time around. This time they put more heat on him, worked on him pretty good. After further investigation, they said, they had further developed physical evidence from the scene of the murder of Rampati Chattergoon. They knew what happened. Mohan had stonewalled police for more than four years, repeatedly denied his guilt in the murder of his wife Yvette, withstood questioning from several detectives. Was it the time he had logged in jail that pushed Mohan over the edge? The Bronx detectives?

Kevin Tracy and his NYPD badge.

They offered him a scenario that perhaps he found attractive, gave him an out. It wasn't his fault, he was just defending himself. Is that right? Maybe you were in the Chattergoon's home, Mohan. Maybe she got a little angry with you—she often did, right? Yes, Mohan agreed, yes, he had been in the apartment, there had been an argument. The death of Rampati Chattergoon had been self-defense. It wasn't Mohan's fault, he was pushed, and attacked. In fact, she pulled a knife on me, Mohan said.

Finally, he cracked. Mohan confessed. He did it. He killed Rampati Chattergoon. Self-defense, he agreed, he had no choice. Mohan paced the room as he spoke, agitated. Steve Kelly put the

258 Jon Wells

paper in front of Mohan. Sign the statement confirming you just said that. Mohan refused. No signing. The confession was a big step, but without a signed statement, Kelly felt it was doubtful if they could get the case before a grand jury to seek an indictment.

In one sense, given what Mohan had admitted to Kelly, the Rampati Chattergoon homicide was no longer just a circumstantial case. He had what the Ontario detectives had never been able to get in their case from him—an admission of responsibility for the victim's death. But in a court of law in New York, a verbal hearsay statement, even via two detectives, would be almost worthless.

The detectives left the prison, chased down more information. Interviewed a couple of people in the Mississauga area. Flew to Miami to interview a person who had been friends with Mohan down there after the Bronx murder. Waited for a DNA profile to be developed from the forensic evidence, for comparison to Mohan's DNA blueprint on file with Hamilton Police. Meanwhile, the Chattergoon family waited in anticipation in the Bronx for the case to get to court. Mohan's brother remained married to one of Rampati's daughters. The Chattergoon and Ramkissoon families read the news, reported in a four-week series in the *Spectator,* that Mohan had allegedly confessed to killing Rampati. It divided both families. How could the Chattergoons look at Mohan's relatives the same way again?

* * *

Mohan Ramkissoon had another day in court for the Yvette Budram case, but he did not appear in person. It was at Osgoode Hall in Toronto, for his appeal. Paul Lahaie, Mike Thomas, and Kevin McKenna drove from Hamilton together for the Ontario Court of Appeal decision. Mohan's appeal lawyer, Irwin Koziebrocki, argued before a three-justice appeal panel that he deserved a new trial. The lawyer said Justice Nick Borkovich erred in five areas of law that hurt Mohan's chances for a fair trial. For one, he argued, the judge had not granted a jury request to read transcripts from four trial witnesses before it deliberated on a verdict.

"The judge has a responsibility to accede to the requests of the jury," he said. Acting for the Crown, assistant Crown attorney

David Lepofsky countered that Mohan's trial lawyer, Tom Carey, didn't object to the judge's approach at the time, and that indeed, those transcripts favored the case *against* Ramkissoon.

On October 16, Justice Eleanore Cronk released the appeal panel's decision. The court rejected Mohan's request for a new trial. It meant Mohan would be in jail until 2018, when he would be eligible for parole, at 52 years old. And then? Thomas and Lahaie continued to hope that the New York angle would bear fruit. Thomas dearly hoped a warrant for Mohan's arrest would be on the books for if and when he was released from Canadian prison.

"Then he can go down there and defend himself on that one. He's responsible for that homicide as well and should be held accountable for it. You know what? He's committed two murders—minimum. And, what, he's going to be walking back into our community? We have to look after the people here in Hamilton, that's why we have to keep pushing for that. We don't want him here."

The book on the Bronx murder, as of the fall of 2008, had not yet been closed. Steve Kelly had retired but still hoped the case would be brought before a grand jury based on the evidence he had gathered—the interviews, forensics, Mohan's lies and evasions and his verbal confession. But it remained to be seen if it would go any further.

If nothing else, even if there was no indictment, the fact remained that the murder case had been reopened, NYPD officers had interviwed Mohan twice in prison, they were of the opinion he was guilty, said he admitted it. Paul Lahaie and Mike Thomas knew that if and when Mohan's opportunity for release arose, it would all be a nice body of information to bring forward for the parole board, when considering whether he was a danger to re-offend. His quest for freedom would now always be viewed through the prism of what he had done in the Bronx 21 years earlier.

Epilogue

A hard blue sky and blinding sun at daybreak in the village, early fall, the air bracingly cold, an early hint of winter along the northeast shore of Lake Ontario. Trees shimmer with the colors—gold, burnt orange, crimson. Near the ferry dock, where Millhaven Creek flows into the lake, wisps of vapor hover over the water like an army of ghosts rising from below. Across the road, up a hill, take the right fork at the end of a winding driveway, and there is the low-rise gray concrete building, black iron gates. Sunlight cracks off twisted razor wire.

His eyes open inside the cell in the federal jail called Millhaven Institution. The eyes are so dark, the pupil and iris seem nearly indistinguishable. Mohan Ramkissoon was up 30 minutes before sunrise. What did that matter, though? He could not see the sun, the colors, in J Unit, home to some of Canada's hardest criminals. There are books in his cell, a television. He never did watch much TV when he was a free man, and still doesn't. Mostly just the news. Just enough to keep up to date on what's going on outside. At night he will dream, he claims, of Yvette and his family. And her death? Does he have nightmares about the murder, whoever is guilty of it? The bludgeoning, the dumping of his wife's body? No. He says he does not dream of that.

Why did he kill his wife? She called the shots in the marriage, sometimes belittled him. Maybe he was fine with that, though. He loved Yvette. Did he love her too much? Was it the brazen affair? The final domestic fight? Her vow to divorce him? A man pushed, and pushed some more, past the breaking point? No. It's insufficient. There must be more to it. But Mohan does not permit explanations. He contests the premise.

"I'm innocent," Mohan says to a journalist visitor. "I'm paying for someone else's actions."

He said his prayers that morning. The Hindu faith he follows is polytheistic—there are many gods to pray to, it is up to the individual to choose which deity to focus on. Which Hindu prayer does the convicted killer recite?

"*Loose us from the yoke of the sins of our fathers/And also from those we ourselves have committed. Release your servant, as a thief is set free/From his crime or as a calf is loosed from its cord.*"

Would a man pray to be set free from his sins if he truly believed he was not guilty? Mohan still does not waver in his position that the one who killed Yvette is free: Harjeet (Happy) Singh. He shakes his head. The other guys here, the other prisoners in J Unit, he imagines they live in relative peace, resigned to their fate, aware of their guilt. They don't enjoy the numbing trappings of prison life, no, but they go through them with resignation. But Mohan? That's different. He is suffering the consequences for someone else. Puts him on edge all the time, he says. He should not be here. Mohan still argues his case forcefully, his face earnest, steeped in the story he has told repeatedly in the past. He is not a large man. Could he have lifted Yvette into the trunk of his car, and dumped her by himself?

"Hell, no," he says, a look of incredulity on his face. He loved his wife, never raised a hand to her. She disappeared. Happy killed her. He is a smart guy, Happy. And an evil one. The police have done this to him. They didn't investigate Happy properly.

"Hey, police have been known to take liberties in the past, right?"

He says he wants justice. For who?

"For me and Yvette ... I miss her every day."

Tears well in his eyes. All he ever wanted was a quiet life, he says. Loved his family, worked hard, didn't smoke, didn't drink, didn't party, didn't really have any friends, that was fine by him. The visitor asks how anyone could live with himself after murdering their wife and dumping her body in a field.

"You'd have to ask Happy that. He's not a human being. The forensic pathologist said there was probably more than one person involved, so where is the mysterious friend?"

A fate determined by God will be Happy's ultimate sentence for what he has done, he says.

Yvette Budram on her trip to Chile.

"Have you heard of karma? It follows you. It follows you. He can run and hide, but you can't hide from that. You can't hide from the guy up there."

The visitor puts a picture in front of Mohan, a photocopy of a family photo of Yvette. It is from her trip to Chile when she was in her early 30s, perhaps at the height of her optimism for her future. She looks radiant. Mohan has seen the photo before. He takes the paper, studies it for a long time, anger creases his face.

"Where did you get this picture? I told the kids not to give out the pictures."

The visitor, aware that Mohan has been interviewed by detectives from the NYPD, and asked about the Bronx homicide, asks about the rumor that many years ago he murdered a woman in New York. The dark eyes stare unblinkingly at the question, his face empty.

Is it true?

"Hell, no," Mohan says, a smile crossing his face.

Have you heard of this rumor before?

"No."

Mohan says he lives in fear. You follow the rules of the prison, but also the unwritten rules of the inmates. Better to get a reprimand in your inmate record than go against the flow. Don't anger inmates, do what the others are doing, keep your mouth shut, follow the pack, or you'll end up abused or dead. Don't make friends, follow the group.

As Mohan speaks to the visitor a tall, muscled inmate with dreadlocks passes before sitting down with a girlfriend, or a wife. The man looks at Mohan and nods.

"Hey bro," Mohan says.

Mohan stands to leave the visitor. His handshake is neutral. He will wait for the heavy steel door to let him into a holding area, then enter through another door into J Unit. There he will be searched by rubber-gloved hands to make sure he has smuggled nothing from a visitor. He dreads the full-body strip search every time. It is, Mohan reflects, the most awful, degrading thing you can imagine.

"Jail is a horrible thing, man," Mohan says in a quiet voice. "It's the path to hell."

* * *

Today, seven years after their mother's body was found, Yvette's two youngest kids now live with family friends near Toronto. Kevin approaches his teens, by accounts a good kid. Preet marked her sixteenth birthday recently and looks more like her mother with each year, the long hair, dark eyes. A beautiful girl. She is a straight-A high school student with dreams of becoming an oncologist. The children still visit their father on occasion, but not as often as when he was first incarcerated.

Family tried to steer the kids clear of learning the details surrounding Yvette's murder, but that has been made no easier by TV documentaries that have been made about the Yvette Budram investigation. One evening, Yvette's eldest daughter, Lisa Budram, whom she had raised back in Guyana, watched part of one program about the case on a Canadian news magazine show. Lisa had years before told police she wanted to view her mother's remains when the body had been identified, but Detective Mike Thomas had talked her out of it. It's not how you want to remember your mother, he said. Lisa heeded the advice. And now this TV show flashed graphic evidence photos of her mother's remains. She burst into tears and did not stop crying for a long time.

When Lisa had first dreamt of her mother in the fall of 2000, she believed, correctly, that it was a bad omen. But much later, after the trial ended, she dreamt of her again, and this time she was holding Lisa in her arms. "I love you," Mom said. Ultimately, Lisa had to see it, had to visit the place off the country road outside Hamilton where her mother had lain for seven months. Lisa was not much of a churchgoer, but felt she was a spiritual person, certainly believed the soul goes somewhere after death. She wondered, would she feel something? Some kind of connection at that place? One day she stood on the soft shoulder of the 8th Concession in Flamborough. She could see the spot, and the brush and the rolling cornfield beyond. But she experienced nothing cosmic. No. All she could do was wonder about the final horrible moments in her mother's life. And then she wept.

Yvette's funeral was held nearly four years after her death, soon after Mohan had been convicted of her murder. That morning was foggy, the air warm and moist at the cemetery in Mississauga west of Toronto. Yvette had been cremated for burial. She had been raised a Hindu in her native Guyana, but in Canada had eventually sought spiritual advice from a Christian minister she befriended. Lisa had asked that minister to preside over the funeral. It was a traditional Christian service, offering words of spiritual comfort that Yvette had not been afforded on the day her life had come to a violent end.

"Yea, though I walk through the valley of the shadow of death, I will fear no evil, for thou art with me."

Preet and Kevin, at the time of the funeral just 12 and nine years old, each said a few words at graveside. Mom loved us very much, they said. We miss you. We love you. The minister continued with that theme, how much Yvette cared for her kids. The words lingered in Lisa's mind.

Who was Yvette Budram? The police worked a long time to discover her name when her identity was unknown. And later Lisa embarked on her own search, of a different sort. She reflected on Yvette's life: Married at 16. The abuse. Her pride, her drive to make it, her temper, stormy relationships. Yvette was a complex woman with her own inner demons. Bottom line? To Lisa, it was that Yvette loved her children, wanted the best for them. Over time Lisa put the pieces together, came to a fuller understanding in a way she never had as a teenager.

There wasn't a day that went by that Lisa didn't regret failing to reconcile with her while she was alive. And she craved hearing Mom say she loved her just one more time.

"Earth to earth, ashes to ashes, dust to dust."

As the funeral concluded in the heavy air, Lisa felt cool drops kiss her skin. Maybe it was a sign, a symbol, she thought, after all the ugliness, of cleansing. She was looking for small blessings, and found one in the gentle rain escorting her mother on a final passage from this world.